Artificial Intelligence in Agriculture

Andrea Apicella

Artificial Intelligence in Agriculture

Technological Foundations, Adoption Drivers and Labor Market Implications

Springer

Andrea Apicella
Pisa, Italy

ISBN 978-3-032-26579-1 ISBN 978-3-032-26580-7 (eBook)
https://doi.org/10.1007/978-3-032-26580-7

This Springer imprint is published by the registered company Springer Nature Switzerland AG
The registered company address is: Gewerbestrasse 11, 6330 Cham, Switzerland

Preface

The growing integration of Artificial Intelligence (AI) into agri-food systems is profoundly affecting production processes, decision-making practices, and the organization of work. More broadly, it is challenging established ways in which knowledge is generated, interpreted, and applied across agricultural value chains. This volume arises from the need to examine these changes as part of a structural transformation involving technologies, skills, organizational arrangements, and institutions, and to provide interpretive tools capable of making sense of this evolving landscape.

The book is designed to offer an integrated perspective on AI in agriculture, moving beyond purely technological approaches as well as narrowly normative interpretations. Its distinctive contribution lies in the combined analysis of the functional configurations of AI, adoption processes, implications for work and skills, and the governance conditions under which digital innovation takes shape. In this respect, the volume is positioned at the intersection of studies on digitalization, agricultural economics, and the social sciences, fostering dialogue across disciplinary boundaries.

The volume addresses a broad yet clearly defined audience. Researchers and scholars will find a coherent conceptual framework for interpreting the evolution of AI in agri-food systems; policy makers and institutional actors may use it as an analytical reference to reflect on the trajectories of digital transition; professionals, consultants, and extension services will find insights into how intelligent technologies are reshaping operational practices; and advanced students and practitioners may use it as an in-depth resource on a rapidly developing field.

From a structural perspective, the chapters have been conceived as relatively autonomous analytical contributions. This choice reflects the complexity of the issues addressed and the need to examine different dimensions—technological, organizational, occupational, and institutional—without reducing them to cursory overviews or fragmenting the analysis into overly specialized treatments. Some conceptual references recur across the volume; this is intentional and aims to ensure interpretive coherence while allowing each chapter to develop its own analytical focus.

Overall, the volume draws on an extensive body of scientific literature and major international frameworks. Rather than advancing prescriptive solutions, it seeks to provide conceptual tools for understanding an ongoing process of transformation and for identifying the conditions under which AI can contribute to an evolution of agriculture that is attentive to economic, social, and environmental dimensions.

Pisa, Italy Andrea Apicella

Competing Interests The author has no competing interests to declare that are relevant to the content of this manuscript.

Contents

1 The Digital Transformation of Agriculture: From Mechanization to Generative AI 1
1.1 Introduction 1
1.2 The Four Waves of Technological Transformation 3
1.2.1 The First Wave: Mechanization and Industrial Agriculture 4
1.2.2 The Second Wave: Precision Agriculture and Sensing Technologies 7
1.2.3 The Third Wave: Artificial Intelligence and Cognitive Automation 10
1.2.4 The Fourth Wave: Generative Artificial Intelligence and Language-Based Systems 12
1.3 Terminology and Operational Definitions 13
1.4 Artificial Intelligence in Agriculture: Impacts, Conditions of Effectiveness, and Emerging Challenges 18
1.4.1 Agricultural Productivity and Resource Sustainability 18
1.4.2 Digital Inequalities and Enabling Conditions 19
1.4.3 Algorithmic Governance, Ethics, and Decision-Making Power 20
1.4.4 Generative AI: Opportunities and Ambivalences 20
1.5 Conclusions and Roadmap of the Volume 21
References 22

2 Functional Configurations of AI in Agriculture 29
2.1 Introduction 29
2.2 Application Functions of AI: The M–D–P–A Model 31
2.2.1 Monitoring 31
2.2.2 Diagnosis 33
2.2.3 Prediction 34
2.2.4 Automation 35

2.3 Enabling Technologies and Emerging Models 37
2.4 Adoption Inequalities and Emerging Configurations 39
2.4.1 M–D–P–A Configurations Across Agricultural Contexts 40
2.4.2 Evolutionary Trajectories of Computational Agricultural Ecosystems 41
2.5 Conclusions 42
References 43

3 Adoption of AI in Agriculture: A Technology-Organization-Environment Perspective 49
3.1 Introduction 49
3.2 The TOE as an Interpretative Lens for AI Adoption Processes in Agriculture 51
3.2.1 Technological Factors in the Adoption of AI in Agriculture 51
3.2.2 Organizational Factors in the Adoption of AI in Agriculture 52
3.2.3 Environmental Factors in the Adoption of AI in Agriculture 53
3.3 Adoption Configurations of AI in Agriculture: Scalable Efficiency and Adaptive Resilience 56
3.3.1 Systemic Risks and Inclusive Strategies in the Adoption of AI in Agriculture 58
3.3.2 Technological Vulnerabilities: Data, Models, and Operational Reliability 59
3.3.3 Organizational Vulnerabilities: Absorptive Capacity, Skills, and Technical Dependencies 60
3.3.4 Environmental Vulnerabilities: Infrastructures, Data Governance, and Territorial Inequalities 61
3.3.5 Inclusive Strategies for Risk Mitigation 62
3.4 Conclusions 64
References 64

4 Digitalization, Automation, and Agricultural Labor: Tasks, Roles, and Inequality 69
4.1 Introduction 69
4.2 Transformations of Roles and Tasks in Smart Agriculture 71
4.2.1 Substitution and Fragmentation of Operational Work 72
4.2.2 Emergence of Hybrid Roles and New Cognitive Value Chains 74
4.2.3 Organizational Recomposition and the Polarization of Skills 75

4.3 Gender and Generational Inequalities in Digital Agricultural Labor ... 76
4.3.1 Digital Divide and Differential Access to Resources ... 79
4.3.2 Youth and Generational Transition ... 80
4.3.3 Gender Gap and Female Leadership ... 81
4.3.4 Migrant Labor and Systemic Vulnerability ... 82
4.4 Policies for a Fair Employment Transition ... 83
4.4.1 From Fragmentation to Equity in Knowledge and Access to Technologies ... 84
4.4.2 Instruments for Inclusion and Reskilling ... 85
4.4.3 Hybrid Ecosystems and Multi-Actor Partnerships ... 86
4.5 Conclusions ... 87
References ... 88

5 Digital Skills, AI, and Learning Agriculture ... 93
5.1 Introduction ... 93
5.2 Policy and International Frameworks for Digital and AI Skills in Agriculture ... 95
5.3 Digital Skills and AI: A Multilevel Interpretive Framework ... 98
5.3.1 Digital Systems Thinking and Data Awareness ... 102
5.3.2 Continuous and Adaptive Learning ... 103
5.3.3 Integration of Hybrid Knowledge and Reflective Professional Identity ... 105
5.3.4 Digital Collaboration and Intelligent Communities ... 108
5.3.5 Digital Literacy and Advanced Technological Mastery ... 109
5.4 Conclusions ... 111
References ... 112

6 Governing Artificial Intelligence in Agriculture: Institutions, Infrastructures, and Future Scenarios ... 117
6.1 Introduction ... 117
6.2 Algorithmic Governance and Digital Rights ... 118
6.2.1 Data Quality, Bias, and Fairness ... 120
6.2.2 Transparency, Explainability, and Accountability ... 121
6.2.3 Privacy, Data Ownership, and Privacy-Preserving Solutions ... 123
6.2.4 Systemic Security, Interoperability, and Data Governance ... 124
6.3 Scenarios 2045 and Operational Roadmap: Methodological Approach ... 126
6.3.1 Methodological Framework: The Generic Foresight Process Framework ... 126
6.3.2 Drivers, Critical Uncertainties, and Generative Logics ... 127
6.3.3 Typological Positioning of the Scenarios ... 128
6.3.4 Function of Scenarios in the Digital Agri-food Governance Process ... 128

6.4 Scenarios Extended to 2045 129
6.4.1 The Logic of the Trajectories to 2045 133
6.4.2 Operational Roadmap 2025–2045 134
6.4.3 Actors, Responsibilities, and SDG Metrics 138
6.5 Conclusions 140
References 141

Index 145

Abbreviations

AI	Artificial Intelligence
AI DMST	Artificial Intelligence–Based Decision-Making Support Tool
AKIS	Agricultural Knowledge and Innovation Systems
CNNs	Convolutional Neural Networks
DE4A	*Digital Economy for Africa*
DigComp	Digital Competence Framework for Citizens
DMST	Digital Management Support Tools
EIP-AGRI	European Innovation Partnership for Agricultural Productivity and Sustainability
FAO	Food and Agriculture Organization
GANs	Generative Adversarial Networks
GDPR	General Data Protection Regulation
GFPP	Generic Foresight Process Framework
GIS	Geographic Information Systems
GNSS	Global Navigation Satellite Systems
HSI	Hyperspectral Imaging
ICT	Information and Communication Technologies
IFAD	International Fund for Agricultural Development
IoT	Internet of Things
ISO	International Organization for Standardization
JRC	Joint Research Centre
LLMs	Large Language Models
M–D–P–A model	Monitoring, Diagnosis, Prediction, Automation Model
NIRS	Near-Infrared Spectroscopy
OECD	Organisation for Economic Co-operation and Development
RRI	Responsible Research and Innovation
SDGs	Sustainable Development Goals
SERS	Surface-Enhanced Raman Scattering

TOE	Technology-Organization-Environment
VRT	Variable-Rate Technologies
XAI	eXplainable AI
YOLO	*You Only Look Once*

Chapter 1
The Digital Transformation of Agriculture: From Mechanization to Generative AI

Abstract This chapter traces the evolution of technological change in agriculture through a four-wave periodization—mechanization, precision agriculture, predictive artificial intelligence (AI), and generative AI—offering a historical lens on the shift from systems grounded in mechanical power to socio-technical configurations centered on the algorithmic processing and production of knowledge. The analysis highlights both continuities and ruptures along this trajectory, showing how each wave has reshaped the relationship between labor, capital, information, and production ecosystems. The chapter also introduces an operational glossary to clarify the technical terminology used throughout the volume, with particular attention to normative definitions of digitalization, AI, and generative models. A synthesis then distills three critical dimensions of digital transformation—productivity and resource sustainability, infrastructural and cognitive inequalities, and algorithmic governance—bringing into focus opportunities, ambivalences, and emerging risks. The chapter concludes by outlining the structure of the volume and its thematic linkages, providing a multilevel conceptual framework for interpreting the dynamics of agricultural digitalization and the socio-economic implications of AI in contemporary agri-food systems.

Keywords Agricultural mechanization · Digital agriculture · Precision agriculture · AI agriculture · Generative AI

1.1 Introduction

Agriculture is currently undergoing a far-reaching transformation driven by the growing integration of digital technologies into production, management, and decision-making practices. Over the past two decades, this process has intensified, making it increasingly inadequate to frame it as a simple technological upgrade, particularly in a sector such as agriculture—one of the world's oldest productive activities, long grounded in cumulative practical knowledge and situated forms of expertise. In this context, digital technologies gain relevance without displacing the

A. Apicella, *Artificial Intelligence in Agriculture*,
https://doi.org/10.1007/978-3-032-26580-7_1

centrality of farming practices and experiential know-how, instead becoming part of an evolving assemblage of tools, skills, and decision-making processes. Technologies ranging from sensing and monitoring systems to cognitive automation, from digital platforms to generative artificial intelligence (AI) models, are reshaping the boundaries between human labor, computational processes, and the biophysical environment. While these developments open substantial opportunities, they also introduce new risks and tensions that are beginning to redefine how agricultural systems are organized and governed.

This evolution has not unfolded uniformly. Digital innovation in agriculture has instead followed distinct trajectories, unfolding through successive phases that have reshaped the sector's operational logics over time. Mechanization represented the first break with manual farming practices. Precision agriculture subsequently shifted attention toward within-field variability, enabled by sensors, Global Navigation Satellite Systems (GNSS), and advanced monitoring tools. AI further expanded the capacity to interpret multi-source data and to support increasingly complex decision-making processes. More recently, generative models have begun to reconfigure how agronomic knowledge is produced and organized, raising new questions related to autonomy, transparency, and data governance.

These transformations have been neither homogeneous nor universally accessible. The ways in which digital technologies spread and are taken up in agriculture are deeply shaped by geographic, socio-economic, infrastructural, and cultural conditions, leading to adoption paths that vary considerably across contexts and, at times, diverge markedly. At the same time, the accelerating pace of digitalization brings a set of critical challenges. It can widen existing inequalities, reinforce dependence on proprietary platforms, intensify pressures on environmental sustainability, and raise unresolved questions about algorithmic transparency. Addressing these issues requires careful, multidimensional analysis.

Within this context, the present chapter serves an introductory and orienting role for the volume. It reconstructs the main stages in the evolution of agricultural digitalization through a four-wave technological periodization, proposed as an interpretive framework for understanding the complexity of ongoing processes while explicitly acknowledging overlaps and non-linear dynamics. In parallel, the chapter clarifies the core concepts employed throughout the book, showing why a clear terminological distinction among digitalization, digital transformation, AI, and generative models is an essential analytical prerequisite in a rapidly evolving field. Technical language, in this sense, does more than describe technologies: it helps set priorities, shape investment decisions, and inform policy, and therefore calls for careful and disciplined use.

A third objective of the chapter is to synthesize the impacts of digital technologies in agriculture as documented in international literature. The discussion focuses on three closely interconnected domains—productivity, resource sustainability, and data governance—which are treated as key interpretive lenses for understanding both the opportunities and the ambivalences of the ongoing transition. The aim is not to provide an exhaustive review, but rather to outline the dynamics that form the shared background against which the contributions of the subsequent chapters are developed.

Overall, this introductory section seeks to establish a historical, conceptual, and methodological framework within which the digital transformation of agriculture can be situated. It provides readers with a shared interpretive ground from which to explore, in the chapters that follow, the technological, social, and economic implications of AI in contemporary agri-food systems.

Placing the digital transformation of agriculture within a historical perspective is therefore essential to understanding the nature of the discontinuities observed today. Current technologies, including advanced forms of AI, represent the latest outcome of a long-term process through which tools, infrastructures, and bodies of knowledge have progressively reshaped the relationship between agricultural activity, technical power, and informational capacity. A more precise interpretation of the contemporary phase thus requires reconstructing the trajectories that have structured the sector's evolution, paying attention to moments of acceleration as well as to breaks and continuities. The following section develops this perspective through a four-wave technological periodization, which provides a systematic way to examine the proliferation of digital functions and their growing integration into agricultural production systems.

1.2 The Four Waves of Technological Transformation

The technological transformation of agriculture can be interpreted as a sequence of socio-technical configurations that, over the past two centuries, have reshaped the relationship between labor, knowledge, and the environment. These configurations, described here as four distinct waves, should not be understood as rigidly sequential stages. Rather, they represent periods of concentrated innovation in which new operational principles emerged, reorganizing the interactions among tools, practices, and institutions. Viewed in comparative perspective, these waves reveal how agriculture has progressively shifted from systems grounded in mechanical power to arrangements centered on information processing and, more recently, on the algorithmic generation of knowledge.

The first wave is associated with mechanization and the systematic introduction of motive power into agricultural production, which reduced reliance on manual labor and strengthened the integration of farming within the broader industrial apparatus. The second wave is identified with precision agriculture, enabled by sensing technologies, geolocation, and Geographic Information Systems (GIS), which made it possible to treat the field as a measurable and internally differentiated space. The third wave corresponds to the diffusion of non-generative AI, whose predictive models expanded the capacity to process heterogeneous data streams and to support complex operational decisions. The fourth wave, finally, is marked by the emergence of generative AI, which enables the production of texts, images, and autonomous computational representations, thereby reshaping the very nature of agronomic knowledge and decision-making practices.

Although these waves have often overlapped and spread unevenly across different regions of the world, their analytical distinction helps to illuminate both continuities and discontinuities in agricultural innovation processes. This historical perspective also provides an essential interpretive foundation for understanding contemporary dynamics of digitalization and their implications for labor, sustainability, and the governance of agri-food systems.

1.2.1 The First Wave: Mechanization and Industrial Agriculture

Mechanization is one of the key processes underpinning the transformation of modern agriculture. Between the nineteenth century and the mid-twentieth century, it took on a historically specific configuration, translating into profound changes in the sector's techno-productive organization (Binswanger, 1986; Matson et al., 1997; Mazoyer and Roudart, 2006; Ruttan, 2000). According to the definition proposed by the Food and Agriculture Organization (FAO), mechanization consists in the systematic application of tools, equipment, and power sources aimed at making agricultural production feasible and efficient (Clarke, 2000).

In this historical phase, mechanization did not coincide with the mere introduction of machinery, but referred to a broader process of reorganization of production operations. The growing use of mechanical power, as a substitute for or complement to human labor, was associated with increased dependence on industrial inputs, infrastructure, and specialized services (Ruttan, 2000). Within this framework, mechanization did not simply affect individual field operations; it took the form of a systemic transformation reshaping labor organization, cost structures, and the relationship between agriculture and the industrial apparatus. Precisely because of this systemic character, its diffusion was conditioned by technical, economic, and institutional factors that shaped both the intensity and the configuration of adoption across different contexts.

The United States case reconstructed by Rasmussen (1982) provides a useful reference for understanding the scale of this first mechanization-driven transformation. In the second half of the nineteenth century, approximately 64% of the national workforce was employed in agriculture; a century later, this share had fallen to 3%. Over the same period, labor productivity increased markedly: by around 1950, a single farmer was able to produce enough food for approximately 78 people, compared with four in 1850 (Rasmussen, 1982). These figures reflect a profound reorganization of the material foundations of agricultural production.

This transformation did not result from a single technological leap, but from a cumulative sequence of innovations. Improvements in manual tools were followed by the introduction of animal-drawn equipment and, subsequently, by the diffusion of mechanical reapers and threshers. The transition toward fully modern mechanization consolidated with the adoption of internal combustion tractors, which led to the progressive displacement of animal traction.

At the same time, mechanization brought about a significant increase in capital intensity. Between 1850 and 1880, average investment per farm rose from 7 to 26 dollars, indicating a growing demand for equipment, infrastructure, and technical skills, as well as a closer integration of agriculture with the mechanical, energy, and chemical sectors (Rasmussen, 1982). Because these inputs and services were largely produced outside the farm, the adoption of machinery was accompanied by a broader reorganization of the production system and by an increasing dependence on external markets for the provision of inputs and services.

In light of these transformations, mechanization can be interpreted as a central component of a broader process of agricultural industrialization. Machinery operates within a wider technological constellation that includes synthetic fertilizers, improved crop varieties, irrigation systems, transport and energy infrastructures, as well as facilities for the storage and processing of agricultural products. Taken together, these elements form an integrated system that simultaneously reshapes agronomic practices, labor organization, and the configuration of agri-food value chains (Pingali, 2007).

Mechanization trajectories have nevertheless been highly differentiated across countries (Binswanger, 1986). Operations requiring large amounts of continuous power, such as plowing or transport, have generally been mechanized at relatively early stages, whereas activities involving fine-grained control of field conditions have exhibited a more delayed mechanizability (Pingali et al., 1987; Pingali, 2007). These technical differences have interacted with specific agronomic and institutional arrangements, giving rise to non-uniform sequences of adoption.

In low-income countries, particularly in sub-Saharan Africa, the diffusion of mechanical technologies has often proceeded in a discontinuous manner, constrained by low levels of cropping intensity, limited infrastructure, and underdeveloped service markets (Binswanger, 1986; FAO & AUC, 2018; Pingali et al., 1987). In the absence of effective demand for mechanization services, utilization levels sufficient to sustain investment, and local chains for maintenance and supply, machinery frequently remains underutilized or is abandoned within a short time span (Diao et al., 2016). In other settings, such as South and East Asia, the diffusion of lightweight equipment and hiring-service networks has enabled more gradual forms of access to mechanical power, allowing the coexistence of multiple energy sources within agricultural operations (Binswanger, 1978; Pingali, 2007).

The increase in available power made a decisive contribution to the growth of agricultural productivity, but it also generated significant pressures on ecological systems, including soil compaction, erosion, and the exploitation of marginal lands (Foley et al., 2011; Matson et al., 1997; Tilman et al., 2002). These effects are particularly pronounced in the absence of management practices oriented toward resource conservation (Clarke, 2000; FAO, 2016).

Taken as a whole, mechanization processes profoundly transformed the structure and functioning of agricultural systems, expanding their operational capacity and strengthening their integration with the industrial apparatus, while at the same time making evident structural tensions related to environmental sustainability. The dynamics observed during this first wave of mechanization thus provide an essential interpretative basis for analyzing subsequent technological transitions and the implications of contemporary forms of innovation in the agricultural sector.

Box 1.1 Mechanization as a Response to Structural Constraints

The diffusion of agricultural mechanization can be interpreted as the outcome of structural pressures that vary according to the relative endowments of land, labor, and capital, as well as to the institutional capacity of production systems to govern technical change (Ruttan, 2002). Observed trajectories do not follow a linear or universal model; rather, they reflect the adaptation of technologies to local constraints and to the economic incentives that shape adoption decisions. From this perspective, mechanization does not represent an inevitable stage of technological progress, but a selective outcome shaped by relative prices, agronomic constraints, and institutional coordination mechanisms. The theory of induced innovation provides a key analytical reference for interpreting this heterogeneity: the direction of technical change depends on the interaction between factor prices and the ability of institutions to translate scientific and engineering knowledge into solutions consistent with local conditions (Hayami and Ruttan, 1970; Ruttan, 1977).

Agricultural technologies thus embody specific trade-offs among production factors. In systems characterized by abundant land and scarce labor, labor-saving innovations tend to emerge, whereas in contexts marked by high population density and limited land availability, innovations oriented toward land-saving strategies and labor-intensive farming practices prevail (Boserup, 1965; Hayami and Ruttan, 1970). Empirical evidence supports this logic: mechanization tends to consolidate where the substitution of human labor with mechanical power allows for reductions in operating costs or helps meet stringent timing constraints imposed by cropping cycles and factor endowments (Binswanger, 1986). At the same time, demand for mechanization also depends on the presence of institutional preconditions—such as service markets, maintenance systems, technical infrastructure, and access to credit—that enable sustained rather than episodic use of technologies. Interpreting mechanization as a response to structural constraints therefore provides a coherent way to account for the diversity of historical trajectories and to avoid deterministic readings that portray the diffusion of mechanical power as an inevitable outcome of agricultural development.

1.2.2 The Second Wave: Precision Agriculture and Sensing Technologies

From the second half of the twentieth century onward, the second wave of agricultural transformation shifted the center of innovation from mechanical power to information processing. While the first wave expanded farms' operational capacity through the systematic introduction of machinery and energy sources, digitalization inaugurated a new phase in which agricultural production became increasingly grounded in the collection, integration, and strategic use of data. Precision agriculture represents the paradigmatic outcome of this reconfiguration. Rather than focusing solely on the mechanization of farming operations, it entails the progressive digitalization of decision-making processes, supported by the algorithmic processing of environmental, agronomic, and livestock-related information (Gebbers and Adamchuk, 2010).

Over time, the international literature has progressively broadened the meaning of precision agriculture, moving beyond an initial understanding centered on localized techniques toward a more comprehensive management system. In this expanded view, precision agriculture is oriented toward the rational use of inputs, environmental sustainability, and productive efficiency, integrating technological, organizational, and informational dimensions within a unified operational framework (Bongiovanni and Lowenberg-Deboer, 2004; National Research Council, 1998; Pierce and Nowak, 1999; Zha, 2020; Zhang et al., 2002).

The conceptual roots of precision agriculture can be traced back to early experimental practices of differentiated soil sampling developed in the first decades of the twentieth century. As early as the 1920s, Linsley & Bauer (1929), for example, proposed non-uniform input management strategies tailored to local soil characteristics, anticipating a core principle of the site-specific approach: intra-field heterogeneity as an informational resource. For a long time, however, such practices remained isolated, largely due to the lack of precise measurement tools and reliable georeferencing mechanisms. It was only in the 1980s and 1990s that this intuition was translated into a systemic approach, alongside the diffusion of GNSS, GIS, on-board and in-field sensors, and the first digital platforms for data processing and analysis (Pierce and Nowak, 1999; Zhang et al., 2002).

During this phase, a fully-fledged techno-decisional infrastructure takes shape. On the hardware side, precision agriculture integrates optical and multispectral sensors, electronic control devices, high-precision GNSS receivers, drones, and variable-rate technologies (VRT) (Auernhammer, 2001; Gebbers and Adamchuk, 2010; Zhang et al., 2002). On the software side, increasingly sophisticated GIS platforms, agronomic and environmental models, prescriptive algorithms, and decision-support systems become widespread, enabling large volumes of heterogeneous information to be transformed into actionable guidance (McBratney et al., 2005; Pierce and Nowak, 1999).

Early map-based approaches rely on the production and overlay of soil maps, yield maps, and field surveys to delineate agronomically homogeneous zones. Sensor-based approaches, by contrast, adjust inputs in real time on the basis of localized measurements of crop physiology or soil properties (Adamchuk et al., 2004; Gebbers and Adamchuk, 2010). Despite these differences, the underlying objective is shared: to replace uniform interventions with spatially and temporally differentiated decisions that reflect intra-field variability and translate it into improved managerial efficiency.

It is at this stage of technological and conceptual maturation that precision agriculture comes to be recognized as an integrated management paradigm. The definition proposed by the International Society of Precision Agriculture (ISPA, 2024) captures the endpoint of this trajectory, describing precision agriculture as an approach aimed at optimizing productivity, quality, sustainability, and profitability through the spatial and temporal analysis of crop- and livestock-related variables. This formulation reflects not only the evolution of digital technologies, but also the growing centrality of information as a productive resource within contemporary agricultural systems.

Digitalization thus introduces a logic of datafication, whereby the agricultural field is reconfigured as an informational surface in which soil, crops, and microclimatic conditions are continuously monitored, modeled, and translated into operational prescriptions (Michels et al., 2020). Differentiated management increasingly depends on the quality of the data collected, the robustness of sensing and analytical systems, and the availability of interfaces capable of rendering information intelligible and actionable for farmers (McBratney et al., 2005). Precision, therefore, should not be understood as a purely technical attribute, but rather as a systemic property of the entire process linking data acquisition, storage, analysis, and decision-making.

From an adoption perspective, precision agriculture technologies display pronounced geographic and structural heterogeneity. In Northern and Western Europe, the combination of relatively larger average farm sizes, well-established digital infrastructures, and supportive public policies has fostered a broader and more sustained diffusion of innovation (European Parliament, 2016). Over the same period, structural transformation within European agriculture has accelerated the decline of small-scale farms and the contraction of the agricultural labor force, reinforcing processes of productive concentration. These dynamics intersect with an unfavorable demographic profile: the high proportion of farmers aged over 65 and the limited presence of younger cohorts constrain the sector's capacity to absorb complex technologies and to renew the technical skill base required for digital farm management (European Parliament, 2016).

In the Global South, barriers to adoption are even more pronounced. Limited connectivity infrastructure, high costs of access to digital services, low levels of technological literacy, and persistent gender inequalities constrain the inclusion of rural communities in innovation processes (UNDP, 2021). In response to these constraints, a range of collective solutions has emerged, including cooperative arrangements, machinery and technology rental services, shared digital platforms, and community-based learning networks. These models help lower entry costs and support more equitable access to digital technologies (UNDP, 2021).

In technologically advanced countries such as the United States, the adoption of individual precision agriculture tools follows a selective pattern. McFadden et al. (2023) show that, in 2019, automated guidance systems were used on more than 70% of sorghum acreage and on 64% of cotton acreage, whereas more complex technologies—such as yield mapping or VRT—were adopted by fewer than one quarter of farms in major field crops including wheat, cotton, and rice. This evidence points to a stratified adoption model, in which tools characterized by lower cognitive complexity and immediate, observable benefits diffuse more rapidly than solutions that require advanced analytical capabilities, continuous technical support, or significant economies of scale.

This digital restructuring has profound implications for the organization of agricultural labor. The diffusion of precision agriculture technologies entails a shift away from predominantly manual tasks toward managerial, analytical, and techno-digital roles, requiring advanced competencies in information and communication technologies (ICT), precision agronomy, environmental management, and data analysis (Pre Agri Project Consortium, 2022). Farmers are no longer merely operators of machinery but increasingly act as interpreters of indicators and algorithmic recommendations, with a growing need for training, advisory services, and specialized technical support.

At the same time, new forms of dependence on digital platforms are emerging. A growing share of predictive analytics, automated prescription services, and integrated farm management solutions is provided by private actors through proprietary systems. This process of platformization reshapes the distribution of informational power within agri-food value chains, shifting decision-making capacity and data control away from farmers and toward technology firms endowed with specialized expertise and financial resources (Carolan, 2017; Rotz et al., 2019b). Issues of data ownership, algorithmic governance, and contractual arrangements therefore become central to understanding the risks and opportunities associated with digitally mediated agricultural systems (Rotz et al., 2019b).

From a broader perspective, the second wave of agricultural transformation can be understood as a complex socio-technical transition in which technological, organizational, and environmental factors interact (Klerkx et al., 2019). Whereas mechanization reconfigured the relationship between labor and land, precision digitalization restructures the relationship between knowledge, power, and the environment, inaugurating a management paradigm grounded in the algorithmic extension of cognitive functions and in the growing centrality of information flows within decision-making processes.

1.2.3 *The Third Wave: Artificial Intelligence and Cognitive Automation*

From the early twenty-first century onward, the third wave of technological transformation in agriculture is associated with the diffusion of non-generative AI applications designed to identify recurring patterns, generate inferences, and support operational decision-making through the analysis of multi-source data (Ruiz-Real et al., 2020). Unlike the second wave, which focused on managing spatial variability through sensors and information systems, this phase introduces a qualitative shift in the relationship between data, knowledge, and decision-making. The objective is no longer limited to improving the precision of agronomic operations, but rather to extending the cognitive capacity of the technical system through inferential models capable of processing complex and not directly observable information.

The most widespread systems fall within the domain of supervised learning and include artificial neural networks, deep learning methods, fuzzy logic, and classification and regression algorithms applied to yield prediction, early detection of crop diseases, and input optimization (Javaid et al., 2023; Kamilaris and Prenafeta-Boldú, 2018; Oliveira and de Souza e Silva, 2023). Their diffusion has been supported by the evolution of agricultural digital infrastructures, including IoT sensor networks, cloud platforms, high-precision positioning systems, real-time analytical environments, and remote monitoring services, which have enabled the systematic integration of heterogeneous environmental, meteorological, and crop-related data (Eastwood et al., 2019; Tsakiridis et al., 2020). Within this framework, non-generative AI finds applications across the entire agri-food value chain, ranging from soil assessment and irrigation management to post-harvest activities such as shelf-life estimation and logistics planning (Ben Ayed and Hanana, 2021; Elbasi et al., 2023; Ryan et al., 2023).

Computer vision technologies are playing an increasingly prominent role within this landscape. Through automated image analysis, they enable the identification of foliar diseases, weeds, and phenotypic anomalies with levels of accuracy that are difficult to achieve through visual inspection alone (Mohanty et al., 2016). The integration of imaging systems with environmental sensors and agronomic models enhances the timeliness of diagnoses and broadens the available informational scope (Ben Ayed and Hanana, 2021). At the same time, operational solutions such as Agroview or specialized robots for selective weeding illustrate the transition toward forms of cognitive automation that intervene directly in the day-to-day management of agricultural operations (Oliveira and de Souza e Silva, 2023; Ryan et al., 2023).

The potential effects of this evolution are substantial, including gains in productivity, reductions in the use of chemical inputs, improved informational continuity along the value chain, and contributions to environmental sustainability (Benos et al., 2021; Liakos et al., 2018; Wu and Zhong, 2025). Nevertheless, the diffusion of agricultural AI remains uneven and strongly conditioned by structural factors (Van Es and Woodard, 2017; Wolfert et al., 2017). Data quality constitutes a critical constraint: fragmented, non-standardized, or non-interoperable datasets limit the robustness of complex models and hinder their large-scale adoption (Klerkx et al., 2019). Similarly, limited interoperability among agricultural machinery, digital platforms, and analytical models constrains the development of coherent technical ecosystems (van der Burg et al., 2021). Finally, disparities in techno-digital skills contribute to heterogeneous adoption trajectories, reinforcing pre-existing divides (Ben Ayed and Hanana, 2021; Ryan et al., 2023).

Beyond these structural conditions, the third wave introduces deeper transformations in the production of agricultural knowledge. Non-generative AI systems do not merely support predefined choices but actively contribute to the construction of computed representations of agro-ecological phenomena, which acquire a prescriptive role within management practices (Elbasi et al., 2024). Agricultural knowledge increasingly shifts toward computational forms capable of aggregating, filtering, and selecting multi-source data, thereby reshaping how farmers interpret and engage with their productive environments (Bronson and Knezevic, 2016). This process entails a redistribution of cognitive authority: actors who control digital platforms, infrastructures, and decision-making models gain an increasingly influential role in defining priorities and efficiency criteria, while local knowledge and tacit competencies—often difficult to formalize within algorithmic models—tend to lose centrality (Sauvagerd et al., 2024).

The opacity of complex models further reinforces this dynamic. Architectures such as deep neural networks can deliver highly accurate outputs while remaining difficult for end users to interpret (Hassija et al., 2024; Ryo, 2022). Tools developed within the field of explainable AI (XAI) seek to mitigate this opacity by making inferential processes more transparent through visualizations and diagnostic indicators (Mohan et al., 2024). Nevertheless, they introduce an additional layer of mediation that reduces—without fully eliminating—the structural non-transparency of computational systems (Ali et al., 2023; Burrell, 2016; Molnar, 2020). In this sense, algorithmic outputs do not merely describe reality, but actively orient decision-making processes and contribute to defining what is considered operationally relevant.

Taken together, these elements show that the third wave is defined not merely by technological maturity, but by the capacity of AI to restructure the relationships between data, decision-making, and knowledge. The effectiveness of cognitive systems depends on the alignment among digital infrastructures, organizational capabilities, interoperability standards, and data governance arrangements, as well as on the ability to manage the epistemic distance that separates agricultural actors from inferential models. Understanding these dynamics is therefore a crucial step for critically interpreting both the opportunities and the challenges associated with the fourth wave, centered on generative AI.

1.2.4 The Fourth Wave: Generative Artificial Intelligence and Language-Based Systems

From the early 2020s onward, the fourth wave of technological transformation in agriculture is marked by the diffusion of generative AI, driven by large language models (LLMs) and multimodal architectures capable of producing text, images, and numerical representations from instructions expressed in natural language (Pallottino et al., 2025; Shahriar et al., 2025). This phase introduces a qualitative shift relative to the previous one, as it moves the focus from pattern recognition to the autonomous generation of content, transforming agronomic representation into an output produced by the model rather than a mere inference derived from data. The discontinuity lies not only in increased computational power, but in the extension of the linguistic and semantic capabilities of digital systems. Generative AI systems can now synthesize heterogeneous bodies of knowledge, formulate technical explanations, translate complex concepts into natural language, and integrate visual, geospatial, and numerical information within a single computational framework (Huang et al., 2024; Li et al., 2025).

These emerging capabilities are reflected in the ways generative systems are progressively integrated into agricultural digital infrastructures. The convergence of generative models and digital twins enables the construction of dynamic representations of cropping processes and the simulation of conditions that are difficult to observe directly, producing counterfactual scenarios that are valuable for training, planning, and ex ante evaluation (Liu et al., 2023). In parallel, the generation of synthetic imagery is gaining prominence as a means of strengthening computer vision systems, particularly where real-world datasets are incomplete or imbalanced. Conditional generative networks, diffusion models, generative adversarial networks (GANs), and Vision Transformers are increasingly employed to expand the range of observable situations and to improve classification reliability by simulating phenological development or the spread of pathogens and weeds (Deepak et al., 2025; Majumder et al., 2024). Taken together, these developments illustrate how generative AI is beginning—albeit in still-evolving ways—to reorganize the relationship between direct observation, modeling, and visual representation.

Alongside simulation-oriented applications, another area of experimentation concerns conversational systems based on LLMs. Tools such as *Farmer.CHAT* or *Jugalbandi* deploy LLMs trained on context-specific agronomic knowledge to deliver personalized recommendations in local languages through messaging-based interfaces (Sai et al., 2025). When supported by appropriate mechanisms of supervision and verification, such applications can help reduce informational, linguistic, and geographic barriers, particularly in rural contexts characterized by low levels of digital literacy. At the same time, their adoption raises important questions regarding the quality of recommendations, the risk of excessive simplification, and potential forms of interpretive dependence—issues that become especially salient when algorithmic representations partially replace local forms of agronomic knowledge (Sai et al., 2025).

These technical and applicative dynamics are accompanied by deeper transformations in the production of agricultural knowledge. The ability to generate text, images, and simulations endows generative models with a representational and interpretive function that extends beyond decision support, introducing new forms of mediation among actors, data, and the environment (Bommasani et al., 2021).

To interpret the evolution of the fourth wave, Krupitzer (2024) identifies three key dimensions that define its degree of maturity: integration, explainability, and trust. Integration refers to the ability of generative models to operate coherently within agricultural digital infrastructures, combining data, simulations, and decision-making processes. Explainability highlights the need to preserve traceability and human oversight over inferential chains, ensuring that linguistic automation does not undermine the operational intelligibility of recommendations. Trust, finally, depends on institutional and organizational conditions such as interoperability, cybersecurity, and the availability of appropriate professional skills—factors that are widely corroborated by the analyses presented in the CAST report (2025).

From an economic perspective, according to McKinsey & Company (2024), the systemic adoption of generative AI could generate up to USD 100 billion in direct "on-the-acre" value and an additional USD 150 billion across the agri-food value chain, provided that models are embedded within decision-making and organizational structures capable of translating generated representations into coherent action. In the absence of such structures, generative AI risks producing fragmented solutions or amplifying informational and decision-making asymmetries, particularly in more vulnerable agricultural contexts.

Overall, the fourth wave does not merely expand computational capacities, but intervenes in the symbolic and cognitive dimensions of agricultural production, reshaping the relationship between language, representation, and decision-making. Taken together, the four waves outline a trajectory that extends from physical mechanization to the algorithmic production of knowledge. Table 1.1 synthesizes these trajectories, providing a schematic overview of the four waves of agricultural innovation.

1.3 Terminology and Operational Definitions

The evolution of digital technologies applied to agriculture has produced a complex and constantly evolving lexicon, in which closely related terms are often used in overlapping ways. Establishing a shared operational vocabulary is therefore a necessary prerequisite for ensuring conceptual coherence throughout the volume. A foundational distinction concerns the concepts of *digitalization* and *digital transformation*. The former refers to the conversion of analog content, processes, or tools into digital formats, whereas the latter denotes a systemic form of change that integrates technologies, data, and innovation into organizational, institutional, and productive processes. As noted by the FAO, digital transformation in agriculture requires enabling digital infrastructures, coherent policy frameworks, e-government

Table 1.1 Four waves of agricultural innovation: technologies, functions, and constraints

Wave	Period	Dominant technologies	Core function	Key constraint addressed	Main ambivalences
Mechanization	Nineteenth–mid-twentieth century	Agricultural machinery; energy and chemical inputs	Expansion of operational capacity	Labor scarcity; productivity limits	Farm concentration; labor displacement; environmental pressures
Precision agriculture	1980s–present	GNSS; sensors; GIS; digital platforms	Site-specific management	Agronomic variability; environmental constraints	Uneven adoption; digital dependency
Non-generative AI	2000s–present	Machine learning; computer vision; predictive models	Cognitive automation	Data complexity; need for optimization	Opacity; skill gaps; informational asymmetries
Generative AI	2020–present	Large language models; multimodal systems	Knowledge generation and mediation	Access to expertise; decision complexity	Epistemic power shifts; reliability risks

systems, and an interoperable ecosystem of services capable of supporting large-scale innovation dynamics (FAO, 2019a; FAO, 2023).

Within the domain of AI, the ISO/IEC 22989:2022 standard provides a shared definitional framework. It describes an *AI system* as "an engineered system that generates outputs such as content, forecasts, recommendations or decisions for a given set of human-defined objectives," while an *AI agent* is defined as "an automated entity that senses and responds to its environment and takes actions to achieve its goals." The same standard characterizes *artificial intelligence* as the "research and development of mechanisms and applications of AI systems."

Within this framework, *machine learning* techniques are systematized by International Organization for Standardization (ISO) and defined as "a type of artificial intelligence in the field of computer science that often uses statistical techniques to give computers the ability to 'learn' with data, without being explicitly programmed" (ISO, 2025b). *Deep learning*, as an advanced component of these techniques, is described as "a subset of machine learning and artificial intelligence: a technique of training computers to mimic the way neurons in the human brain process and learn information" (ISO, 2025a). Among the architectures of particular relevance are *GANs*, defined by ISO/IEC TR 24372:2021 as "a neural network architecture comprised of one or more generators and one or more discriminators that compete to improve model performance." Within such models, the *generator* is "a neural network that produces samples usually to be classified by a discriminator," while the *discriminator* is "a neural network that classifies samples usually produced by a generator."

In parallel, the Organisation for Economic Co-operation and Development (OECD) defines *generative AI* as "a category of AI that can create new content such as text, images, videos, and music" (OECD, 2024). Within this domain, *LLMs* constitute a central class of tools and are described by the European Commission's Knowledge Centre as "a type of artificial intelligence model trained through deep learning algorithms to recognize, generate, translate, and/or summarize vast quantities of written human language and textual data" (Knowledge Centre, 2023).

The increasing architectural complexity of AI systems has also intensified attention toward *XAI*, defined by the European Data Protection Supervisor as the "ability of AI systems to provide clear and understandable explanations for their actions and decisions" (EDPS, 2023).

Enabling Technologies and Digital Agricultural Paradigms

Recent developments in agricultural practices have reinforced the role of precision agriculture. As defined in Sect. 1.2.2, precision agriculture is understood here as a data-driven management strategy that supports differentiated decision-making through the systematic collection, processing, and analysis of spatially and temporally explicit information (ISPA, 2024).

Within this framework, particular importance is assumed by technologies for data collection, management, and analysis. Among these, GNSS are described by NASA as "a space geodesy technique that provides autonomous geospatial positioning with global coverage" (NASA, 2025a), while environmental sensors contribute to the real-time measurement of key agronomic parameters—such as moisture, temperature, and soil properties—thereby providing a decision-making basis for differentiated management practices (FAO, 2019b). GIS perform a fundamental analytical function and are defined by NASA as "a computer system that analyzes and displays geographically referenced information from a variety of data sources to map and examine changes on Earth" (NASA, 2025b). These tools are complemented by prescription software capable of processing large volumes of agronomic data to generate operational maps and management recommendations based on variability (FAO, 2023), as well as by computer vision techniques that support object recognition, image classification, and automated crop monitoring (FAO, 2021).

The progressive consolidation of these technologies has fostered the emergence of the broader paradigm of *digital agriculture*, which encompasses data interoperability, cloud platforms, digital services for farmers, distributed forms of AI, and new modes of algorithmic governance across the agri-food value chain (FAO, 2019a; FAO, 2021; FAO, 2023). Within this context, *multimodal architecture* also plays a key role and is identified by the FAO as a model capable of integrating heterogeneous data—such as images, signals, textual information, and geospatial data—to support complex analyses and decision-making processes (FAO, 2023). Another cross-cutting concept is that of the *digital twin*, defined by the UK government as "a virtual model of an object, a system, or a process, connected to its real-world counterpart by a 2-way flow of right-time data, meaning it mimics it in all aspects" (GOV.UK, 2024). Finally, *digital platforms*, understood by the OECD as core infrastructures of the data-driven economy, shape market access, modes of work organization, and value distribution through mechanisms of algorithmic intermediation (OECD, 2020).

In conclusion, the operational glossary presented in Box 1.2 summarizes the key definitions adopted throughout the chapter, providing a terminological reference that is consistent with the objectives of the volume.

Box 1.2 Operational Glossary of Key Terms

Artificial Intelligence (AI): "research and development of mechanisms and applications of AI systems." (ISO/IEC 22989:2022);
AI System: "an engineered system that generates outputs such as content, forecasts, recommendations or decisions for a given set of human-defined objectives." (ISO/IEC 22989:2022);
AI Agent: "an automated entity that senses and responds to its environment and takes actions to achieve its goals." (ISO/IEC 22989:2022);
Machine Learning (ML): "a type of artificial intelligence in the field of computer science that often uses statistical techniques to give computers the ability to 'learn' with data, without being explicitly programmed." (ISO, 2025);

Deep Learning (DL): "a subset of machine learning and artificial intelligence: a technique of training computers to mimic the way neurons in the human brain process and learn information." (ISO, 2025);
Generative Adversarial Network (GAN): "a neural network architecture comprised of one or more generators and one or more discriminators that compete to improve model performance." (ISO/IEC TR 24372:2021);

> Generator: "a neural network that produces samples usually to be classified by a discriminator.";
> Discriminator: "a neural network that classifies samples usually produced by a generator." (ISO/IEC TR 24372:2021).

Generative AI (GenAI): "a category of AI that can create new content such as text, images, videos, and music." (OECD, 2024);
Large Language Model (LLM): "a type of artificial intelligence model trained through deep learning algorithms to recognize, generate, translate, and/or summarize vast quantities of written human language and textual data." (Knowledge Centre on Translation and Interpretation, 2023);
Explainable Artificial Intelligence (XAI): "the ability of AI systems to provide clear and understandable explanations for their actions and decisions." (EDPS, 2023);

> Transparency: "the ability for a specific model to be understood";
> Interpretability: "the degree of human comprehensibility of a given 'black box' model or decision."
> Explainability: "providing clear and coherent explanations for specific model predictions or decisions." (EDPS, 2023);

Cyber-Physical System (CPS): "engineered systems that are built from, and depend upon, the seamless integration of computation and physical components" (NSF, 2024);
Multimodal Architectures: AI models that combine heterogeneous data—such as images, signals, text, and geospatial data—to support complex analyses (FAO, 2023);
Digital Twin: "a virtual model of an object, a system, or a process, connected to its real-world counterpart by a 2-way flow of right-time data, meaning it mimics it in all aspects" (GOV.UK, 2024);
GNSS (Global Navigation Satellite Systems): "a space geodesy technique that provides autonomous geospatial positioning with global coverage" (NASA, 2025a);
Environmental Sensors: Devices that measure parameters such as moisture, temperature, light, or soil conditions in real time (FAO, 2019b);
GIS (Geographic Information System): "a computer system that analyzes and displays geographically referenced information from a variety of data sources to map and examine changes on Earth" (NASA, 2025b);

Prescription Software: Tools that generate operational maps and agronomic recommendations based on variability (FAO, 2023);
Computer Vision: AI techniques for the automated analysis of images or video (FAO, Computer Vision 2021);
Digital Platform: A digital infrastructure that connects users, services, and data, enabling forms of algorithmic intermediation (OECD, 2020).

1.4 Artificial Intelligence in Agriculture: Impacts, Conditions of Effectiveness, and Emerging Challenges

Building on the conceptual framework outlined in the previous sections, AI has become a central driver of the digital transformation of agricultural systems. The growing integration of inferential and generative applications into agricultural infrastructures affects not only how information is processed, but also how decisions are formulated, implemented, and governed. These impacts extend to productivity, resource management, access to technologies, and the distribution of decision-making authority, while remaining highly contingent on enabling conditions and governance arrangements.

Against this background, the section examines four interconnected domains: impacts on productivity and sustainability; digital inequalities and enabling conditions; issues of algorithmic governance; and the ambivalences introduced by generative AI. These dimensions are not treated exhaustively but provide an interpretative backdrop for the applied and adoption-focused analyses developed in the chapters that follow.

1.4.1 Agricultural Productivity and Resource Sustainability

The literature indicates that the use of machine learning, deep learning, and computer vision techniques is associated with improvements in yield estimation, early disease detection, input modulation, and the automation of crop operations, both in high-tech farming contexts and in small-scale systems (EPRS, 2023; Kamilaris and Prenafeta-Boldú, 2018; Liakos et al., 2018; Songol et al., 2021). Targeted applications in irrigation management, fertilization, and livestock farming further suggest a potential contribution to the more rational use of water, fertilizers, and plant protection products, generating combined economic and environmental benefits (FAO, 2021; Getahun et al., 2024; Padhiary et al., 2025).

At the same time, recent analyses highlight the ambivalent nature of these developments. Models oriented toward yield maximization or the optimization of narrowly defined sets of variables may overlook relevant ecological interdependencies, producing unintended effects on biodiversity, nutrient cycles, and soil quality, and reproducing—in algorithmic form—pressures already observed during earlier phases of agricultural intensification (Omotayo et al., 2025; Tzachor et al., 2022). As a result, the sustainability of agricultural AI cannot be inferred automatically from its technical performance alone, but depends on design choices, institutional arrangements, and regulatory frameworks, which are examined in greater depth in the chapters that follow. The following chapters examine these conditions across three analytical layers: the techno-infrastructural prerequisites that enable reliable AI deployment (Chaps. 2 and 3); the organizational and labor reconfigurations through which environmental and economic effects are mediated (Chaps. 4 and 5); and the governance frameworks—encompassing data rights, accountability, interoperability, and risk management—necessary to align agricultural AI with long-term sustainability objectives (Chap. 6).

1.4.2 Digital Inequalities and Enabling Conditions

The adoption of AI reflects—and in some cases amplifies—existing differences in infrastructural endowments, access to information, and human capital across regions, farm types, and production systems (Omotayo et al., 2025; Rijswijk et al., 2021). Limitations in connectivity, energy access, and the availability of digital devices constrain, in many low–and middle-income countries, the very possibility of deploying machine learning–based applications or advanced decision-support systems (Ahmad et al., 2024). These constraints are compounded by challenges related to data quality, availability, and standardization, which affect the capacity to train reliable models and to adapt them to specific agro-ecological conditions (FAO, 2019a; FAO, 2021).

Digital skills and cultural conditions constitute additional determinants. The perceived ability to master digital technologies often proves more influential than a generally favorable attitude in shaping adoption intentions (Mohr and Kühl, 2021). At the same time, design approaches primarily oriented toward dominant languages and contexts tend to exclude users operating in local languages or under conditions of low digital literacy (FAO, 2021). These adoption constraints are examined in greater depth in the chapters that follow, which analyze the infrastructural and technological conditions enabling AI deployment (Chaps. 2 and 3) and the organizational, skill-related, and labor mediations through which digital technologies are integrated into agricultural systems (Chaps. 4 and 5).

1.4.3 Algorithmic Governance, Ethics, and Decision-Making Power

The integration of AI in agriculture takes place within a context characterized by significant informational asymmetries between end users and the actors who design and manage digital infrastructures, algorithms, and platforms (EPRS, 2023; Rotz et al., 2019a; Ryan, 2020). The combination of opaque models, restrictive contractual arrangements, and concentrated control over data raises critical questions concerning data ownership, access, and reuse, as well as the actual capacity to challenge inappropriate or misleading algorithmic recommendations (EPRS, 2023; FAO, 2021).

From an ethical perspective, recent contributions emphasize the need to address more systematically issues such as transparency, bias, accountability, and contestability, which remain relatively marginal in analyses of agricultural AI compared to the prominence given to agronomic and economic dimensions (Ryan, 2022). Approaches including XAI, open-source models, and participatory design practices are increasingly discussed as potential means to make innovation more equitable and subject to human control (Carolan, 2017; Doshi-Velez and Kim, 2017; Rotz et al., 2019a), although their practical implementation remains an ongoing challenge. These issues are revisited in the chapters that follow, which first examine the socio-technical implications of algorithmic mediation (Chaps. 4 and 5) and then address, in a dedicated section, the governance of agricultural AI, including data rights, accountability, transparency, and systemic risk management (Chap. 6).

1.4.4 Generative AI: Opportunities and Ambivalences

Generative AI introduces a substantial extension of the analytical and communicative capabilities of intelligent systems, enabling the automated production of linguistic, visual, and simulative content from instructions expressed in natural language (Krupitzer, 2024; Shahriar et al., 2025). LLMs are being experimentally applied in digital extension activities, technical writing, and the translation of specialized knowledge into more accessible forms, including through tools that integrate curated corpora of agronomic documents (CAST, 2025; Samuel et al., 2025; Yang et al., 2025).

At the same time, the literature highlights emerging risks associated with the "opaque plausibility" of generated outputs, the difficulty of verifying content produced with high levels of expressive confidence, and increasing dependence on digital infrastructures and computational capacities concentrated in a limited number of actors (Aijaz et al., 2025; Niszczota and Rybicka, 2023; Tzachor et al., 2022). These ambivalences suggest that the use of generative AI in agriculture requires strengthened forms of validation, oversight, and local adaptation, as well as governance strategies aimed at ensuring transparency, security, and contestability

(Alexander et al., 2024; Chen, 2025; Girmay et al., 2025; Reitano et al., 2025). These issues are examined in greater depth in Chap. 6, which focuses on the governance of generative AI in agri-food systems, with particular attention to risks related to opaque decision-making, infrastructural concentration, and the institutional mechanisms required to ensure transparency, oversight, and long-term sustainability.

1.5 Conclusions and Roadmap of the Volume

The digital transformation of agriculture, as outlined in this chapter, cannot be reduced to a purely technological phenomenon. Rather, it constitutes a systemic restructuring that affects modes of production, forms of agronomic knowledge, organizational relationships, and the cognitive infrastructures underpinning agricultural activity. The proposed periodization—articulated around four waves, from mechanization to generative AI—has enabled this evolution to be situated historically, showing how each phase has profoundly reshaped the relationship between technology, labor, and the environment.

Alongside this historical perspective, terminological clarification has proven essential, highlighting the performative nature of technical language and the importance of a precise taxonomy for understanding and steering ongoing processes. The analysis of documented impacts has brought to the fore three critical axes of transformation—productivity, sustainability, and data governance—revealing both the opportunities and the structural tensions generated by the adoption of digital technologies. In particular, challenges related to connectivity, cognitive inequalities, algorithmic transparency, and environmental contradictions call for an integrated interpretative approach.

Building on this framework, the volume is structured into five chapters that address, in thematically distinct yet theoretically coherent ways, the key issues introduced in this opening chapter. Chapter 2 examines the main application domains of AI in agriculture, reconstructing the current technological state of the art and discussing adoption inequalities across geographic, infrastructural, and institutional contexts. Chapter 3 focuses on the factors shaping technology adoption, comparing small–and large-scale farms and analyzing the systemic risks associated with cognitive automation. Chapter 4 addresses impacts on agricultural labor, documenting task reconfiguration, emerging inequalities, and policy measures for an inclusive employment transition. Chapter 5 is devoted to digital skills and training, proposing a multilevel framework and illustrating effective educational tools and practices, with particular attention to persistent barriers. Finally, Chap. 6 integrates the preceding analyses into a structured foresight exercise grounded in principles of equity, sustainability, and transparency, presenting three development scenarios up to 2045 alongside a strategic roadmap.

Taken together, the chapters that follow do not seek to offer a single prescriptive model for the adoption of AI in agriculture. Instead, they provide interpretative tools and practical orientations to support a digital transition that is genuinely inclusive, contextually grounded, and socially legitimate.

References

Adamchuk, V. I., Hummel, J. W., Morgan, M. T., & Upadhyaya, S. K. (2004). On-the-go soil sensors for precision agriculture. *Computers and Electronics in Agriculture, 44*(1), 71–91. https://doi.org/10.1016/j.compag.2004.03.002

Ahmad, A., Liew, A. X. W., Venturini, F., Kalogeras, A., Candiani, A., Di Benedetto, G., & Martos, V. (2024). AI can empower agriculture for global food security: Challenges and prospects in developing nations. *Frontiers in Artificial Intelligence, 7*, 1328530. https://doi.org/10.3389/frai.2024.1328530

Aijaz, N., Lan, H., Raza, T., Yaqub, M., Iqbal, R., & Pathan, M. S. (2025). Artificial intelligence in agriculture: Advancing crop productivity and sustainability. *Journal of Agriculture and Food Research, 20*, 101762. https://doi.org/10.1016/j.jafr.2025.101762

Alexander, C. S., Yarborough, M., & Smith, A. (2024). Who is responsible for 'responsible AI'?: Navigating challenges to build trust in AI agriculture and food system technology. *Precision Agriculture, 25*(1), 146–185. https://doi.org/10.1007/s11119-023-10063-3

Ali, S., Abuhmed, T., El-Sappagh, S., Muhammad, K., Alonso-Moral, J. M., Confalonieri, R., & Herrera, F. (2023). Explainable artificial intelligence (XAI): What we know and what is left to attain trustworthy artificial intelligence. *An International Journal on Information Fusion, 99*(101805), 101805. https://doi.org/10.1016/j.inffus.2023.101805

Auernhammer, H. (2001). Precision farming—The environmental challenge. *Computers and Electronics in Agriculture, 30*(1–3), 31–43. https://doi.org/10.1016/s0168-1699(00)00153-8

Ben Ayed, R., & Hanana, M. (2021). Artificial intelligence to improve the food and agriculture sector. *Journal of Food Quality, 2021*, 1–7. https://doi.org/10.1155/2021/5584754

Benos, L., Tagarakis, A. C., Dolias, G., Berruto, R., Kateris, D., & Bochtis, D. (2021). Machine learning in agriculture: A comprehensive updated review. *Sensors (Basel, Switzerland), 21*(11), 3758. https://doi.org/10.3390/s21113758

Binswanger, H. P. (1978). *The economics of tractors in South Asia*. International Crops Research Institute for the Semi-Arid Tropics.

Binswanger, H. P. (1986). Agricultural mechanization: A comparative historical perspective. *The World Bank Research Observer, 1*(1), 27–56.

Bommasani, R., Hudson, D. A., Adeli, E., Altman, R., Arora, S., von Arx, S., & Liang, P. (2021). On the opportunities and risks of foundation models. Preprint Retrieved from http://arxiv.org/abs/2108.07258.

Bongiovanni, R., & Lowenberg-Deboer, J. (2004). Precision agriculture and sustainability. *Precision Agriculture, 5*(4), 359–387. https://doi.org/10.1023/b:prag.0000040806.39604.aa

Boserup, E. (1965). *The conditions of agricultural growth: The economics of agrarian change under population pressure*. George Allen & Unwin.

Bronson, K., & Knezevic, I. (2016). Big data in food and agriculture. *Big Data & Society, 3*(1), 1–5. https://doi.org/10.1177/2053951716648174

Burrell, J. (2016). How the machine "thinks": Understanding opacity in machine learning algorithms. *Big Data & Society, 3*(1), 1–12. https://doi.org/10.1177/2053951715622512

Carolan, M. (2017). Publicising food: Big data, precision agriculture, and co-experimental techniques of addition. *Sociologia Ruralis, 57*(2), 135–154. https://doi.org/10.1111/soru.12120

CAST (2025). AI in agriculture: Opportunities, challenges, and recommendations. Council for agricultural science and technology. Retrieved September 7, 2025, from https://www.cast-science.org/publication/ai-in-agriculture/

Chen, X. (2025). The role of modern agricultural technologies in improving agricultural productivity and land use efficiency. *Frontiers in Plant Science, 16*(1675657), 1675657. https://doi.org/10.3389/fpls.2025.1675657

Clarke, L. (2000). *Strategies for agricultural mechanization developmen. The role of the private sector and the governmentt*. AGST, FAO.

Deepak, L., Nisarga, H. D., Pradvith, K. J., Sinchana, A., & Jayanna, H. S. (2025). Leveraging generative AI for accurate crop disease detection. In *Proceedings of the 3rd International Conference on Smart Systems for Electrical Sciences (ICSSES)*. IEEE. https://doi.org/10.1109/ICSSES64899.2025.11009749

Diao, X., Silver, J., & Takeshima, H. (2016). Agricultural mechanization and agricultural transformation. Background paper for African transformation report. IFPRI/ACET/JICA-RI.

Doshi-Velez, F., & Kim, B. (2017). Towards a rigorous science of interpretable machine learning. Preprint Retrieved from https://doi.org/10.48550/arXiv.1702.08608.

Eastwood, C., Ayre, M., Nettle, R., & Dela Rue, B. (2019). Making sense in the cloud: Farm advisory services in a smart farming future. *NJAS: Wageningen Journal of Life Sciences, 90–91*(1), 1–10. https://doi.org/10.1016/j.njas.2019.04.004

EDPS. (2023). *TechDispatch on explainable artificial intelligence*. European Data Protection Supervisor EDPS.

Elbasi, E., Mostafa, N., AlArnaout, Z., Zreikat, A. I., Cina, E., Varghese, G., & Zaki, C. (2023). Artificial intelligence technology in the agricultural sector: A systematic literature review. *IEEE Access: Practical Innovations, Open Solutions, 11*, 171–202. https://doi.org/10.1109/access.2022.3232485

Elbasi, E., Mostafa, N., Zaki, C., AlArnaout, Z., Topcu, A. E., & Saker, L. (2024). Optimizing agricultural data analysis techniques through AI-powered decision-making processes. *Applied Sciences (Basel, Switzerland), 14*(17), 8018. https://doi.org/10.3390/app14178018

European Parliament. (2016). *Precision agriculture and the future of farming in Europe: Scientific foresight study*. European Parliamentary Research Service.

EPRS (2023). Artificial intelligence in the Agri-food sector: Applications, risks and impacts. European Parliamentary Research Service. PE 734.711.

FAO & AUC. (2018). *Sustainable agricultural mechanization: A framework for Africa*. FAO & AUC.

FAO. (2016). *Agricultural mechanization: A key input for sub-Saharan African smallholders. Integrated crop management series* (Vol. 23). FAO.

FAO. (2019a). *Digital agriculture transformation and digital innovation: Transforming ideas into value in a sustainable way for #ZeroHunger*. FAO IT Division.

FAO. (2019b). *Digital technologies in agriculture and rural areas: Briefing paper*. FAO.

FAO. (2021). *Digital agriculture in action: artificial intelligence for agriculture*. FAO and ITU.

FAO. (2023). Advancing the digital transformation of agriculture and rural areas through national strategies, e-government systems, and digital villages: Update for Europe and Central Asia. European Commission on Agriculture, Forty-third Session, Budapest, 27–28 September 2023. FAO.

Foley, J. A., Ramankutty, N., Brauman, K. A., Cassidy, E. S., Gerber, J. S., Johnston, M., & Zaks, D. P. M. (2011). Solutions for a cultivated planet. *Nature, 478*(7369), 337–342. https://doi.org/10.1038/nature10452

Gebbers, R., & Adamchuk, V. I. (2010). Precision agriculture and food security. *Science* (New York, N.Y.), 327(5967), 828–831. doi:https://doi.org/10.1126/science.1183899.

Getahun, S., Kefale, H., & Gelaye, Y. (2024). Application of precision agriculture technologies for sustainable crop production and environmental sustainability: A systematic review. *The ScientificWorldJournal, 2024*, 2126734. https://doi.org/10.1155/2024/2126734

Girmay, M. B., Droste, J., Deters, H., & Doerr, J. (2025). Explainability needs in agriculture: Exploring dairy farmers' user personas. Preprint Retrieved from https://doi.org/10.48550/arXiv.2509.16249.

GOV.UK (2024, January). What a digital twin is and how you can contribute, department for business & trade. Published 29 November 2023; Updated 12 January 2024. Retrieved June 20, 2025, from https://www.gov.uk/government/publications/what-a-digital-twin-is-and-how-you-can-contribute/what-a-digital-twin-is-and-how-you-can-contribute

Hassija, V., Chamola, V., Mahapatra, A., Singal, A., Goel, D., Huang, K., & Hussain, A. (2024). Interpreting black-box models: A review on explainable artificial intelligence. *Cognitive Computation, 16*(1), 45–74. https://doi.org/10.1007/s12559-023-10179-8

Hayami, Y., & Ruttan, V. W. (1970). Agricultural productivity differences among countries. *The American Economic Review, 60*(5), 895–911.

Huang, D., Yan, C., Li, Q., & Peng, X. (2024). From large language models to large multimodal models: A literature review. *Applied Sciences (Basel, Switzerland), 14*(12), 5068. https://doi.org/10.3390/app14125068

ISPA. (2024). *Precision agriculture definition.* International society of precision agriculture. https://www.ispag.org/resources/definition

ISO. (2022). *ISO 22989:2022 information technology—Artificial intelligence concepts and terminology.* International Organization for Standardization.

ISO. (2025a). *Deep learning: The mechanics of magic.* International Organization for Standardization. https://www.iso.org/artificial-intelligence/deep-learning

ISO. (2025b). *Machine learning (ML): All there is to know.* International Organization for Standardization. https://www.iso.org/artificial-intelligence/machine-learning

ISO/IEC. (2021). *TR 24372:2021. Information technology—Artificial intelligence (AI)—Overview of computational approaches for AI systems.* International Organization for Standardization.

Javaid, M., Haleem, A., Khan, I. H., & Suman, R. (2023). Understanding the potential applications of artificial intelligence in agriculture sector. *Advanced Agrochem, 2,* 15–30. https://doi.org/10.1016/j.aac.2022.10.001

Kamilaris, A., & Prenafeta-Boldú, F. X. (2018). Deep learning in agriculture: A survey. *Computers and Electronics in Agriculture, 147,* 70–90. https://doi.org/10.1016/j.compag.2018.02.016

Klerkx, L., Jakku, E., & Labarthe, P. (2019). A review of social science on digital agriculture, smart farming and agriculture 4.0: New contributions and a future research agenda. *NJAS–Wageningen Journal of Life Sciences, 90–91,* 100315. https://doi.org/10.1016/j.njas.2019.100315

Knowledge Centre. (2023). *What is a large language model?*Knowledge Centre. https://knowledge-centre-translation-interpretation.ec.europa.eu/en/news/what-large-language-model.

Krupitzer, C. (2024). Generative artificial intelligence in the Agri-food value chain—Overview, potential, and research challenges. *Frontiers in Food Science and Technology, 4,* 1473357. https://doi.org/10.3389/frfst.2024.1473357

Li, H., Wu, H., Li, Q., & Zhao, C. (2025). A review on enhancing agricultural intelligence with large language models. *Artificial Intelligence in Agriculture, 15*(4), 671–685. https://doi.org/10.1016/j.aiia.2025.05.006

Liakos, K. G., Busato, P., Moshou, D., Pearson, S., & Bochtis, D. (2018). Machine learning in agriculture: A review. *Sensors (Basel, Switzerland), 18*(8), 2674. https://doi.org/10.3390/s18082674

Linsley, C. M., & Bauer, F. C. (1929). *Test your soil for acidity.* Circular 346, University of Illinois Agricultural Experiment Station.

Liu, J., Zhou, Y., Li, Y., Li, Y., Hong, S., Li, Q., & Wang, X. (2023). Exploring the integration of digital twin and generative AI in agriculture. In *2023 15th international conference on intelligent human-machine systems and cybernetics (IHMSC) (pp. 223–228).* https://doi.org/10.1109/ihmsc58761.2023.00059

Majumder, S., Khandelwal, Y., & Sornalakshmi, K. (2024). Computer vision and generative ai for yield prediction in digital agriculture. In *Proceedings of the 2nd international conference on networking and communications (ICNWC).* IEEE. https://doi.org/10.1109/ICNWC60771.2024.10537337

Matson, P. A., Parton, W. J., Power, A. G., & Swift, M. J. (1997). Agricultural intensification and ecosystem properties. *Science* (New York, N.Y.), 277(5325), 504–509. doi:https://doi.org/10.1126/science.277.5325.504.

Mazoyer, M., & Roudart, L. (2006). *A history of world agriculture: From the neolithic age to the current crisis.* NYU Press.

McBratney, A., Whelan, B., Ancev, T., & Bouma, J. (2005). Future directions of precision agriculture. *Precision Agriculture, 6*(1), 7–23. https://doi.org/10.1007/s11119-005-0681-8

McFadden, J., Njuki, E., & Griffin, T. (2023). Precision agriculture in the digital era: Recent adoption on U.S. farms. (Economic Information Bulletin No. 248). U.S. Department of Agriculture, Economic Research Service.

McKinsey & Company. (2024, 10 June). From bytes to bushels: How gen AI can shape the future of agriculture. McKinsey &, 10 June 2024. Retrieved July 1, 2025, from https://www.mckinsey.com/industries/agriculture/our-insights/from-bytes-to-bushels-how-gen-ai-can-shape-the-future-of-agriculture

Michels, M., Fecke, W., Feil, J.-H., Musshoff, O., Pigisch, J., & Krone, S. (2020). Smartphone adoption and use in agriculture: Empirical evidence from Germany. *Precision Agriculture, 21*(2), 403–425. https://doi.org/10.1007/s11119-019-09675-5

Mohan, R. N. V. J., Rayanoothala, P. S., & Sree, R. P. (2024). Next-gen agriculture: Integrating AI and XAI for precision crop yield predictions. *Frontiers in Plant Science, 15*, 1451607. https://doi.org/10.3389/fpls.2024.1451607

Mohanty, S. P., Hughes, D. P., & Salathé, M. (2016). Using deep learning for image-based plant disease detection. *Frontiers in Plant Science, 7*, 1419. https://doi.org/10.3389/fpls.2016.01419

Mohr, S., & Kühl, R. (2021). Acceptance of artificial intelligence in German agriculture: An application of the technology acceptance model and the theory of planned behavior. *Precision Agriculture, 22*(6), 1816–1844. https://doi.org/10.1007/s11119-021-09814-x

Molnar, C. (2020). Interpretable machine learning. Retrieved August 30, 2025, from https://christophm.github.io/interpretable-ml-book/

NASA. (2025a). GNSS–global navigation satellite system. https://www.earthdata.nasa.gov/data/space-geodesy-techniques/gnss

NASA. (2025b). About GIS at NASA. https://www.earthdata.nasa.gov/learn/gis/about

National Research Council. (1998). *Precision agriculture in the 21st century: Geospatial and information technologies in crop management.* NRC National Academy of Sciences.

Niszczota, P., & Rybicka, I. (2023). The credibility of dietary advice formulated by ChatGPT: Robo-diets for people with food allergies. *Nutrition, 112*(112076). https://doi.org/10.1016/j.nut.2023.112076

NSF. (2024). NSF 24–581: Cyber-physical systems (CPS). Program Solicitation. Directorate for Computer and Information Science and Engineering. NSF. https://new.nsf.gov/funding/opportunities/cyber-physical-systems-cps.

OECD. (2020). Regulating platform work in the digital age. OECD Going Digital Toolkit Notes, No. 1. OECD Publishing. doi:https://doi.org/10.1787/181f8a7f-en.

OECD. (2024). Generative AI.. Organisation for Economic Co-operation and Development. https://www.oecd.org/en/topics/generative-ai.html

Oliveira, R. C. D., & de Souza Silva, R. D. D. S. (2023). Artificial intelligence in agriculture: Benefits, challenges, and trends. *Applied Sciences, 13*(13), 7405. https://doi.org/10.3390/app13137405

Omotayo, A. O., Adediran, S. A., Omotoso, A. B., Olagunju, K. O., & Omotayo, O. P. (2025). Artificial intelligence in agriculture: Ethics, impact possibilities, and pathways for policy. *Computers and Electronics in Agriculture, 239*(110927), 110927. https://doi.org/10.1016/j.compag.2025.110927

Padhiary, M., Kumar, A., & Sethi, L. N. (2025). Emerging technologies for smart and sustainable precision agriculture. *Discover. Robotics, 1*(1). https://doi.org/10.1007/s44430-025-00006-0

Pallottino, F., Violino, S., Figorilli, S., Pane, C., Aguzzi, J., Colle, G., & Ortenzi, L. (2025). Applications and perspectives of generative artificial intelligence in agriculture. *Computers*

and Electronics in Agriculture, 230(109919), 109919. https://doi.org/10.1016/j.compag.2025.109919
Pierce, F. J., & Nowak, P. (1999). Aspects of precision agriculture. In *Advances in agronomy. Advances in agronomy (pp. 1–85)*. https://doi.org/10.1016/s0065-2113(08)60513-1
Pingali, P. L. (2007). Agricultural mechanization: Adoption patterns and economic impact. In R. Evenson & P. Pingali (Eds.), *Handbook of agricultural economics* (Vol. 3, pp. 2779–2805). Elsevier. https://doi.org/10.1016/S1574-0072(06)03054-4
Pingali, P. L., Bigot, Y., & Binswanger, H. (1987). *Agricultural mechanization and the evolution of faring systems in sub-Saharan Africa*. The World Bank.
Pre Agri Project Consortium. (2022). Precision agriculture handbook for beginners. Project Code: 2020–1–EL01–KA202–078806. Erasmus + Programme, Strategic Partnerships for Vocational Education and Training.
Rasmussen, W. D. (1982). The mechanization of agriculture. *Scientific American, 247*(3), 76–89.
Reitano, M., Segovia, M. S., & Nayga, R. M., Jr. (2025). A systematic review on the impact of artificial intelligence in the Agri-food supply chain. *Food Policy, 137*(102983), 102983. https://doi.org/10.1016/j.foodpol.2025.102983
Rijswijk, K., Klerkx, L., Bacco, M., Bartolini, F., Bulten, E., Debruyne, L., & Brunori, G. (2021). Digital transformation of agriculture and rural areas: A socio-cyber-physical system framework to support responsibilisation. *Journal of Rural Studies, 85*, 79–90. https://doi.org/10.1016/j.jrurstud.2021.05.003
Rotz, S., Duncan, E., Small, M., Botschner, J., Dara, R., Mosby, I., & Fraser, E. D. G. (2019a). The politics of digital agricultural technologies: A preliminary review. *Sociologia Ruralis, 59*(2), 203–229. https://doi.org/10.1111/soru.12233
Rotz, S., Gravely, E., Mosby, I., Duncan, E., Finnis, E., Horgan, M., & Fraser, E. (2019b). Automated pastures and the digital divide: How agricultural technologies are shaping labour and rural communities. *Journal of Rural Studies, 68*, 112–122. https://doi.org/10.1016/j.jrurstud.2019.01.023
Ruiz-Real, J. L., Uribe-Toril, J., Torres Arriaza, J. A., & de Pablo Valenciano, J. (2020). A look at the past, present and future research trends of artificial intelligence in agriculture. *Agronomy (Basel, Switzerland), 10*(11), 1839. https://doi.org/10.3390/agronomy10111839
Ruttan, V. W. (1977). Induced innovation and agricultural development. *Food Policy, 2*(3), 196–216.
Ruttan, V. W. (2000). *Technology, growth, and development: An induced innovation perspective*. OUP Catalogue.
Ruttan, V. W. (2002). Productivity growth in world agriculture: Sources and constraints. *Journal of Economic Perspectives, 16*(4), 161–184.
Ryan, M. (2020). Agricultural big data analytics and the ethics of power. *Journal of Agricultural & Environmental Ethics, 33*(1), 49–69. https://doi.org/10.1007/s10806-019-09812-0
Ryan, M. (2022). The social and ethical impacts of artificial intelligence in agriculture: Mapping the agricultural AI literature. *AI & SOCIETY, 38*, 2473–2485. https://doi.org/10.1007/s00146-021-01377-9
Ryan, M., Isakhanyan, G., & Tekinerdogan, B. (2023). An interdisciplinary approach to artificial intelligence in agriculture. *NJAS: Impact in Agricultural and Life Sciences, 95*(1). https://doi.org/10.1080/27685241.2023.2168568
Ryo, M. (2022). Explainable artificial intelligence and interpretable machine learning for agricultural data analysis. *Artificial Intelligence in Agriculture, 6*, 257–265. https://doi.org/10.1016/j.aiia.2022.11.003
Sai, S., Kumar, S., Gaur, A., Goyal, S., Chamola, V., & Hussain, A. (2025). Unleashing the power of generative AI in agriculture 4.0 for smart and sustainable farming. *Cognitive Computation, 17*(1). https://doi.org/10.1007/s12559-025-10420-6
Samuel, D. J., Skarga-Bandurova, I., Sikolia, D., & Awais, M. (2025). AgroLLM: Connecting farmers and agricultural practices through large language models for enhanced knowledge transfer and practical application. Preprint Retrieved from 10.48550/ARXIV.2503.04788.

Sauvagerd, M., Mayer, M., & Hartmann, M. (2024). Digital platforms in the agricultural sector: Dynamics of oligopolistic platformisation. *Big Data & Society, 11*(4). https://doi.org/10.1177/20539517241306365

Shahriar, S., Corradini, M. G., Sharif, S., Moussa, M., & Dara, R. (2025). The role of generative artificial intelligence in digital Agri-food. *Journal of Agriculture and Food Research, 20*(101787), 101787. https://doi.org/10.1016/j.jafr.2025.101787

Songol, M., Awuor, F., & Maake, B. (2021). Adoption of artificial intelligence in agriculture in the developing nations: A review. *Journal of Language, Technology & Entrepreneurship in Africa, 12*(2), 208–229. https://doi.org/10.4314/jolte.v12i2

Tilman, D., Cassman, K. G., Matson, P. A., Naylor, R., & Polasky, S. (2002). Agricultural sustainability and intensive production practices. *Nature, 418*(6898), 671–677. https://doi.org/10.1038/nature01014

Tsakiridis, N. L., Diamantopoulos, T., Symeonidis, A. L., Theocharis, J. B., Iossifides, A., Chatzimisios, P., & Kouvas, D. (2020). Versatile internet of things for agriculture: An explainable AI approach. *IFIP Advances in Information and Communication Technology*, 180–191. https://doi.org/10.1007/978-3-030-49186-4_16

Tzachor, A., Devare, M., King, B., Avin, S., & Ó hÉigeartaigh, S. (2022). Responsible artificial intelligence in agriculture requires systemic understanding of risks and externalities. *Nature Machine Intelligence, 4*(2), 104–109. https://doi.org/10.1038/s42256-022-00440-4

UNDP. (2021). *Precision agriculture for smallholder farmers.* United Nations Development Programme.

van der Burg, S., Kloppenburg, S., Kok, E. J., & van der Voort, M. (2021). Digital twins in Agri-food: Societal and ethical themes and questions for further research. *NJAS: Impact in Agricultural and Life Sciences, 93*(1), 98–125. https://doi.org/10.1080/27685241.2021.1989269

Van Es, H., & Woodard, J. (2017). Innovation in agriculture and food systems in the digital age. *The Global Innovation Index, 99.*

Wolfert, S., Ge, L., Verdouw, C., & Bogaardt, M.-J. (2017). Big data in smart farming–a review. *Agricultural Systems, 153*, 69–80. https://doi.org/10.1016/j.agsy.2017.01.023

Wu, P., & Zhong, Y. (2025). Artificial intelligence in sustainable agriculture: Towards a socio-technical roadmap. *Smart Agricultural Technology, 12*(101578), 101578. https://doi.org/10.1016/j.atech.2025.101578

Yang, B., Zhang, Y., Feng, L., Chen, Y., Zhang, J., Xu, X., & Li, S. (2025). AgriGPT: A large language model ecosystem for agriculture. Preprint Retrieved from https://doi.org/10.48550/arXiv.2508.08632.

Zha, J. (2020). Artificial intelligence in agriculture. *Journal of Physics. Conference Series, 1693*(1), 012058. https://doi.org/10.1088/1742-6596/1693/1/012058

Zhang, N., Wang, M., & Wang, N. (2002). Precision agriculture—A worldwide overview. *Computers and Electronics in Agriculture, 36*(2–3), 113–132. https://doi.org/10.1016/S0168-1699(02)00096-0

Chapter 2
Functional Configurations of AI in Agriculture

Abstract This chapter examines the current state of artificial intelligence (AI) in agriculture through a functional classification of applications based on the M–D–P–A model: monitoring, diagnosis, prediction, and automation. Drawing on a systematic review of the scientific and technical literature published between 2015 and 2025, the chapter shows how AI has become embedded—albeit with differing levels of maturity—in the processes of perception, interpretation, and actuation that structure digital agri-food systems. It analyzes the enabling technologies underpinning these developments—including IoT ecosystems, cloud–edge architectures, specialized sensing technologies, analytical platforms, and robotic solutions—highlighting the critical role of interoperability, data quality, and service-based models (AI-as-a-Service) in shaping scalability. In the final part, the focus shifts to territorial and institutional inequalities in adoption, emphasizing the coexistence of highly integrated M–D–P–A configurations in agro-industrial systems and more selective or experimental implementations in contexts with intermediate or low levels of digital infrastructure, particularly in the Global South. The chapter thus frames agricultural AI as a set of differentiated computational ecosystems that constitute the context within which adoption processes, transformations of work, and emerging skill requirements—addressed in subsequent chapters—take place.

Keywords Functional configurations · M–D–P–A model · Agricultural AI technologies

2.1 Introduction

Artificial Intelligence (AI) is assuming an increasingly significant role in the digital transformation of agriculture, contributing—though with varying intensity across contexts—to the reorganization of the ways in which firms and institutions produce, exchange, and use agronomic information. The expansion of sensor technologies, the integration of Internet of Things (IoT) networks and continuous data acquisition platforms, and the diffusion of advanced analytical systems have expanded the capacity to

A. Apicella, *Artificial Intelligence in Agriculture*,
https://doi.org/10.1007/978-3-032-26580-7_2

observe crop, environmental, and livestock-related phenomena, fostering the development of more structured forms of decision support and automation (Akhter & Sofi, 2022; De Baerdemaeker, 2023; Rajak et al., 2023). In parallel, multi-actor initiatives combining AI, IoT, remote sensing, blockchain, and robotics point to the emergence of innovative configurations along agri-food value chains, which are supported unevenly by cloud–edge infrastructures and by policies aimed at the creation of interoperable data spaces (Elbehri & Chestnov, 2021; Rauch et al., 2025; World Economic Forum, 2025).

The literature depicts a broad and fragmented application landscape in which heterogeneous techniques—ranging from computer vision to predictive models and autonomous robotics—are deployed across the entire crop cycle (Wakchaure et al., 2023). To interpret this heterogeneity, the chapter adopts a functional classification that organizes AI applications into four main groups: monitoring, diagnosis, prediction, and automation (the M–D–P–A model). This model does not derive from a pre-existing disciplinary taxonomy; rather, it was developed through a systematic review of the scientific and technical literature produced between 2015 and 2025, a period marked by the emergence of models based on advanced algorithms, distributed sensor networks, and robotic solutions for agricultural applications. The selection of contributions combined three main criteria:

- functional relevance, including studies that explicitly describe the cognitive or operational tasks performed by AI systems;
- disciplinary diversity, through the consultation of publications in digital agronomy, systems engineering, applied computer science, agricultural economics, and data science;
- empirical or implementation-based validation, prioritizing applications tested in field conditions, on farms, or in pilot environments, complemented by technical reports and white papers from international initiatives.

The four functions do not represent sequential or independent stages, but rather elements of a possible cognitive pipeline, whose concrete configuration varies according to information infrastructures, agro-ecological conditions, and organizational capacities (De Baerdemaeker, 2023; Elbehri & Chestnov, 2021). In contexts characterized by mature digital ecosystems, these components tend to be integrated into more complex technical systems; elsewhere, they remain isolated, reflecting differences in technological endowments, professional skills, and levels of connectivity (Rauch et al., 2025; Wolfert et al., 2017).

In light of these considerations, the chapter aims to describe the main application functions of agricultural AI according to the M–D–P–A model (Sect. 2.2), to analyze the enabling technologies and computational architectures underpinning these applications (Sect. 2.3), and to examine the geography of adoption as well as the socio-economic and institutional implications associated with the diffusion of AI in agricultural systems (Sect. 2.4).

2.2 Application Functions of AI: The M–D–P–A Model

Applications of AI in agricultural systems can be analytically organized around four core functions that describe how information is handled within decision-making processes: monitoring, diagnosis, prediction, and automation. Adopted here as the M–D–P–A model, this framework is grounded in an operational distinction between types of data processing and modes of algorithmic intervention, rather than in crop stages or production phases (De Baerdemaeker, 2023; Elbehri & Chestnov, 2021).

Each function captures a specific role played by AI systems. Monitoring refers to the observational acquisition of data; diagnosis involves the classification of states or anomalies; prediction extends available information over time through inferential models; and automation translates assessments or predictions into executable actions. Considered jointly, these functions provide a common analytical lens through which applications with different objectives and contexts of use can be compared.

Sections 2.2.1, 2.2.2, 2.2.3 and 2.2.4 examine each function with reference to the type of processing required, the outputs generated, and the main constraints shaping their operational performance.

2.2.1 Monitoring

Monitoring represents one of the functions through which AI can contribute to the development of a digitally extended agriculture, expanding the capacity to observe and interpret agricultural systems (Elbasi et al., 2023; Misra et al., 2022; Sharma et al., 2023). Proximal, mobile, and remote sensing technologies generate heterogeneous information flows that, when appropriately processed, can be translated into representations that are meaningful for management purposes. In this sense, AI tends to operate not as a substitute for sensing technologies, but as a cognitive extension of detection devices, contributing to the transformation of raw data into more interpretable information (Demissie et al., 2026; Kumari et al., 2025; Wolfert et al., 2017).

Wireless sensor networks and IoT architectures currently constitute the most consolidated component of this landscape. Sensors dedicated to monitoring soil moisture, temperature, gaseous compounds, or animal activity, supported by low-energy communication protocols, enable the continuous collection of information (Jha et al., 2019). AI can support these processes through noise filtering, data normalization, and the identification of recurring patterns, thereby improving information quality and reducing the need for manual supervision. As noted by Misra et al. (2022), such pipelines tend to require a variable combination of local–and cloud-based processing, and are fueling growing interest in forms of distributed computing that may be particularly relevant in rural contexts characterized by intermittent connectivity.

Alongside static sensing infrastructures, mobile systems based on drones and autonomous vehicles can further expand observational capacity by providing data with high spatial and temporal resolution. The use of RGB-D cameras, LiDAR sensors, and advanced image analysis techniques makes it possible to reconstruct the three-dimensional structure of plants, estimate biomass and vigor, and identify early signals of stress (Sharma & Shivandu, 2024). Computer vision algorithms can support the extraction of metrics from complex datasets, making information available that is often timelier than that obtained through manual surveys. These developments are consistent with international assessments that identify autonomous aerial and ground systems as tools capable of strengthening precision agriculture practices, particularly in contexts characterized by high spatial variability (World Economic Forum, 2021).

At the territorial scale, satellite remote sensing provides an additional layer of monitoring that is useful for integrating and contextualizing locally collected data. The Sen2-Agri system offers an example of how the automated processing of multispectral imagery can contribute to the production of crop maps, vegetation indicators, and phenological information with increasing levels of accuracy (Defourny et al., 2019). Such tools, when adopted within multilateral initiatives, can facilitate transparency in agricultural markets and support early warning systems (Elbehri & Chestnov, 2021).

An emerging perspective concerns agricultural digital twins, understood as dynamic virtual models that seek to integrate data streams from sensors, robots, and satellite platforms to represent crop development in an up-to-date manner (Shamia et al., 2023). Although these tools are still in a phase of maturation, they display potential to support the simulation of management scenarios and predictive analysis, in continuity with trends identified in studies on advanced decision-support systems (Rauch et al., 2025).

The diffusion of monitoring systems nevertheless remains shaped by uneven techno-organizational factors (Aubert et al., 2012; Vecchio et al., 2020; Vijayakumar et al., 2025). Variables such as connectivity continuity, protocol heterogeneity, device robustness in harsh environments, implementation costs, and the skills required for data interpretation can significantly influence the adoption of digital solutions (Ge et al., 2025; Misra et al., 2022). The resulting picture is a heterogeneous one, in which mature technologies coexist with experimental systems, and in which the integration of AI into monitoring processes varies according to productive, infrastructural, and institutional contexts.

Taken together, these elements depict an agricultural monitoring domain in transition, supported by multi-layer architectures—proximal, mobile, satellite, and virtual—connected through algorithms that can facilitate the transformation of complex data into operational information. AI thus emerges as a potential coordinating element within a knowledge system that is still consolidating, yet already oriented toward expanding the capacity to observe and understand agricultural systems.

2.2.2 Diagnosis

Diagnosis constitutes a central function in digital agriculture systems, as it enables the transformation of data availability into the capacity to identify biological anomalies, plant diseases, pest infestations, and behavioral alterations in animals. In this domain, AI can play a significant interpretative role by contributing to the automation of processes traditionally reliant on expert observation and, under favorable conditions, by offering greater timeliness, repeatability, and integration with decision-support systems (Ferentinos, 2018; Mohanty et al., 2016; Sladojevic et al., 2016).

In the crop domain, diagnosis relies predominantly on computer vision techniques. Convolutional neural networks (CNNs) represent a well-established approach, owing to their ability to learn hierarchical representations directly from pixel data and to reduce the need for manual intervention in feature engineering (Jafar et al., 2024; Shehu et al., 2025). The pipelines described in the literature typically include stages of image acquisition, segmentation, feature extraction, and classification, achieving accuracy levels that, under controlled conditions, tend to exceed those of traditional visual assessment (Bhargava et al., 2024; Lee et al., 2020; Mohanty et al., 2016). Consistent with these findings, Jha et al. (2019) document the integration of CNNs into advanced monitoring systems, highlighting how such models can contribute to the automated diagnosis of crops.

A rapidly developing line of research concerns the early detection of pest infestations. For critical pests such as *Tuta absoluta*, models based on lightweight CNNs and optimized variants of the *You Only Look Once* (YOLO) architecture have been developed, designed to operate on edge devices with limited computational resources (Shehu et al., 2025). These solutions show potential for strengthening early warning systems, while still requiring larger datasets and validation across heterogeneous operational contexts, in which environmental conditions can significantly affect model performance.

In livestock farming, digital diagnosis follows complementary trajectories. Systems based on behavioral sensors, such as accelerometers and smart collars, can support the automated identification of alterations in movement patterns associated with specific physiological states, including estrus, calving, or early signs of lameness (Subeesh & Mehta, 2021). In parallel, video analysis techniques and anomaly detection based on computer vision models are gaining relevance, although their levels of maturity remain uneven (Nasirahmadi et al., 2017). Available experimental evidence points to the need for further validation under real operating conditions, particularly with regard to model robustness and their integration with on-farm infrastructures (Gan et al., 2021). Assessments from the Artificial Intelligence–based Decision-Making Support Tool (AI DMST) project, for example, indicate that edge processing applied to animal diagnosis represents a capability still in a phase of consolidation rather than a fully widespread practice (Rauch et al., 2025).

Alongside crop–and livestock-related applications, non-visual diagnosis is assuming an increasingly important role within the agri-food value chain. Techniques based on hyperspectral imaging (HSI), near-infrared spectroscopy (NIRS), and surface-enhanced Raman scattering (SERS) sensors, when integrated with deep learning models, offer opportunities for the identification of mycotoxins, chemical residues, and contaminants with high levels of sensitivity (Ge et al., 2025). However, much of the available evidence is derived from studies conducted under laboratory conditions, pointing to the need for technical and procedural adaptations for deployment in real production environments, which are characterized by greater variability (Deng et al., 2025; Yao et al., 2025).

The sources converge in identifying several structural constraints that may affect the diffusion of AI-based diagnostic solutions. These include the still limited availability of annotated and representative datasets (Jafar et al., 2024; Jha et al., 2019), the reduced generalizability of models in uncontrolled scenarios (Shehu et al., 2025), difficulties in integration with edge and IoT architectures in rural contexts (Misra et al., 2022; Rauch et al., 2025), and the complexity of adapting hyperspectral techniques to field operations (Ge et al., 2025).

Overall, AI-based diagnosis emerges as a consolidating component of digital agriculture, with the potential to extend observational capabilities across the entire value chain. Its maturation, however, requires further methodological, infrastructural, and organizational advances in order for these solutions to achieve stable and reliable application across heterogeneous production contexts.

2.2.3 Prediction

Prediction represents a relevant function within the digital agricultural ecosystem, as it can contribute to anticipating productive dynamics or risk conditions through the algorithmic processing of historical, biological, and environmental data (Atzberger, 2013). From this perspective, AI plays an increasingly important role in transforming heterogeneous observations—originating from field sensors, remote sensing platforms, IoT systems, or climate models—into indications that can support agronomic decision-making in contexts characterized by growing uncertainty (Jabed & Azmi Murad, 2024; Mahdizadeh Gharakhanlou & Perez, 2024).

An initial application domain concerns the prediction of yields and crop conditions. The literature shows that machine learning and deep learning models can estimate variables such as productivity, biomass, or nutritional stress by integrating proximal data, climatic parameters, and spectral or hyperspectral information (Abbas et al.2020; Ge et al., 2025; Shawon et al., 2025). These models are often grounded in vegetation indices, spectral signatures, and bioclimatic measurements, offering opportunities for prediction at the farm or territorial scale and, potentially, for supporting operational planning and input allocation (Shawon et al., 2025).

A second application domain concerns the prediction of phytosanitary risks. Analyses reported by Elbehri and Chestnov (2021) indicate that neural networks and probabilistic models can be employed within early warning systems to anticipate the spread of pests and pathogens through the integration of meteorological data, dispersion models, and field observations. Subsequent studies further show that the combination of IoT, computer vision, and predictive algorithms can enhance the timeliness of detecting crop anomalies or conditions conducive to disease development, with potential benefits for more sustainable risk management (Aijaz et al., 2025; Nyakuri et al., 2025; Upadhyay et al., 2025).

The climatic dimension represents a further pillar of predictive applications. Deep learning models applied to environmental data and microclimatic observations can be used to estimate precipitation patterns, thermal variations, and local weather conditions with increasing granularity (Zanchi et al., 2023). As emphasized by Elbehri and Chestnov (2021), such data-driven approaches can support adaptive irrigation strategies and contribute to mitigating the impacts of extreme events. Aijaz et al. (2025) further highlight that the integration of distributed IoT data with advanced climate models can enable high-resolution forecasting, with applications ranging from water management to the planning of crop operations in scenarios characterized by high variability.

Despite these developments, literature highlights significant limitations. The availability of large and representative datasets remains limited, particularly for yield estimation in heterogeneous agronomic contexts (Ge et al., 2025). Model generalizability is constrained by variability in environmental conditions and data quality, while the integration of IoT sensors, climate models, and edge-based analytical systems requires infrastructures that are not yet uniformly available (Aijaz et al., 2025). Moreover, several predictive models exhibit high performance under controlled conditions but require further evaluation in complex operational scenarios, where factors such as microclimatic variability or data uncertainty can substantially affect reliability (Hernández Hernández et al., 2025; Zarbakhsh et al., 2025).

Taken together, these findings outline a development trajectory toward predictive systems capable of supporting more anticipatory and resilient agronomic practices. Despite still differentiated levels of maturity, the integration of AI, advanced sensing technologies, and climate modeling offers agricultural actors potentially relevant tools for addressing increasing environmental uncertainty, with particularly significant implications in contexts more exposed to climatic and phytosanitary vulnerabilities.

2.2.4 Automation

Automation represents the point of convergence of the M–D–P–A model, as it enables the translation of the outcomes of monitoring, diagnosis, and prediction processes into action. Within this perspective, agricultural systems increasingly take on the characteristics of cyber-physical environments in which sensors, algorithms, and machines cooperate with varying degrees of autonomous coordination. Contemporary automation therefore does not coincide solely with mechanization; rather, it incorporates perceptual and decision-making capabilities that can render crop operations more responsive to environmental and operational conditions, and potentially less dependent on direct human oversight (Jiang et al., 2025).

The literature indicates that this evolution is supported by the convergence of mobile robotics, distributed sensing, and advanced computer vision techniques (Ghazal et al., 2024; Padhiary et al., 2025). Documented applications include precision weeding and seeding, assisted harvesting, and the autonomous management of protected environments, made possible by the ability of robotic systems to interpret field variability through deep neural networks trained to recognize crops, weeds, and obstacles (Jha et al., 2019; Saleem et al., 2021). Increasing model maturity enables the association of perceptual functions with basic operational decisions, such as regulating travel speed or modulating implements in real time (Ahmed et al., 2025).

A distinctive feature of recent trajectories concerns the development of distributed architectures in which operational intelligence is partitioned between cloud and edge layers. The integration of IoT infrastructures with machine learning algorithms enables local processing of data generated by sensors installed on machines, crops, or animals, reducing dependence on continuous connectivity and allowing the autonomous execution of recurrent tasks (Tariq et al., 2025). Within this framework are automated irrigation and fertigation solutions, assisted guidance systems, and tools for livestock physiological monitoring, in which the continuous availability of data can enable more adaptive responses to changing conditions (Subeesh & Mehta, 2021).

The vision of automation at a broader agricultural scale is further informed by studies exploring the progressive integration of robotics, learning algorithms, and environmental monitoring devices. Recent evidence suggests that such technologies may facilitate production models characterized by reduced human supervision, in which autonomous robotic platforms interact with climatic sensors and predictive models to modulate crop interventions and resource management under variable or difficult-to-predict environmental conditions (Aijaz et al., 2025; Łągiewska & Panek-Chwastyk, 2025). This trajectory nevertheless remains constrained by significant limitations: the intrinsic complexity of agricultural environments, the variability of observed data, the scarcity of annotated datasets, and the lack of consolidated interoperability standards continue to hinder the extension and scalability of advanced solutions (Atapattu et al., 2024).

There also remains a gap between the growing perceptual capabilities of systems and their effective decision-making autonomy. As several studies indicate, the transition from vision-based algorithms to models capable of formulating reliable choices in dynamic contexts is still the subject of ongoing research and requires advances in learning techniques, as well as broader reflection on the safety and reliability conditions of autonomous systems in agriculture (Adam et al., 2026; Sarker, 2022; Spagnuolo et al., 2025).

Overall, the current landscape suggests a possible evolutionary trajectory toward agricultural machines conceived as cyber-physical systems endowed with integrated sensing, decision-making, and actuation capabilities. This evolution does not unfold uniformly and encounters technical, infrastructural, and organizational obstacles; nevertheless, it represents one of the most dynamic fronts of digital agriculture, within which AI, robotics, and sensing technologies jointly contribute to redefining operational practices and, more broadly, production models.

The functional reading offered by the M–D–P–A model shows how AI is now integrated—albeit with differing levels of maturity—across the phases of perception, interpretation, anticipation, and actuation within agricultural processes. This integration has not yet resulted in a fully coherent ecosystem: applications remain heterogeneous in terms of technical requirements, standardization, and interoperability potential, with marked differences between crop and livestock domains. The outcome is a landscape undergoing advanced transformation, yet still characterized by vertical solutions and limitations in scalability.

Table 2.1 summarizes the main functions of the M–D–P–A model, highlighting application domains, the technologies involved, and application objectives. This representation helps to capture both the complementarities among functions and the constraints that shape their adoption. Precisely in order to examine the infrastructures and enabling conditions underpinning these applications, Sect. 2.3 discusses the technologies that frame agriculture as a distributed computational ecosystem.

2.3 Enabling Technologies and Emerging Models

The adoption of AI in agriculture depends on a complex set of enabling technologies that support its operation and shape its potential application domains. The maturity of the solutions described by the M–D–P–A model is, in fact, inseparable from the digital infrastructures, computational architectures, and integration mechanisms that render data flows operational across the entire production cycle (Assimakopoulos et al., 2024; Elbasi et al., 2023; Nautiyal et al., 2025). The gradual transition from isolated applications to computational agricultural ecosystems points to the growing relevance of distributed configurations, in which sensors, algorithms, and actuators interact in a coordinated manner, albeit with uneven levels of maturity.

The evolution of IoT ecosystems described in the literature shows that agricultural monitoring is grounded in low-power technologies, dedicated communication protocols, and cloud platforms oriented toward scalable data management (Elbasi et al., 2023). Solutions such as ZigBee, LoRaWAN, RFID, and NB-IoT networks constitute the primary infrastructure for transmitting information from environmental and livestock sensors, while the quality of data flows depends on device robustness and network continuity—factors that are particularly critical in rural areas characterized by intermittent connectivity (Nautiyal et al., 2025). In parallel, several technical contributions document configurations in which part of the processing is performed locally, reducing reliance on the cloud and mitigating latency constraints. This is the case for robotic platforms used in greenhouse management (Uzhinskiy, 2023) and for traceability solutions integrated with IoT devices that feed near–real-time decision-making processes (Misra et al., 2022), pointing to a broader shift toward distributed computing paradigms associated with edge and fog architectures.

Alongside infrastructural aspects, interoperability emerges as a critical technical requirement that remains largely unresolved. Sensor heterogeneity, the use of proprietary protocols, and the absence of shared standards constrain the integration of data

Table 2.1 Digital technologies applications according to the M–D–P–A model

Function	Domain	AI and digital technologies	Application objective	Application example	Source
Monitoring	Crops (farm scale)	IoT, WSN, environmental sensors, ML	Microclimatic and soil monitoring	WSN-based field sensing	Jha et al. (2019)
Monitoring	Crops (territorial scale)	Earth observation, spectral models, classification algorithms	Crop mapping and vegetation indicators (e.g., LAI)	Multispectral satellite data processing	Defourny et al. (2019)
Diagnosis	Crops	CNNs, lightweight deep learning, computer vision	Plant disease detection	Image-based diagnostic pipelines	Jafar et al. (2024)
Diagnosis	Post-harvest	Deep learning, hyperspectral imaging	Quality and contamination detection	Hyperspectral anomaly analysis	Ge et al. (2025)
Prediction	Crops	ML, deep learning, proximal and EO data	Yield, growth, and stress prediction	Data-driven crop performance models	Abbas et al. (2020)
Prediction	Operations	ML, edge computing, IoT data streams	Microclimatic and operational risk forecasting	Edge-based micro-forecasting	Aijaz et al. (2025)
Automation	Crops	Mobile robotics, deep learning, machine vision	Precision field operations	Vision-guided agricultural robots	Saleem et al. (2021)
Automation	Livestock	AIoT, distributed ML	Automated behavioral monitoring	Edge-enabled wearable systems	Subeesh and Mehta (2021)

acquisition and analysis pipelines, limiting the ability to coherently combine multi-source data (Elbasi et al., 2023). Hardware vulnerabilities, network discontinuities, and platform incompatibilities further undermine system continuity and may compromise the quality of diagnostic and predictive analyses (Nautiyal et al., 2025). These challenges are particularly pronounced in contexts where automation depends on the synchronization of heterogeneous sensory data streams, as is the case in robotic systems or advanced decision-support processes.

The evolution of AI techniques applied in agriculture reflects a gradual transition from rule-based approaches to machine learning and deep learning models capable of handling highly variable data, such as multispectral imagery, climatic time series, and animal behavioral signals (Jha et al., 2019; Nautiyal et al., 2025). Within this context, emerging applications of generative AI—discussed in the McKinsey & Company (2024)—focus on the use of models capable of integrating heterogeneous information and generating contextualized recommendations. While these developments highlight potential economic impacts across the agri-food value chain, they also require high-quality data foundations, continuous updating, and validation procedures adapted to diverse operational contexts.

Data availability remains a cross-cutting constraint. Incomplete, noisy, or unstructured datasets hinder model training and reduce generalizability, particularly in regions characterized by limited sensing infrastructures (Elbasi et al., 2023). Recent trends point to an increasing reliance on simulation techniques, data augmentation, and multimodal integration, with the aim of building training pipelines that are more robust and resilient to environmental variability (Waqas et al., 2025). In this case as well, the maturity of solutions remains strongly conditioned by the quality and continuity of empirical observations.

At the value-chain level, the integration of blockchain and IoT technologies represents a development trajectory aimed at strengthening mechanisms of trust and transparency. Misra et al. (2022) show how such combinations enable continuous product traceability and the automated verification of information along the value chain, while Assimakopoulos et al. (2024) emphasize the role of distributed ledgers and smart contracts in certification and quality control processes. The association of sensor-generated data with immutable records and automated verification procedures opens up prospects for more accountability-oriented governance models, while at the same time requiring reliable digital infrastructures and dedicated competencies.

Despite the potential outlined above, the realization of a fully interoperable computational agriculture remains constrained by infrastructural limitations, the high costs of advanced technologies, skills gaps, and data security risks (Elbasi et al., 2023; Nautiyal et al., 2025). McKinsey's analyses (2024) further highlight the risk that these dynamics may exacerbate digital inequalities across operators and territories. Cooperative strategies, targeted investments in local capabilities, and delivery models based on AI-as-a-Service or shared platforms (Adão et al., 2025) are identified as possible pathways to support a more inclusive and scalable transition.

2.4 Adoption Inequalities and Emerging Configurations

The application functions described by the M–D–P–A model are not distributed uniformly across agricultural systems. Their presence, combination, and level of maturity vary according to the structure of production systems, the degree of digital transformation, and the availability of technical infrastructures capable of supporting continuous monitoring, automated diagnosis, advanced prediction, and process automation. This section therefore shifts the focus from individual use cases to the overall configuration of AI applications, with particular attention to geographical differences and the evolutionary trajectories of computational agricultural ecosystems.

2.4.1 M–D–P–A Configurations Across Agricultural Contexts

Market analyses indicate that the adoption of AI-based technologies in agriculture is currently concentrated in specific areas of the Global North, where the presence of mature digital infrastructures and consolidated technological ecosystems facilitates the integration of multiple functions of the M–D–P–A model into relatively coherent systems (Grand View Research, 2023; MarketsandMarkets, 2025). In North America and Western Europe, sectoral growth is estimated to expand from approximately USD 1.9 billion in 2023 to more than USD 9 billion by 2030 (Grand View Research, 2023), driven in particular by the combined use of distributed sensing, analytical platforms, and automation applications in both crop and livestock domains (Chowdhury et al., 2025; Manzoor et al., 2025). In these contexts, monitoring and diagnosis functions tend to be integrated with predictive models and, increasingly, with automation systems that translate algorithmic outputs into operational actions.

However, such patterns are not uniform across the Global North. Within Europe, for instance, several countries exhibit comparatively lower levels of precision agriculture and more limited integration of AI technologies than the continent's main hubs. This variation highlights how M–D–P–A configurations are shaped not only by current infrastructural endowments but also by uneven trajectories of agricultural modernization, even within broadly comparable macroeconomic contexts (Popa, 2011). In these cases, digital monitoring may be relatively advanced, while predictive and automation components remain less widespread.

The Asia–Pacific region represents a second dynamic pole, characterized by high growth rates but marked internal heterogeneity. In some technologically advanced economies within the region, configurations comparable to those observed in North America can be identified, with digital ecosystems that combine monitoring, prediction, and automation; in other contexts, applications remain more narrowly focused on specific functions, such as satellite remote sensing or crop monitoring platforms (Chowdhury et al., 2025). This pattern suggests that the sequence through which M–D–P–A components are adopted may vary substantially depending on the structure of production systems and the infrastructures available.

In agricultural economies of the Global South, the presence of the four functions is more uneven. Across large areas of sub-Saharan Africa and South Asia, documented initiatives indicate a predominance of solutions oriented toward monitoring and diagnosis, often implemented through lightweight applications, offline tools, or smartphone-based systems that rely on simplified forms of computer vision or classification (Ofosu-Ampong et al., 2025; Songol et al., 2021). In these contexts, prediction and automation are more selectively deployed and tend to be concentrated in pilot projects or organized value chains, pointing to an adoption pattern that advances through experimental clusters rather than through systemic integration.

Overall, the geography of agricultural AI adoption can be interpreted as a map of the uneven penetration of M–D–P–A functions. In highly digitalized agro-industrial systems, the four functions tend to coexist and to underpin integrated computational architectures; in contexts with intermediate levels of infrastructural development, selective combinations prevail, often centered on monitoring and prediction; in low digital-intensity economies, applications are concentrated primarily on forms of monitoring and diagnosis adapted to technical and informational constraints (World Economic Forum, 2021). This diversity does not define a linear hierarchy, but rather a plurality of configurations in which AI functions are embedded within specific technological and production ecosystems.

2.4.2 Evolutionary Trajectories of Computational Agricultural Ecosystems

The differences described above concern not only the level of diffusion of applications, but also the ways in which they are combined over time. A first trajectory—more clearly observable in contexts with high digital intensity—is characterized by a transition from vertical solutions to more integrated pipelines. In these cases, monitoring systems based on IoT, remote sensing, or in-field sensing feed diagnostic and predictive models that can, in turn, be connected to partial or full automation systems, for example for irrigation, fertigation, or selected crop operations (Elbehri & Chestnov, 2021; Rauch et al., 2025). Market-oriented studies suggest that the projected growth of the agricultural AI segment is closely associated with the expansion of such functional integrations along the value chain (Global Market Insights, 2025; Grand View Research, 2023).

A second trajectory, more frequently observed in contexts with intermediate levels of infrastructural development, is instead characterized by the persistence of point solutions, in which one or two functions of the M–D–P–A model are introduced without full integration with the others. This applies, for example, to yield or climate risk forecasting systems that operate on remotely sensed data but are not yet connected to field-level automation devices, or to visual diagnostic applications that do not feed in a structured manner into broader predictive or decision-support tools (Mansoor et al., 2025; McFadden et al., 2022). In this configuration, AI contributes to the production of additional information but does not consistently translate into a restructuring of operational processes.

A third trajectory emerges in agricultural systems characterized by low connectivity, where the combination of distributed architectures, edge processing, and intermittent synchronization enables a context-adapted use of AI, primarily within monitoring and diagnosis functions (Ge et al., 2025; Shehu et al., 2025). In these cases, the adoption of low-power devices and lightweight models makes it possible to deploy intelligent functionalities in the absence of continuous cloud infrastructures, outlining modes of use that differ from the data-intensive configurations described for agro-industrial systems.

Available evidence converges in showing that the evolution of computational agricultural ecosystems follows multiple pathways, in which M–D–P–A functions are embedded in different combinations depending on technical resources and the structure of production systems (Assimakopoulos et al., 2024; Elbasi et al., 2023; Nautiyal et al., 2025). In some cases, the trajectory points toward integrated cyber-physical systems, in which sensors, models, and actuators operate as components of a coordinated decision-making environment; in others, AI remains confined to specific tasks of observation, classification, or prediction, without translating into a broader transformation of operational practices.

In summary, agricultural AI currently presents itself as a set of differentiated functional configurations of the M–D–P–A cycle rather than as a uniform application model. It is within these configurations—shaped by varying degrees of integration among monitoring, diagnosis, prediction, and automation—that the adoption processes examined in the following chapter take shape.

2.5 Conclusions

The analysis developed in this chapter has shown that applications of AI in agriculture can be interpreted through four recurring functions—monitoring, diagnosis, prediction, and automation—which describe distinct modes of information production and use. The reconstruction of the M–D–P–A model highlights that these functions do not constitute linear stages, but rather combinable components that give rise to variable configurations depending on the technical capabilities available and the operational constraints of different production systems.

The discussion of enabling technologies has shown that the integration of the four functions depends on heterogeneous infrastructures, encompassing IoT ecosystems, cloud–edge architectures, specialized sensing technologies, analytical platforms, and interoperability mechanisms that are still in the process of consolidation. These elements constitute the technical framework within which applications of the M–D–P–A model are situated, shaping their scalability, reliability, and degree of informational continuity.

The examination of the geography of adoption has further highlighted differentiated configurations: agro-industrial systems that integrate all components of the M–D–P–A cycle; contexts with intermediate levels of infrastructural development in which selective combinations prevail, particularly between monitoring and prediction; and low digital-intensity contexts characterized by the use of lightweight solutions centered on functions of observation or classification. These trajectories confirm that agricultural AI takes multiple forms and that digital transformation unfolds along non-uniform pathways.

Overall, the chapter has outlined an evolving technical and application landscape in which the potential of AI is expressed through distinct functional configurations, strongly shaped by infrastructural resources, organizational capacities, and institutional conditions. These elements provide the starting point for the analysis of adoption processes, drivers, and barriers that influence the integration of AI into agricultural systems, which are addressed in the following chapter.

References

Abbas, F., Afzaal, H., Farooque, A. A., & Tang, S. (2020). Crop yield prediction through proximal sensing and machine learning algorithms. *Agronomy (Basel, Switzerland), 10*(7), 1046. https://doi.org/10.3390/agronomy10071046

Adam, M., Anisi, D. A., & Ribeiro, P. (2026). A verification methodology for safety assurance of RAS. In *Lecture notes in computer science* (pp. 281–294). https://doi.org/10.1007/978-3-032-01486-3_23

Adão, T., Lopes, R. D., Silva, N., Pascoal, D., Morais, R., & Peres, E. (2025). Artificial intelligence as-a-service in agriculture: Sketching a scalable platform for multipurpose decision support. *Procedia Computer Science, 263*, 156–166. https://doi.org/10.1016/j.procs.2025.07.020

Ahmed, D., Imran, B. M., Churuvija, M., & Karkee, M. (2025). An integrated visual servoing framework for precise robotic pruning operations in modern commercial orchard. Preprint retrieved from https://doi.org/10.48550/ARXIV.2504.07309.

Aijaz, N., Lan, H., Raza, T., Yaqub, M., Iqbal, R., & Pathan, M. S. (2025). Artificial intelligence in agriculture: Advancing crop productivity and sustainability. *Journal of Agriculture and Food Research, 20*(101762), 101762. https://doi.org/10.1016/j.jafr.2025.101762

Akhter, R., & Sofi, S. A. (2022). Precision agriculture using IoT data analytics and machine learning. *Journal of King Saud University–Computer and Information Sciences, 34*(8), 5602–5618. https://doi.org/10.1016/j.jksuci.2021.05.013

Assimakopoulos, F., Vassilakis, C., Margaris, D., Kotis, K., & Spiliotopoulos, D. (2024). Artificial intelligence tools for the agriculture value chain: Status and prospects. *Electronics, 13*(22), 4362. https://doi.org/10.3390/electronics13224362

Atapattu, A. J., Perera, L. K., Nuwarapaksha, T. D., Udumann, S. S., & Dissanayaka, N. S. (2024). Challenges in achieving artificial intelligence in agriculture. In *Artificial Intelligence Techniques in Smart Agriculture* (pp. 7–34). Springer Nature Singapore. https://doi.org/10.1007/978-981-97-5878-4_2

Atzberger, C. (2013). Advances in remote sensing of agriculture: Context description, existing operational monitoring systems and major information needs. *Remote Sensing, 5*(2), 949–981. https://doi.org/10.3390/rs5020949

Aubert, B. A., Schroeder, A., & Grimaudo, J. (2012). IT as enabler of sustainable farming: An empirical analysis of farmers' adoption decision of precision agriculture technology. *Decision Support Systems, 54*(1), 510–520. https://doi.org/10.1016/j.dss.2012.07.002

Bhargava, A., Shukla, A., Goswami, O. P., Alsharif, M. H., Uthansakul, P., & Uthansakul, M. (2024). Plant leaf disease detection, classification, and diagnosis using computer vision and artificial intelligence: A review. *IEEE Access: Practical Innovations, Open Solutions, 12*, 37443–37469. https://doi.org/10.1109/access.2024.3373001

Chowdhury, K., Rahman, M. A., Mallik, S. K., Chowdhury, L. N., & Nova, N. A. (2025). Bridging the global digital divide in agriculture: The role of AI in equitable technology access. *International Journal of Sustainable Development and Planning, 20*(6), 2469–2481. https://doi.org/10.18280/ijsdp.200616

De Baerdemaeker, J. (2023). Artificial intelligence in the Agri-food sector: Applications, risks and impacts. European Parliamentary Research Service (EPRS) , Scientific Foresight Unit (STOA). PE 734.711.

Defourny, P., Bontemps, S., Bellemans, N., Cara, C., Dedieu, G., Guzzonato, E., & Koetz, B. (2019). Near real-time agriculture monitoring at national scale at parcel resolution: Performance assessment of the Sen2-Agri automated system in various cropping systems around the world. *Remote Sensing of Environment, 221*, 551–568. https://doi.org/10.1016/j.rse.2018.11.007

Demissie, W. A., Sebastiani, L., & Rossetto, R. (2026). Integration of artificial intelligence and remote sensing for crop yield prediction and crop growth parameter estimation in Mediterranean agroecosystems: Methodologies, emerging technologies, research gaps, and future directions. *European Journal of Agronomy: The Journal of the European Society for Agronomy, 173*(127894), 127894. https://doi.org/10.1016/j.eja.2025.127894

Deng, J., Mei, C., & Jiang, H. (2025). Enhancing the application of near-infrared spectroscopy in grain mycotoxin detection: An exploration of a transfer learning approach across contaminants and grains. *Food Chemistry, 480*(143854), 143854. https://doi.org/10.1016/j.foodchem.2025.143854

Elbasi, E., Mostafa, N., AlArnaout, Z., Zreikat, A. I., Cina, E., Varghese, G., & Zaki, C. (2023). Artificial intelligence technology in the agricultural sector: A systematic literature review. *IEEE Access: Practical Innovations, Open Solutions, 11*, 171–202. https://doi.org/10.1109/access.2022.3232485

Elbehri, A., & Chestnov, R. (2021). *Digital agriculture in action—Artificial intelligence for agriculture.* Food and Agriculture Organization of the United Nations (FAO) and International Telecommunication Union (ITU).

Ferentinos, K. P. (2018). Deep learning models for plant disease detection and diagnosis. *Computers and Electronics in Agriculture, 145*, 311–318. https://doi.org/10.1016/j.compag.2018.01.009

Gan, H., Ou, M., Zhao, F., Xu, C., Li, S., Chen, C., & Xue, Y. (2021). Automated piglet tracking using a single convolutional neural network. *Biosystems Engineering, 205*, 48–63. https://doi.org/10.1016/j.biosystemseng.2021.02.010

Ge, C., Zhang, G., Wang, Y., Shao, D., Song, X., & Wang, Z. (2025). Research status and development trends of artificial intelligence in smart agriculture. *Agriculture, 15*(21), 2247. https://doi.org/10.3390/agriculture15212247

Ghazal, S., Munir, A., & Qureshi, W. S. (2024). Computer vision in smart agriculture and precision farming: Techniques and applications. *Artificial Intelligence in Agriculture, 13*, 64–83. https://doi.org/10.1016/j.aiia.2024.06.004

Global Market Insights (2025). AI in agriculture market size–by component, by technology, by application, by deployment mode, by farm size, forecast 2025–2034. In Global market insights Inc. Retrieved October 21, 2025, from https://www.gminsights.com/industry-analysis/ai-in-agriculture-market

Grand View Research, (2023). Artificial intelligence in agriculture market size report, 2030. https://www.grandviewresearch.com/industry-analysis/artificial-intelligence-in-agriculture-market.

Hernández Hernández, G. C., Gómez Gómez, J., & Jiménez-Cabas, J. (2025). Predictive models based on artificial intelligence to estimate crop yield: A literature review. *Agriculture, 15*(23), 2438. https://doi.org/10.3390/agriculture15232438

Jabed, M. A., & Azmi Murad, M. A. (2024). Crop yield prediction in agriculture: A comprehensive review of machine learning and deep learning approaches, with insights for future research and sustainability. *Heliyon, 10*(24), e40836. https://doi.org/10.1016/j.heliyon.2024.e40836

Jafar, A., Bibi, N., Naqvi, R. A., Sadeghi-Niaraki, A., & Jeong, D. (2024). Revolutionizing agriculture with artificial intelligence: Plant disease detection methods, applications, and their limitations. *Frontiers in Plant Science, 15*, 1356260. https://doi.org/10.3389/fpls.2024.1356260

Jha, K., Doshi, A., Patel, P., & Shah, M. (2019). A comprehensive review on automation in agriculture using artificial intelligence. *Artificial Intelligence in Agriculture, 2*, 1–12. https://doi.org/10.1016/j.aiia.2019.05.004

Jiang, L., Xu, B., Husnain, N., & Wang, Q. (2025). Overview of agricultural machinery automation technology for sustainable agriculture. *Agronomy (Basel, Switzerland), 15*(6), 1471. https://doi.org/10.3390/agronomy15061471

Kumari, K., Mirzakhani Nafchi, A., Mirzaee, S., & Abdalla, A. (2025). AI-driven future farming: Achieving climate-smart and sustainable agriculture. *AgriEngineering, 7*(3), 89. https://doi.org/10.3390/agriengineering7030089

Łągiewska, M., & Panek-Chwastyk, E. (2025). Integrating remote sensing and autonomous robotics in precision agriculture: Current applications and workflow challenges. *Agronomy (Basel, Switzerland), 15*(10), 2314. https://doi.org/10.3390/agronomy15102314

Lee, S. H., Goëau, H., Bonnet, P., & Joly, A. (2020). New perspectives on plant disease characterization based on deep learning. *Computers and Electronics in Agriculture, 170*(105220), 105220. https://doi.org/10.1016/j.compag.2020.105220

Mahdizadeh Gharakhanlou, N., & Perez, L. (2024). From data to harvest: Leveraging ensemble machine learning for enhanced crop yield predictions across Canada amidst climate change. *The Science of the Total Environment, 951*(175764), 175764. https://doi.org/10.1016/j.scitotenv.2024.175764

Mansoor, S., Iqbal, S., Popescu, S. M., Kim, S. L., Chung, Y. S., & Baek, J.-H. (2025). Integration of smart sensors and IOT in precision agriculture: Trends, challenges and future prospectives. *Frontiers in Plant Science, 16*, 1587869. https://doi.org/10.3389/fpls.2025.1587869

Manzoor, F., Wei, L., Siraj, M., Lu, X., & Qiyang, G. (2025). Digital agriculture technology adoption in low and middle-income countries—A review of contemporary literature. *Frontiers in Sustainable Food Systems, 9*(1621851). https://doi.org/10.3389/fsufs.2025.1621851

MarketsandMarkets. (2025). *Artificial intelligence in agriculture market size, share, trends and industry growth–2033*. MarketsandMarkets. https://www.marketsandmarkets.com/Market-Reports/ai-in-agriculture-market-159957009.html

McFadden, J., Casalini, F., Griffin, T., & Anton, J. (2022). The digitalisation of agriculture: A literature review and emerging policy issues. In *OECD food, agriculture and fisheries papers, no. 176*. OECD Publishing. https://doi.org/10.1787/285cc27d-en

McKinsey & Company (2024, June 10). From bytes to bushels: How gen AI can shape the future of agriculture. McKinsey & Company, 10 June 2024. Retrieved October 2, 2025, from https://www.mckinsey.com/industries/agriculture/our-insights/from-bytes-to-bushels-how-gen-ai-can-shape-the-future-of-agriculture#/

Misra, N. N., Dixit, Y., Al-Mallahi, A., Bhullar, M. S., Upadhyay, R., & Martynenko, A. (2022). IoT, big data, and artificial intelligence in agriculture and food industry. *IEEE Internet of Things Journal, 9*(9), 6305–6324. https://doi.org/10.1109/jiot.2020.2998584

Mohanty, S. P., Hughes, D. P., & Salathé, M. (2016). Using deep learning for image-based plant disease detection. *Frontiers in Plant Science, 7*, 1419. https://doi.org/10.3389/fpls.2016.01419

Nasirahmadi, A., Edwards, S. A., Matheson, S. M., & Sturm, B. (2017). Using automated image analysis in pig behavioural research: Assessment of the influence of enrichment substrate provision on lying behaviour. *Applied Animal Behaviour Science, 196*, 30–35. https://doi.org/10.1016/j.applanim.2017.06.015

Nautiyal, M., Joshi, S., Hussain, I., Rawat, H., Joshi, A., Saini, A., & Kumar, S. (2025). Revolutionizing agriculture: A comprehensive review on artificial intelligence applications in enhancing properties of agricultural produce. *Food Chemistry: X, 29*(102748), 102748. https://doi.org/10.1016/j.fochx.2025.102748

Nyakuri, J. P., Nkundineza, C., Gatera, O., Nkurikiyeyezu, K., & Mwitende, G. (2025). AI and IoT-powered edge device optimized for crop pest and disease detection. *Scientific Reports, 15*(1), 22905. https://doi.org/10.1038/s41598-025-06452-5

Ofosu-Ampong, K., Abera, W., Mesfin, T., & Abate, T. (2025). Digital agro-advisory tools in the global south: A behavioural analysis of impacts, and future directions. *Discover. Agriculture, 3*(1). https://doi.org/10.1007/s44279-025-00190-y

Padhiary, M., Kumar, A., & Sethi, L. N. (2025). Emerging technologies for smart and sustainable precision agriculture. *Discover Robotics, 1*(1). https://doi.org/10.1007/s44430-025-00006-0

Popa, C. (2011). Adoption of artificial intelligence in agriculture. *Bulletin of University of Agricultural Sciences and Veterinary Medicine Cluj-Napoca Agriculture, 68*(1). https://doi.org/10.15835/buasvmcn-agr:6454

Rajak, P., Ganguly, A., Adhikary, S., & Bhattacharya, S. (2023). Internet of things and smart sensors in agriculture: Scopes and challenges. *Journal of Agriculture and Food Research, 14*(100776), 100776. https://doi.org/10.1016/j.jafr.2023.100776

Rauch, B., Matar, R., & Dörr, J. (2025). AI-enabled decision-making support tools (AI DMST) for agriculture: Analysis of market dynamics, technical requirements and stakeholder perspectives. Fraunhofer IESE. Study prepared for the European Commission, DG CNECT.

Saleem, M. H., Potgieter, J., & Arif, K. M. (2021). Automation in agriculture by machine and deep learning techniques: A review of recent developments. *Precision Agriculture, 22*(6), 2053–2091. https://doi.org/10.1007/s11119-021-09806-x

Sarker, I. H. (2022). AI-based modeling: Techniques, applications and research issues towards automation, intelligent and smart systems. *SN Computer Science, 3*(2), 158. https://doi.org/10.1007/s42979-022-01043-x

Shamia, D., Suganyadevi, S., Satheeswaran, V., & Balasamy, K. (2023). Digital twins in precision agriculture monitoring using artificial intelligence. In *Digital twin for smart manufacturing* (pp. 243–265). https://doi.org/10.1016/b978-0-323-99205-3.00004-3

Sharma, K., & Shivandu, S. K. (2024). Integrating artificial intelligence and internet of things (IoT) for enhanced crop monitoring and management in precision agriculture. *Sensors International, 5*(100292), 100292. https://doi.org/10.1016/j.sintl.2024.100292

Sharma, S., Verma, K., & Hardaha, P. (2023). Implementation of artificial intelligence in agriculture. *Journal of Computational and Cognitive Engineering, 2*(2), 155–162. https://doi.org/10.47852/bonviewJCCE2202174

Shawon, S. M., Ema, F. B., Mahi, A. K., Niha, F. L., & Zubair, H. T. (2025). Crop yield prediction using machine learning: An extensive and systematic literature review. *Smart Agricultural Technology, 10*(100718), 100718. https://doi.org/10.1016/j.atech.2024.100718

Shehu, H. A., Ackley, A., Mark, M., & Eteng, O. E. (2025). Artificial intelligence for early detection and management of Tuta absoluta-induced tomato leaf diseases: A systematic review. *European Journal of Agronomy: The Journal of the European Society for Agronomy, 170*(127669), 127669. https://doi.org/10.1016/j.eja.2025.127669

Sladojevic, S., Arsenovic, M., Anderla, A., Culibrk, D., & Stefanovic, D. (2016). Deep neural networks based recognition of plant diseases by leaf image classification. *Computational Intelligence and Neuroscience, 2016*, 3289801. https://doi.org/10.1155/2016/3289801

Songol, M., Awuor, F., & Maake, B. (2021). Adoption of artificial intelligence in agriculture in the developing nations: A review. *Journal of Language, Technology & Entrepreneurship in Africa, 12*(2), 208–229. https://doi.org/10.4314/jolte.v12i2

Spagnuolo, M., Todde, G., Caria, M., Furnitto, N., Schillaci, G., & Failla, S. (2025). Agricultural robotics: A technical review addressing challenges in sustainable crop production. *Robotics, 14*(2), 9. https://doi.org/10.3390/robotics14020009

Subeesh, A., & Mehta, C. R. (2021). Automation and digitization of agriculture using artificial intelligence and internet of things. *Artificial Intelligence in Agriculture, 5*, 278–291. https://doi.org/10.1016/j.aiia.2021.11.004

Tariq, M. U., Saqib, S. M., Mazhar, T., Khan, M. A., Shahzad, T., & Hamam, H. (2025). Edge-enabled smart agriculture framework: Integrating IoT, lightweight deep learning, and agentic AI for context-aware farming. *Results in Engineering, 28*(107342), 107342. https://doi.org/10.1016/j.rineng.2025.107342

Upadhyay, A., Chandel, N. S., Singh, K. P., Chakraborty, S. K., Nandede, B. M., Kumar, M., & Elbeltagi, A. (2025). Deep learning and computer vision in plant disease detection: A comprehensive review of techniques, models, and trends in precision agriculture. *Artificial Intelligence Review, 58*(3). https://doi.org/10.1007/s10462-024-11100-x

Uzhinskiy, A. (2023). Advanced technologies and artificial intelligence in agriculture. *AppliedMath, 3*(4), 799–813. https://doi.org/10.3390/appliedmath3040043

Vecchio, Y., Agnusdei, G. P., Miglietta, P. P., & Capitanio, F. (2020). Adoption of precision farming tools: The case of Italian farmers. *International Journal of Environmental Research and Public Health, 17*(3), 869. https://doi.org/10.3390/ijerph17030869

Vijayakumar, S., Murugaiyan, V., Ilakkiya, S., Kumar, V., Sundaram, R. M., & Kumar, R. M. (2025). Opportunities, challenges, and interventions for agriculture 4.0 adoption. *Discover Food, 5*(1). https://doi.org/10.1007/s44187-025-00576-3

Wakchaure, M., Patle, B. K., & Mahindrakar, A. K. (2023). Application of AI techniques and robotics in agriculture: A review. *Artificial Intelligence in the Life Sciences, 3*(100057), 100057. https://doi.org/10.1016/j.ailsci.2023.100057

Waqas, M., Naseem, A., Humphries, U. W., Hlaing, P. T., Dechpichai, P., & Wangwongchai, A. (2025). Applications of machine learning and deep learning in agriculture: A comprehensive review. *Green Technologies and Sustainability, 3*(3), 100199. https://doi.org/10.1016/j.grets.2025.100199

Wolfert, S., Ge, L., Verdouw, C., & Bogaardt, M.-J. (2017). Big data in smart farming—A review. *Agricultural Systems, 153*, 69–80. https://doi.org/10.1016/j.agsy.2017.01.023

World Economic Forum. (2021). *Artificial intelligence for agriculture innovation (AI4AI)*. World Economic Forum.

World Economic Forum. (2025, June 24). How AI can help improve food systems in the agricultural revolution. Retrieved October 7, 2025, from https://www.weforum.org/stories/2025/06/ai-food-systems-agricultural-revolution/

Yao, S., Yu, T., Ramos, A. F. V., Zhang, Z., Rouzi, Z., & Rodriguez-Saona, L. (2025). Toward smart and in-situ mycotoxin detection in food via vibrational spectroscopy and machine learning. *Food Chemistry: X, 31*(103016), 103016. https://doi.org/10.1016/j.fochx.2025.103016

Zanchi, M., Zapperi, S., & La Porta, C. A. M. (2023). Harnessing deep learning to forecast local microclimate using global climate data. *Scientific Reports, 13*(1), 21062. https://doi.org/10.1038/s41598-023-48028-1

Zarbakhsh, S., Fakhrzad, F., Rajkovic, D., Niedbała, G., & Piekutowska, M. (2025). Approaches and challenges in machine learning for monitoring agricultural products and predicting plant physiological responses to biotic and abiotic stresses. *Current Plant Biology, 43*(100535), 100535. https://doi.org/10.1016/j.cpb.2025.100535

Chapter 3
Adoption of AI in Agriculture: A Technology-Organization-Environment Perspective

Abstract This chapter examines the adoption of artificial intelligence (AI) in agriculture through the Technology-Organization-Environment (TOE) framework, showing how the integration of intelligent technologies emerges from the interaction among technical requirements, organizational capacities, and institutional conditions. A systematic review of the literature (2010–2025) indicates that the diffusion of AI is shaped by interdependent factors, including data quality and interoperability, operational complexity, and compatibility with existing practices; human capital, leadership, and financial resources; and digital infrastructures, data governance, value-chain pressures, and socio-cultural dynamics. Comparative analysis of the evidence identifies two recurring adoption configurations—scalable efficiency and adaptive resilience—that capture differentiated modes of AI integration across agricultural firms depending on their level of digital maturity and territorial context. The chapter also discusses systemic risks associated with the three TOE domains, including algorithmic bias, technical dependencies, infrastructural inequalities, and information asymmetries, and outlines inclusive strategies grounded in responsible design, cooperative data governance, and regulated experimental spaces. Overall, AI adoption is conceptualized as a multilevel socio-technical process whose outcomes depend on the alignment among technologies, organizations, and institutions.

Keyword AI adoption agriculture · TOE framework

3.1 Introduction

The adoption of Artificial Intelligence (AI) in agriculture constitutes a complex process shaped by the interaction among technological conditions, organizational resources, and institutional characteristics. To interpret this heterogeneity, it is useful to draw on the Technology-Organization-Environment (TOE) framework developed by Tornatzky and Fleischer (1990), which has been widely applied in studies of organizational innovation to analyze processes of technological adoption. The conceptual flexibility of the model has facilitated its application across diverse productive

A. Apicella, *Artificial Intelligence in Agriculture*,
https://doi.org/10.1007/978-3-032-26580-7_3

contexts and underscores its capacity to capture the multidimensional nature of the digital transformations currently affecting agriculture (Baker, 2011).

The model distinguishes three analytical dimensions: technology, which refers to the requirements, properties, and level of maturity of available solutions; organization, encompassing resources, skills, and managerial arrangements; and environment, which relates to the institutional, infrastructural, and market conditions within which firms operate. This articulation is particularly useful for understanding the adoption of data-driven technologies, in which interoperability, internal capabilities, and external support jointly shape decision-making trajectories. Recent applications of the TOE framework in the agricultural domain indeed confirm the combined role of technical factors, professional competences, and contextual constraints in the diffusion of digital technologies (Li et al., 2024; Lin et al., 2016; Nagy et al., 2025).

The preparation of this chapter was based on a structured review of the literature published between 2010 and 2025, a period during which advanced digital applications—including solutions based on AI—began to consolidate empirically in the agricultural sector at the international level. The review was conducted between July and November 2025 through the consultation of major scientific databases, using combinations of keywords associated with the TOE framework and agricultural digitalization (e.g., "Technology-Organization-Environment," "AI adoption," "smart farming," and "digital agriculture").

The selection of contributions followed a two-stage screening process (title and abstract review, followed by full-text assessment) and prioritized studies meeting three criteria: (i) the explicit use of the TOE framework as an interpretative lens; (ii) diversity of application contexts, encompassing crop production, livestock farming, and agri-food value chains; and (iii) the presence of empirical evidence, based on real-world implementations or decision-making processes observed at the farm level.

The selected articles were analyzed using a thematic coding procedure guided by the conceptual structure of the model, allowing heterogeneous findings to be mapped onto the three TOE dimensions and enabling the identification of recurring factors in the adoption trajectories described in literature.

Evidence from adjacent sectors confirms the relevance of the TOE framework for analyzing the adoption of AI-based technologies, showing how technological conditions, organizational capabilities, and environmental factors interact in shaping innovation processes (Chatterjee et al., 2021; Na et al., 2022; wael Al-Khatib, 2023; Yang et al., 2022). The evidence gathered through the systematic review informs the analysis of the three dimensions of the TOE framework developed in Sect. 3.2. Subsequent sections examine the adoption configurations emerging from the literature (Sect. 3.3) and the main vulnerabilities and strategies characterizing the diffusion of AI within agricultural systems (Sect. 3.4).

3.2 The TOE as an Interpretative Lens for AI Adoption Processes in Agriculture

The analysis developed in this chapter is organized around the three analytical dimensions commonly identified in the literature through the TOE perspective. This framework provides a structured way to examine how technological characteristics, organizational capacities, and environmental conditions shape AI adoption processes in agriculture, as consistently documented across prior studies (Chatterjee et al., 2021; Gangwar et al., 2015; Lin et al., 2016; Wang & Liu, 2014).

Rather than treating adoption as the outcome of isolated determinants, the TOE perspective emphasizes the interdependence among technical properties, firm-level resources, and contextual factors. In doing so, it offers a coherent lens for reading the heterogeneous evidence reviewed in the previous section and for structuring the analysis of adoption configurations and vulnerabilities developed in the sections that follow.

3.2.1 Technological Factors in the Adoption of AI in Agriculture

Within the TOE framework, the technological dimension helps to explain how farmers assess the introduction of AI in relation to their operational needs. AI-based solutions are embedded in the evolutionary trajectory of agricultural digitalization initiated by advanced sensing technologies, IoT, robotics, and precision agriculture platforms, sharing their data-driven logic while extending predictive and decision-support capabilities (Wolfert et al., 2017). In the TOE literature, the perception of relative advantage plays a central role and is closely associated with the potential to reduce production uncertainty, improve efficiency, and support data-informed decision-making. These elements are also highlighted in recent studies on the adoption of advanced smart farming tools (Nagy et al., 2025).

This perception, however, is contingent on several enabling conditions. It depends on the availability of reliable data, the ability to integrate heterogeneous information sources, and the capacity to translate algorithmic outputs into operational guidance that is consistent with existing farm practices.

Alongside the expected benefits, perceived complexity represents a critical factor in adoption processes. The use of predictive models, machine learning algorithms, or integrated platforms requires technical competences that are not always available, making complexity a significant barrier—particularly in contexts characterized by limited digital resources (Eastwood et al., 2017; Yoon et al., 2020). Evidence from the adoption of IoT technologies shows that increasing operational complexity tends to reduce user acceptance, a pattern that is especially pronounced in areas marked by low levels of digital literacy (Li et al., 2024). Due to the more sophisticated nature of its algorithmic and infrastructural components, AI further intensifies this dynamic.

Compatibility with existing infrastructures and farm practices represents a further key factor in adoption processes. Research on smart farming shows that continuity with established routines and seamless integration into on-farm digital systems reduce operational frictions and facilitate the assimilation of new technologies (Yoon et al., 2020). In the case of IoT-based solutions, the availability of reliable sensors, data transmission networks, and interoperable platforms constitutes a fundamental prerequisite for realizing the potential of data-intensive technologies (Li et al., 2024).

AI-based applications further amplify this requirement: data quality, standardization, and interoperability are necessary conditions for algorithms to learn, adapt, and generate reliable predictions. The literature indicates that informational fragmentation substantially constrains the capacity of advanced technologies to create value (Luo et al., 2025).

Overall, the technological dimension highlights that AI adoption results from the interaction between perceived relative advantage, operational complexity, and compatibility with the farm-level digital ecosystem. Although these factors reflect dynamics already observed in the evolution of digital agricultural technologies, AI requires higher levels of infrastructural maturity, data quality, and system integration for its transformative potential to be fully realized in agricultural contexts.

3.2.2 Organizational Factors in the Adoption of AI in Agriculture

Within the TOE framework, organizational factors refer to internal resources, competences, and managerial capabilities that shape the readiness of agricultural firms to engage with AI. The literature on sectoral digitalization shows that the adoption of advanced technologies is strongly influenced by firms' internal structures and by how decision-makers perceive and interpret the risks and opportunities associated with innovation (Nagy et al., 2025; Penone et al., 2024).

A first element concerns human capital, which constitutes a central component of organizational readiness. The deployment of AI-based systems requires adequate levels of digital literacy and prior familiarity with data-driven tools. Studies on IoT adoption confirm that the availability of internal competences facilitates the integration of connected technologies and the processing of complex information (Li et al., 2024; Lin et al., 2016). However, in contexts characterized by consolidated technological service ecosystems, some contributions show that adoption processes can be delegated to external providers, thereby reducing the direct weight of internal competences in shaping innovation outcomes (Yoon et al., 2020).

Leadership support represents a second decisive factor. In agricultural firms—often family-run—the main decision-maker generally coincides with the owner, who shapes the firm's strategic orientation and evaluates the relevance of innovation, in line with the decision-making model outlined by Rogers et al. (2014). Managerial support and openness to innovation are consistently associated with a higher propensity to adopt digital technologies and new management practices (Lin et al., 2016; Penone et al., 2024). Here again, the literature documents' contexts in which the role of individual leadership is attenuated: when systems are extensively outsourced, the availability of professional technical support reduces the centrality of the CEO's profile in adoption-related decisions (Yoon et al., 2020).

Finally, economic and infrastructural resources constitute a further key component of the organizational dimension. The adoption of AI-based solutions entails investments in hardware, software, maintenance, and data management, as well as the procurement of outsourced services (Horvitz & Mulligan, 2015). These costs represent a significant barrier, as observed in studies on Korean smart farming systems (Yoon et al., 2020) and in analyses of small and medium-sized enterprises in developing countries, where financial constraints and limited access to credit affect firms' capacity to innovate (Nagy et al., 2025). The likelihood of adoption increases in organizations that exhibit a sufficient level of digital maturity, understood as the availability of infrastructural assets, operational procedures, and information systems that are consistent with the use of data-intensive technologies (Luo et al., 2025).

Overall, the organizational dimension highlights how the integration of AI depends on the combination of internal competences, leadership orientation, and the availability of economic and infrastructural resources. Even in the presence of technologically mature solutions, adoption remains highly sensitive to organizational readiness; where such readiness is lacking, AI tends to widen the gap between digitally advanced firms and resource-constrained enterprises, contributing to heterogeneous adoption trajectories within the agricultural sector.

3.2.3 Environmental Factors in the Adoption of AI in Agriculture

Within the TOE framework, the environmental dimension encompasses the institutional, infrastructural, and competitive conditions that shape agricultural firms' capacity to adopt AI-based technologies. This perspective is particularly salient in a sector characterized by regulatory constraints, public incentives, and value-chain dynamics, all of which exert a significant influence on firms' innovation orientations (Rijswijk et al., 2021). In the domain of smart farming, the literature depicts a landscape in which such conditions may act either as enablers or as barriers, giving rise to contexts that are more or less conducive to the diffusion of advanced technologies (Klerkx et al., 2019; Klerkx and Rose, 2020).

Among the main environmental factors, institutional support plays a pivotal role. Training programs, financial incentives, dedicated digital infrastructures, and investment-support initiatives foster the adoption of digital technologies, as shown by studies focusing on the Chinese context (Li et al., 2024; Luo et al., 2025). Although these analyses primarily concern IoT-based solutions and digital platforms, they indicate that AI can likewise benefit from policy frameworks capable of reducing adoption-related uncertainty and supporting the technical conditions required for the management of data-intensive systems. The informational nature of AI—grounded in data quality and continuity—makes the institutional environment a particularly salient factor.

A second element concerns competitive and value-chain pressure. The digital evolution of agri-food systems has introduced new informational standards—such as advanced traceability and yield forecasting—that can stimulate the adoption of innovative solutions (Bronson & Knezevic, 2016). Demands originating from downstream actors in the value chain often encourage agricultural firms to equip themselves with technologies capable of producing reliable data and predictive functions (Penone et al., 2024). However, the relevance of such pressures varies according to market structure: studies conducted in less integrated local contexts indicate that competitive pressure tends to be weaker or not statistically significant (Li et al., 2024).

The availability of digital infrastructures represents a further key area. Stable connectivity, cloud services, sensor networks, and management platforms constitute essential prerequisites for the functioning of AI systems, which depend on continuous and interoperable information flows (Miller et al., 2025; Padhiary et al., 2025). In many rural areas, the lack of such infrastructures and the weakness of supporting ecosystems emerge as recurring barriers, constraining both adoption and the perceived value associated with advanced solutions (Nagy et al., 2025; Yoon et al., 2020).

Finally, the environmental dimension also encompasses socio-cultural factors that shape farmers' attitudes toward AI. Concerns related to algorithmic transparency, the loss of decision-making control, or the alignment of intelligent technologies with local practices may generate resistance, particularly in contexts characterized by strong manual traditions or limited familiarity with digital technologies (Nagy et al., 2025).

Overall, the environmental dimension shows that the adoption of AI is closely linked to the institutional, infrastructural, competitive, and socio-cultural configuration of territories. Ecosystems characterized by effective public support, robust digital infrastructures, and active collaborative networks are more likely to integrate AI-based solutions, whereas less structured contexts tend to generate more pronounced adoption gaps, with significant implications for the competitiveness of agricultural firms.

Table 3.1 summarizes the main factors identified in the literature on the adoption of advanced digital technologies in agriculture, interpreted through the lens of the TOE framework. Although many contributions focus on specific solutions, such as IoT systems, intelligent sensing technologies, or farm management platforms, the reported evidence is also relevant to AI, as it frames adoption processes as the outcome of interactions between the technical characteristics of solutions, available internal resources, and institutional and market conditions. The adoption of AI, in fact, requires the convergence of technological, organizational, and environmental elements, giving rise to trajectories in which operational, managerial, and socio-institutional dimensions are tightly interdependent.

Table 3.1 Synthesis of TOE factors in the adoption of advanced digital technologies in agriculture

TOE dimension	Factor	Concise description	Key sources
Technology	Relative advantage	Perceived gains in efficiency, quality, and uncertainty reduction	Nagy et al. (2025); Yoon et al. (2020)
	Perceived complexity	Technical and managerial burdens associated with implementation and use	Li et al. (2024)
	Compatibility	Alignment with existing practices, infrastructures, and organizational routines	Yoon et al. (2020)
	Data availability and quality	Access to accurate, integrated, and reliable data required by data-driven systems	Luo et al. (2025)
Organization	Human capital and skills	Availability of digital competences and technical expertise within the firm	Lin et al. (2016); Li et al. (2024)
	Leadership and innovation orientation	Managerial openness to experimentation and strategic support for innovation	Nagy et al. (2025); Penone et al. (2024)
	Financial resources	Capacity to sustain investments in technologies and related services	Nagy et al. (2025); Yoon et al. (2020)
	Organizational structure	Degree of formalization of management systems and operational processes	Nagy et al. (2025)
Environment	Institutional support	Presence of incentives, training programs, regulation, and public infrastructures	Li et al. (2024); Luo et al. (2025); Yoon et al. (2020)
	Market pressure and value-chain dynamics	External requirements related to traceability, quality, and information disclosure	Li et al. (2024); Penone et al. (2024)
	Digital infrastructures	Availability of connectivity, cloud services, and sensor networks	Luo et al. (2025); Yoon et al. (2020)
	Socio-cultural conditions	Attitudes toward technology, trust, and perceived control over decision-making	Nagy et al. (2025)

From this perspective, the transition toward intelligent systems cannot be interpreted as a purely technological decision, but rather as a process of progressive transformation involving organizational structures, value-chain relationships, and broader regulatory and infrastructural contexts. The TOE framework makes it possible to capture this multilevel nature of digital innovation in agriculture, interpreting the adoption of AI as the outcome of specific systemic configurations. On this basis, the following sections examine the drivers and barriers associated with the three dimensions of the model, offering an analytical reading of the variables that influence the diffusion of AI-based technologies within the agricultural sector.

3.3 Adoption Configurations of AI in Agriculture: Scalable Efficiency and Adaptive Resilience

The review of the literature indicates that the adoption of digital technologies in agriculture does not follow a uniform pathway but instead unfolds through configurations shaped by specific combinations of technological, organizational, and environmental factors. Although existing studies do not converge on a single typology, a comparative reading of the findings reveals two recurrent modes of AI integration that, for analytical purposes, can be interpreted as distinct trajectories: a logic of scalable efficiency, more commonly observed among medium- and large-scale farms, and a logic of adaptive resilience, which is more typical of contexts characterized by limited resources or higher exposure to risk (Bhat et al., 2025; Manzoor et al., 2025; Miller et al., 2025; Sharma & Shivandu, 2024). These trajectories do not represent rigid categories or evolutionary sequences, but rather interpretive configurations constructed on the basis of recurring patterns identified in the literature.

In structurally consolidated firms, the availability of internal skills, digitized infrastructures, and technological partnerships enables the integration of AI within already mature management systems. In this setting, AI is primarily adopted to expand predictive capacity, support process automation, and enhance traceability along the value chain, in continuity with well-established digitalization strategies (Sharma & Shivandu, 2024). Empirical studies show that such organizational and environmental conditions—corresponding to high levels of readiness and favorable infrastructural contexts—promote a planned form of adoption oriented toward improvements in operational efficiency and firm-level sustainability (Nagy et al., 2025; Penone et al., 2024; Yoon et al., 2020). This trajectory therefore reflects configurations in which the three TOE domains converge to support forms of technological scalability.

In smallholder farms and in agricultural systems characterized by more limited resource availability, the introduction of AI takes more selective and context-specific forms. In these settings, the primary objective is not the systemic optimization of processes, but rather the enhancement of the capacity to respond to uncertain operating conditions, such as climate variability or restricted access to critical information

(Dibbern et al., 2025; Junior et al., 2019; Li et al., 2024). Adoption is often guided by principles of compatibility with existing practices and by solutions that require lower levels of managerial complexity (Lin et al., 2016). Moreover, the role of the institutional context proves particularly significant: forms of digital intermediation, public support programs, and local collaborative networks decisively shape the ability to incorporate intelligent technologies (Bisheko and Rejikumar, 2023). This trajectory corresponds to configurations in which the environment partially compensates for limited internal technological and organizational capacities, orienting AI toward resilience-oriented objectives.

The differences between the two trajectories reflect broader tensions in data governance and in the distribution of digital capabilities along agri-food value chains. Several studies indicate that the integration of AI tends to strengthen the position of actors already embedded in advanced technological ecosystems, while potentially constraining the participation of those with more limited resources, with implications for the equity of agricultural information systems (Hackfort, 2021; Omotayo et al., 2025; Sood et al., 2022). Analyses focusing on complementary technologies, such as blockchain and IoT systems, further confirm that the effectiveness of digital innovations depends on the alignment between technical architectures, organizational capacities, and territorial specificities (Asante Boakye et al., 2022).

The body of evidence further suggests that different adoption pathways may lead to functionally equivalent outcomes—according to a logic of equifinality—when combinations of technological, organizational, and environmental factors are aligned with firms' objectives and operating conditions (Luo et al., 2025). Scalable efficiency and adaptive resilience should therefore be interpreted as alternative responses generated by specific configurations of resources, market pressures, and infrastructural availability. These trajectories illustrate how the adoption of AI does not stem from a single logic of technological rationality, but rather from situated socio-technical processes that reflect the diversity of production models and agricultural ecosystems. Identifying these trajectories helps to clarify how different forms of organizational capacity and varying institutional conditions can support heterogeneous digital transitions that nonetheless may converge toward more efficient, robust, and information-rich agricultural systems.

Box 3.1 At the Boundaries of the Agricultural Digital Transition: A Comparison of Two Adoption Models

Based on the evidence synthesized in Sect. 3.3, the adoption of AI in agriculture tends to be structured around two recurring configurations, shaped by firms' differing technological, organizational, and environmental endowments. The comparison presented in Box 3.1 illustrates, in a comparative perspective, how the three dimensions of the TOE framework take differentiated forms in medium- and large-scale farms as opposed to smallholder farms, outlining adoption logics oriented, respectively, toward scalable efficiency and adaptive resilience. This representation is not intended as a classificatory scheme, but rather as a synthetic analytical device that highlights distinctive features useful for interpreting the diversity of agricultural digitalization pathways documented in the literature (Table 3.2).

Table 3.2 Adoption configurations of AI in agriculture: scalable efficiency and adaptive resilience across TOE dimensions

Dimension	Medium- and large-scale farms	Smallholder farms
Primary objective	Optimization, integration, and standardization of processes along the value chain	Risk mitigation, local adaptation, and continuity of production
Technological factor (T)	Integration of AI into complex digital architectures, including data platforms, predictive systems, and intelligent automation solutions	Selective adoption of tools oriented toward addressing specific problems, with limited systemic integration
Organizational factor (O)	Availability of specialized internal skills, algorithmic management capabilities, and formalized decision-making processes	Low absorptive capacity, a strong role of social networks and community-based learning, and reliance on external technical services
Environmental factor (E)	Embeddedness in structured value chains, access to global markets, availability of financial capital, and mature digital infrastructures	Dependence on institutional support, local territorial conditions, and agricultural extension services
Predominant adoption outcome	Scalable efficiency: productivity gains, cost reduction, and enhanced traceability	Adaptive resilience: improved capacity to respond to shocks and to make decisions under conditions of uncertainty

3.3.1 Systemic Risks and Inclusive Strategies in the Adoption of AI in Agriculture

The adoption of AI in agricultural systems entails a set of vulnerabilities arising from the interaction between technological solutions, organizational capacities, and institutional conditions. Consistent with the TOE framework, these risks take different forms depending on firms' levels of digital maturity, the availability of internal skills, and the quality of infrastructures and regulatory arrangements governing information flows (Omotayo et al., 2025; Tzachor et al., 2022).

The purpose of this section is to examine these critical issues by distinguishing among technological, organizational, and environmental dimensions, highlighting how they affect both the reliability of AI systems and the distribution of benefits across different agricultural contexts. Sections 4.1–4.3 analyze the main risks associated with the three TOE dimensions, while the concluding Sect. 4.4 discusses mitigation strategies aimed at fostering a more equitable and sustainable adoption of AI.

3.3.2 Technological Vulnerabilities: Data, Models, and Operational Reliability

The technological dimension of AI in agriculture exhibits vulnerabilities stemming from data quality, model transferability, and the reliability of digital infrastructures. These issues are particularly critical in a sector marked by pronounced ecological heterogeneity, fragmented production structures, and uneven access to information (Tzachor et al., 2022).

A first area of fragility concerns the representativeness and standardization of data. Incomplete datasets, collected in highly mechanized contexts or limited to commercial crops, reduce model generalizability, thereby undermining the accuracy of predictions in polycultural or ecologically variable systems (Atapattu et al., 2024; Assimakopoulos et al., 2024). The lack of shared data formats and the presence of discontinuous information flows further exacerbate this problem, complicating the development of coherent pipelines for model training and validation (FAO, 2024; Songol et al., 2021).

A second critical area concerns algorithmic bias, which may arise from the geographic and socio-economic distribution of available data. Models trained on unbalanced datasets tend to privilege highly technology-intensive production conditions, generating recommendations that are poorly suited to marginal or low-infrastructure contexts (Li et al., 2024). In addition, the opacity of some models deployed in agricultural decision-support systems can reduce process transparency and limit users' ability to interpret or contextualize the guidance provided, with implications for farmers' decision-making autonomy (Sparrow et al., 2021).

A third vulnerability concerns dependence on reliable digital infrastructures. Applications based on IoT sensors, cloud-based analytics, and real-time monitoring require network continuity and computational stability—conditions that are not guaranteed in many rural areas affected by persistent digital divides (McFadden et al., 2022; World Economic Forum, 2021). Intermittent connectivity or limited access to cloud services can degrade model performance, constrain updates, and hinder the integration of field-generated data (Mansoor et al., 2025). These shortcomings give rise to operational risks that may compromise not only the effectiveness of AI solutions, but also their reliability in day-to-day decision-making processes.

Overall, these technological vulnerabilities underscore that the effectiveness of agricultural AI depends on the alignment among data architectures, model quality, and local infrastructural conditions. In the absence of targeted investments in standardization, interoperability, and resilient digital infrastructures, the adoption of AI risks amplifying pre-existing informational and operational inequalities within agricultural systems. These dynamics provide an essential analytical backdrop for the governance-oriented discussion developed in Chap. 6, where issues of data governance, infrastructural concentration, and risk management are examined in greater depth and connected to long-term strategies for inclusive and sustainable AI deployment.

3.3.3 Organizational Vulnerabilities: Absorptive Capacity, Skills, and Technical Dependencies

The organizational dimension constitutes a critical node in assessing the systemic risks associated with the adoption of AI in agriculture. Firms' ability to integrate and effectively use AI-based solutions depends not only on technological availability, but also on levels of absorptive capacity, internal skills, managerial processes, and work organization (Nagy et al., 2025; Penone et al., 2024).

A first area of vulnerability concerns human capital and digital skills, which directly affect users' ability to interpret data, assess algorithmic recommendations, and integrate AI into everyday decision-making processes. As highlighted by Ayre et al. (2019) and Bronson and Knezevic (2016), intelligent technologies require forms of digital literacy that go beyond the instrumental use of platforms, encompassing an understanding of model limitations, the capacity for oversight, and the critical interpretation of outputs. In contexts where such competencies are limited, algorithmic recommendations may be adopted mechanically or misinterpreted, increasing operational vulnerability and the risk of cognitive dependence on digital tools.

A second vulnerability concerns decision-making processes and organizational structures. In firms lacking formalized procedures for data management or dedicated roles for overseeing intelligent systems, the integration of AI tends to be fragmented and reactive (Jouanjean et al., 2020). This can lead to misalignments between expectations and outcomes, particularly when adoption occurs in the absence of long-term strategies or systematic assessments of costs and benefits (Lin et al., 2016). Moreover, the introduction of advanced solutions in organizations with low absorptive capacity may expose firms to partial or unstable implementations, with adverse effects on operational efficiency and the continuity of digital services.

A third area of vulnerability concerns structural dependencies on technology providers. In many agricultural contexts, AI is integrated through outsourced services—ranging from monitoring systems to algorithm maintenance—creating forms of lock-in that constrain firms' ability to modify technical configurations, negotiate terms of use, or develop autonomous solutions (Forney & Epiney, 2022; Yoon et al., 2020). This dependence can be particularly acute in smallholder farms, where limited internal skills and the absence of proprietary infrastructures heighten exposure to external actors, reduce control over data, and increase the risk of service disruption.

Finally, the organizational dimension also encompasses relational vulnerabilities linked to the role of agricultural extension services and intermediary support networks. In many regions, these structures lack the technical capacities required to effectively accompany the adoption of AI, with consequences for the quality of technology transfer and for the ability to adapt tools to local needs (Sher et al., 2025; World Economic Forum, 2021). Insufficient institutional support can thus exacerbate inequalities in access to skills and amplify the risks of inappropriate or ineffective implementation.

Overall, organizational vulnerabilities indicate that the impact of AI is not determined solely by the technical maturity of available solutions, but by the ability of agricultural enterprises to develop adequate skills, managerial processes, and forms of coordination. In the absence of these conditions, AI tends to reinforce existing inequalities and to generate new operational and informational dependencies, ultimately undermining the resilience of production systems and the sustainability of the agricultural digital transition. These dynamics provide a key analytical foundation for the examination of labor, skills, and organizational change developed in Chaps. 4 and 5, and for the integrative assessment of governance challenges and future scenarios presented in Chap. 6.

3.3.4 Environmental Vulnerabilities: Infrastructures, Data Governance, and Territorial Inequalities

The environmental dimension of the TOE framework highlights a set of vulnerabilities arising from the institutional, infrastructural, and market conditions within which the adoption of AI in agriculture takes place. Unlike technological and organizational risks, which manifest primarily within firms, environmental vulnerabilities emerge from the interactions among actors, rules, and infrastructures that govern the agricultural digital ecosystem and shape the distribution of opportunities for innovation.

A first area concerns the quality and maturity of digital infrastructures, which are necessary to ensure continuity of information flows, access to cloud services, and integration across heterogeneous systems. In many regions characterized by intermittent connectivity or fragmented IoT networks, predictive models lack the stable data streams required for effective learning, resulting in less reliable recommendations and increased operational vulnerability for end users (Mansoor et al., 2025; McFadden et al., 2022). The absence of shared infrastructures—such as interoperable platforms or public data certification services—further amplifies informational fragmentation and constrains the development of solutions adapted to local territorial specificities (FAO, 2024; Songol et al., 2021).

A second area of vulnerability concerns the governance of agricultural data, a critical element in AI-based systems. The concentration of data collection and management within a limited number of private platforms can generate significant asymmetries in the distribution of informational power, reducing producers' ability to control data circulation and the conditions under which algorithmic outputs are used (Forney & Epiney, 2022; Jouanjean et al., 2020). These issues are compounded by the lack of shared standards, limited model transparency, and difficulties in assessing data quality or provenance—conditions that may undermine both the accuracy of predictions and farmers' trust in the system (De Baerdemaeker, 2023; Rauch et al., 2025).

A third area concerns competitive pressures and value-chain dynamics, which often shape AI adoption in asymmetric ways. In contexts characterized by structured value chains and globalized markets, demands for traceability, high quality standards, and sustainable production can encourage the introduction of predictive systems and advanced automation (Bronson & Knezevic, 2016; Sharma & Shivandu, 2024). In less integrated contexts, however, these pressures may act as barriers, as firms often lack the resources needed to comply with such standards, thereby widening the gap between digitally intensive producers and more marginal farms (Li et al., 2024). Value-chain dynamics may thus contribute to the emergence of polarized agricultural ecosystems, in which only a subset of actors is able to fully benefit from intelligent technologies.

Finally, the environmental dimension also encompasses socio-cultural factors that shape attitudes toward intelligent technologies. Distrust in algorithms, concerns about the loss of decision-making autonomy, or perceived incompatibilities between digital innovation and local practices constitute significant barriers, particularly in regions characterized by strong manual traditions or low levels of digital experience (Nagy et al., 2025; Sen et al., 2025). These obstacles affect not only initial adoption but also users' ability to sustain informed and critical engagement with AI-based solutions over time.

Overall, environmental vulnerabilities highlight how the effectiveness and equity of AI depend on the presence of robust institutional ecosystems, interoperable infrastructures, and transparent governance arrangements. In their absence, AI tends to consolidate existing divides, generate new forms of informational dependency, and produce benefits that are unevenly distributed along value chains. The issues outlined in this section provide a key analytical basis for the integrative discussion developed in Chap. 6, where environmental constraints and governance conditions are examined in relation to broader adoption dynamics. Section 4.4 examines the inclusive strategies and governance models proposed in the literature to mitigate these risks and to steer the digital transition in agriculture toward more equitable and resilient configurations.

3.3.5 Inclusive Strategies for Risk Mitigation

The technological, organizational, and environmental vulnerabilities identified in the previous sections call for strategies capable of steering the adoption of AI along inclusive trajectories, ensuring a more equitable distribution of the benefits of innovation and mitigating the risk that AI may amplify pre-existing inequalities within agricultural systems. From this perspective, the literature identifies three main lines of intervention: responsible design, cooperative data governance, and regulated experimental spaces. These strategies operate at different levels of the TOE framework, simultaneously acting on the technological, organizational, and environmental dimensions.

A first line of action concerns Responsible Research and Innovation (RRI), which advances a set of principles—anticipation, inclusion, reflexivity, and responsiveness—to guide the design and implementation of emerging technologies (Owen et al., 2012; Stilgoe et al., 2013). Applied to agricultural AI, RRI entails the active involvement of farmers, extension services, public institutions, and local communities in defining objectives, operational constraints, and success metrics (Sparrow et al., 2021; Tzachor et al., 2022). Such participation helps reduce the risk of technologically sophisticated but socially misaligned solutions, fostering closer alignment with ecological conditions and local knowledge systems.

A second area concerns cooperative data governance, which is regarded as a central lever for reducing informational asymmetries and strengthening farmers' autonomy *vis-à-vis* platforms and technology providers (Forney & Epiney, 2022; Jouanjean et al., 2020). Models such as data cooperatives enable shared data management, enhancing producers' ability to define rules for data access, use, and sharing. At the same time, the literature highlights the importance of open standards, interoperability, and independent audit mechanisms that allow for the verification of transparency, provenance, and quality of both datasets and algorithms (De Baerdemaeker, 2023; Rauch et al., 2025). These instruments represent essential prerequisites for ensuring fairness in decision-making processes and for mitigating the risks of technological lock-in.

A third line of intervention is represented by digital sandboxes—regulated experimental environments that allow AI technologies to be tested under real but controlled operating conditions. These spaces foster multi-actor learning processes and enable regulatory institutions to progressively assess the impacts of innovation, adapting rules and standards based on empirical evidence (Rauch et al., 2025; Tzachor et al., 2022). Sandboxes prove particularly valuable in contexts characterized by low levels of digital maturity, where the abrupt introduction of algorithmic solutions could generate organizational or informational risks that are difficult to manage.

Alongside these three pillars, targeted initiatives aimed at strengthening the organizational and cognitive capacities of rural actors play a critical role and are widely regarded as a necessary condition for an inclusive digital transition. Context-specific digital literacy programs, accessible socio-linguistic interfaces (Elbehri & Chestnov, 2021), and renewed agricultural extension services help reduce the cognitive divide that often reinforces infrastructural and economic gaps (Sen et al., 2025; Sher et al., 2025). As emphasized in the literature, the effectiveness of AI depends not only on the technical availability of solutions but also on users' ability to interpret results, assess limitations, and integrate algorithmic outputs into everyday decision-making processes (Cao & Huang, 2022; Ranasinghe et al., 2022).

Overall, the strategies identified indicate that the adoption of AI in agriculture cannot be addressed as a purely technical process, but rather requires the construction of socio-institutional ecosystems capable of integrating innovation and inclusion. Responsible design, cooperative data governance, and regulated experimentation constitute complementary tools for leading AI toward configurations that are more equitable, sustainable, and consistent with the diversity of agricultural systems.

3.4 Conclusions

The analysis shows that the adoption of AI in agriculture follows heterogeneous pathways shaped by the interaction between technological characteristics, organizational capacities, and environmental conditions. The TOE framework provides a useful lens for interpreting this complexity, highlighting that the integration of AI depends not only on the intrinsic properties of algorithms, but also on how digital solutions are embedded in established practices, differentiated production structures, and often uneven institutional and infrastructural configurations.

The distinction between scalable efficiency logics and forms of adaptive resilience shows that AI does not generate uniform outcomes. In organizations characterized by high levels of digital maturity, AI is integrated into already structured management architectures, supporting processes of optimization and standardization. In small-scale contexts or in systems marked by limited resources, adoption instead takes more selective forms, oriented toward managing uncertainty and strengthening the capacity to respond to operational constraints. In both configurations, the observed trajectories derive from the coherence between technical requirements, organizational readiness, and territorial conditions, rather than from a linear or universally replicable adoption model.

The analysis of vulnerabilities highlights that the expansion of AI entails risks related to data quality and representativeness, model transferability, the continuity of digital infrastructures, and asymmetries in information governance. These factors affect both the operational reliability of intelligent systems and the distribution of benefits along agri-food value chains, raising issues of equity, accountability, and transparency. From this perspective, practices of responsible design, cooperative models of data governance, and regulated experimental spaces emerge as relevant instruments for steering the introduction of AI toward more inclusive configurations that are better aligned with local specificities.

Overall, AI emerges as a socio-technical transformation process that reconfigures relationships among technologies, organizations, and institutions. The implications for skills, professional roles, and forms of coordination are examined in the subsequent chapters, together with issues of algorithmic governance and regulation. This chapter has therefore outlined the interpretive premises necessary to understand how AI may contribute to the development of agricultural systems that are more informed, resilient, and consistent with the diversity of production contexts.

References

Asante Boakye, E., Zhao, H., & Ahia, B. N. K. (2022). Blockchain technology prospects in transforming Ghana's economy: a phenomenon-based approach. Information Technology for Development, 1–30. https://doi.org/10.1080/02681102.2022.2073580

Assimakopoulos, F., Vassilakis, C., Margaris, D., Kotis, K., & Spiliotopoulos, D. (2024). Artificial intelligence tools for the agriculture value chain: Status and prospects. *Electronics, 13*(22), 4362. https://doi.org/10.3390/electronics13224362

Atapattu, A. J., Perera, L. K., Nuwarapaksha, T. D., Udumann, S. S., & Dissanayaka, N. S. (2024). Challenges in achieving artificial intelligence in agriculture. In *Artificial intelligence techniques in smart agriculture* (pp. 7–34). Springer Nature Singapore. https://doi.org/10.1007/978-981-97-5878-4_2

Ayre, M., Mc Collum, V., Waters, W., Samson, P., Curro, A., Nettle, R., & Reichelt, N., et al. (2019). Supporting and practising digital innovation with advisers in smart farming. *NJAS: Wageningen Journal of Life Sciences, 90–91*(1), 1–12. https://doi.org/10.1016/j.njas.2019.05.001

De Baerdemaeker, J. (2023). *Artificial intelligence in the agri-food sector: Applications, risks and impacts*. European Parliamentary Research Service (EPRS), Scientific Foresight Unit (STOA). PE 734.711.

Baker, J. (2011). The technology–organization–environment framework. In *Information systems theory* (pp. 231–245). https://doi.org/10.1007/978-1-4419-6108-2_12

Bhat, I. A., Ansarullah, S. I., Ahmad, F., Amir, S., Sidana, S., Sinha, A., & Yazdani, G., et al. (2025). Leveraging artificial intelligence in agribusiness: a structured review of strategic management practices and future prospects. *Discover Sustainability, 6*(1). https://doi.org/10.1007/s43621-025-01260-3

Bisheko, M. J., & Rejikumar. (2023). Major barriers to adoption of improved postharvest technologies among smallholder farmers in sub-Saharan Africa and South Asia: A systematic literature review. *World Development Sustainability, 2*(100070), 100070. https://doi.org/10.1016/j.wds.2023.100070

Bronson, K., & Knezevic, I. (2016). Big data in food and agriculture. *Big Data & Society, 3*(1), 205395171664817. https://doi.org/10.1177/2053951716648174

Cao, S., & Huang, C.-M. (2022). Understanding user reliance on AI in assisted decision-making. *Proceedings of the ACM on Human-Computer Interaction, 6*(CSCW2), 1–23. https://doi.org/10.1145/3555572

Chatterjee, S., Rana, N. P., Dwivedi, Y. K., & Baabdullah, A. M. (2021). Understanding AI adoption in manufacturing and production firms using an integrated TAM–TOE model. *Technological Forecasting and Social Change, 170*, Article 120880. https://doi.org/10.1016/j.techfore.2021.120880

Dibbern, T., Romani, L., & Massruhá, S. (2025). Drivers and barriers to digital agriculture adoption: A mixed-methods analysis of challenges and opportunities in Latin American. *Sustainability, 17*(8), 3676. https://doi.org/10.3390/su17083676

Eastwood, C., Klerkx, L., Ayre, M., & Dela Rue, B. (2017). Managing socio-ethical challenges in the development of smart farming: from a fragmented to a comprehensive approach for responsible research and innovation. *Journal of Agricultural and Environmental Ethics, 32*(5–6), 741–768. https://doi.org/10.1007/s10806-017-9704-5

Elbehri, A., & Chestnov, R. (2021). *Digital agriculture in action—Artificial intelligence for agriculture*. Food and Agriculture Organization of the United Nations (FAO) and International Telecommunication Union (ITU).

FAO. (2024, February 28). *Artificial Intelligence: The next frontier in agrifood systems transformation.* https://www.fao.org/brussels/news/news-detail/artificial-intelligence--the-next-frontier-in-agrifood-systems-transformation/en

Forney, J., & Epiney, L. (2022). Governing farmers through data? Digitization and the question of autonomy in agri-environmental governance. *Journal of Rural Studies, 95*, 173–182. https://doi.org/10.1016/j.jrurstud.2022.09.001

Gangwar, H., Date, H., & Ramaswamy, R. (2015). Understanding determinants of cloud computing adoption using an integrated TAM-TOE model. *Journal of Enterprise Information Management, 28*(1), 107–130. https://doi.org/10.1108/jeim-08-2013-0065

Hackfort, S. (2021). Patterns of inequalities in digital agriculture: A systematic literature review. *Sustainability, 13*(22), 12345. https://doi.org/10.3390/su132212345

Horvitz, E., & Mulligan, D. (2015). Data, privacy, and the greater good. *Science, 349*(6245), 253–255. https://doi.org/10.1126/science.aac4520

Jouanjean, M., Casalini, F., Wiseman, L., & Gray, E. (2020). *Issues around data governance in the digital transformation of agriculture: The farmers' perspective* (OECD Food, Agriculture and Fisheries Papers, No. 146). OECD Publishing.

Junior, C. H., Oliveira, T., & Yanaze, M. (2019). The adoption stages (Evaluation, Adoption, and Routinisation) of ERP systems with business analytics functionality in the context of farms. *Computers and Electronics in Agriculture, 156*, 334–348. https://doi.org/10.1016/j.compag.2018.11.028

Klerkx, L., Jakku, E., & Labarthe, P. (2019). A review of social science on digital agriculture, smart farming and agriculture 4.0: New contributions and a future research agenda. *NJAS: Wageningen Journal of Life Sciences, 90–91*(1), 1–16. https://doi.org/10.1016/j.njas.2019.100315

Klerkx, L., & Rose, D. (2020). Dealing with the game-changing technologies of Agriculture 4.0: How do we manage diversity and responsibility in food system transition pathways? *Global Food Security, 24*, 100347. https://doi.org/10.1016/j.gfs.2019.100347

Li, L., Min, X., Guo, J., & Wu, F. (2024). The influence mechanism analysis on the farmers' intention to adopt Internet of Things based on UTAUT-TOE model. *Scientific Reports, 14*(1), 15016. https://doi.org/10.1038/s41598-024-65415-4

Lin, D., Lee, C. K. M., & Lin, K. (2016). Research on effect factors evaluation of internet of things (IOT) adoption in Chinese agricultural supply chain. In *2016 IEEE International Conference on Industrial Engineering and Engineering Management (IEEM)*. https://doi.org/10.1109/ieem.2016.7797948

Luo, W., Zuo, S., Tang, S., & Li, C. (2025). The formation of new quality productivity of agriculture under the perspectives of digitalization and innovation: A dynamic qualitative comparative analysis based on the "Technology-Organization-Environment" framework. *Sustainability, 17*(2), 597. https://doi.org/10.3390/su17020597

Mansoor, S., Iqbal, S., Popescu, S. M., Kim, S. L., Chung, Y. S., & Baek, J.-H. (2025). Integration of smart sensors and IOT in precision agriculture: Trends, challenges and future prospectives. *Frontiers in Plant Science, 16*, 1587869. https://doi.org/10.3389/fpls.2025.1587869

Manzoor, F., Wei, L., Siraj, M., Lu, X., & Qiyang, G. (2025). Digital agriculture technology adoption in low and middle-income countries—a review of contemporary literature. *Frontiers in Sustainable Food Systems, 9*(1621851). https://doi.org/10.3389/fsufs.2025.1621851

McFadden, J., Casalini, F., Griffin, T., & Anton, J. (2022). *The digitalisation of agriculture: A literature review and emerging policy issues* (OECD Food, Agriculture and Fisheries Papers, No. 176). OECD Publishing. https://doi.org/10.1787/285cc27d-en.

Miller, T., Mikiciuk, G., Durlik, I., Mikiciuk, M., Łobodzińska, A., & Śnieg, M. (2025). The IoT and AI in agriculture: The time is now-A systematic review of smart sensing technologies. *Sensors (Basel, Switzerland), 25*(12), 3583. https://doi.org/10.3390/s25123583

Na, S., Heo, S., Han, S., Shin, Y., & Roh, Y. (2022). Acceptance model of artificial intelligence (AI)-based technologies in construction firms: Applying the technology acceptance model (TAM) in combination with the technology–organisation–environment (TOE) framework. *Buildings, 12*(2), 90. https://doi.org/10.3390/buildings12020090

Nagy, A., Tumiwa, J., Arie, F., László, E., Alsoud, A. R., & Al-Dalahmeh, M. (2025). A meta-analysis of the impact of TOE adoption on smart agriculture SMEs performance. *PLoS ONE, 20*(2), Article e0310105. https://doi.org/10.1371/journal.pone.0310105

Omotayo, A. O., Adediran, S. A., Omotoso, A. B., Olagunju, K. O., & Omotayo, O. P. (2025). Artificial intelligence in agriculture: Ethics, impact possibilities, and pathways for policy. *Computers and Electronics in Agriculture, 239*(110927), Article 110927. https://doi.org/10.1016/j.compag.2025.110927

Owen, R., Macnaghten, P., & Stilgoe, J. (2012). Responsible research and innovation: From science in society to science for society, with society. *Science & Public Policy, 39*(6), 751–760. https://doi.org/10.1093/scipol/scs093

Padhiary, M., Kumar, A., & Sethi, L. N. (2025). Emerging technologies for smart and sustainable precision agriculture. *Discover Robotics, 1*(1). https://doi.org/10.1007/s44430-025-00006-0

Penone, C., Giampietri, E., & Trestini, S. (2024). Exploring farmers' intention to adopt marketing contracts: empirical insights using the TOE framework. *Agricultural and Food Economics, 12*(1). https://doi.org/10.1186/s40100-024-00333-7

Ranasinghe, N., Ramanan, A., Fernando, S., Hameed, P. N., Herath, D., Malepathirana, T., & Halgamuge, S., et al. (2022). *Interpretability and accessibility of machine learning in selected food processing, agriculture and health applications.* Preprint retrieved from https://doi.org/10.48550/ARXIV.2211.16699

Rauch, B., Matar, R., & Dörr, J. (2025). *AI-enabled Decision-Making Support Tools (AI DMST) for agriculture: Analysis of market dynamics, technical requirements and stakeholder perspectives.* Fraunhofer IESE. Study prepared for the European Commission, DG CNECT.

Rijswijk, K., Klerkx, L., Bacco, M., Bartolini, F., Bulten, E., Debruyne, L., Dessein, J., Scotti, I., & Brunori, G. (2021). Digital transformation of agriculture and rural areas: A socio-cyber-physical system framework to support responsibilisation. *Journal of Rural Studies, 85*, 79–90. https://doi.org/10.1016/j.jrurstud.2021.05.003

Rogers, E. M., Singhal, A., & Quinlan, M. M. (2014). *Diffusion of innovations. In An integrated approach to communication theory and research* (pp. 432–448). Routledge.

Sen, L. T. H., Phuong, L. T. H., Chou, P., Dacuyan, F. B., Nyberg, Y., & Wetterlind, J. (2025). The opportunities and barriers in developing interactive digital extension services for smallholder farmers as a pathway to sustainable agriculture: A systematic review. *Sustainability, 17*(7), 3007. https://doi.org/10.3390/su17073007

Sharma, K., & Shivandu, S. K. (2024). Integrating artificial intelligence and Internet of Things (IoT) for enhanced crop monitoring and management in precision agriculture. *Sensors International, 5*(100292), Article 100292. https://doi.org/10.1016/j.sintl.2024.100292

Sher, A., Mazhar, S., Rahut, D. B., & Yuan, H. (2025). Leveraging internet use for sustainable agriculture: the impact of digital training on adoption of energy-smart agricultural practices and welfare. *Scientific Reports, 15*(1). https://doi.org/10.1038/s41598-025-16804-w

Songol, M., Awuor, F., & Maake, B. (2021). Adoption of artificial intelligence in agriculture in the developing nations: A review. *Journal of Language, Technology & Entrepreneurship in Africa, 12*(2), 208–229. https://doi.org/10.4314/jolte.v12i2

Sood, A., Sharma, R. K., & Bhardwaj, A. K. (2022). Artificial intelligence research in agriculture: A review. *Online Information Review, 46*(6), 1054–1075. https://doi.org/10.1108/oir-10-2020-0448

Sparrow, R., Howard, M., & Degeling, C. (2021). Managing the risks of artificial intelligence in agriculture. *NJAS: Impact in Agricultural and Life Sciences, 93*(1), 172–196. https://doi.org/10.1080/27685241.2021.2008777

Stilgoe, J., Owen, R., & Macnaghten, P. (2013). Developing a framework for responsible innovation. *Research Policy, 42*(9), 1568–1580. https://doi.org/10.1016/j.respol.2013.05.008

Tornatzky, L. G., & Fleischer, M. (1990). *The processes of technological innovation.* Lexington Books.

Tzachor, A., Devare, M., King, B., Avin, S., & Ó hÉigeartaigh, S. (2022). Responsible artificial intelligence in agriculture requires systemic understanding of risks and externalities. *Nature Machine Intelligence, 4*(2), 104–109. https://doi.org/10.1038/s42256-022-00440-4

wael AL-khatib, A. (2023). Drivers of generative artificial intelligence to fostering exploitative and exploratory innovation: A TOE framework. *Technology in Society, 75*(102403), 102403. https://doi.org/10.1016/j.techsoc.2023.102403

Wang, X., & Liu, N. (2014). The application of internet of things in agricultural means of production supply chain management. *Journal of Chemical and Pharmaceutical Research, 6*(7), 2304–2310.

Wolfert, S., Ge, L., Verdouw, C., & Bogaardt, M.-J. (2017). Big data in smart farming—a review. *Agricultural Systems, 153*, 69–80. https://doi.org/10.1016/j.agsy.2017.01.023

World Economic Forum. (2021). *Artificial intelligence for agriculture innovation (AI4AI)*. World Economic Forum.

Yang, J., Luo, B., Zhao, C., & Zhang, H. (2022). Artificial intelligence healthcare service resources adoption by medical institutions based on TOE framework. *Digital Health, 8*, 20552076221126030. https://doi.org/10.1177/20552076221126034

Yoon, C., Lim, D., & Park, C. (2020). Factors affecting adoption of smart farms: The case of Korea. *Computers in Human Behavior, 108*(106309), Article 106309. https://doi.org/10.1016/j.chb.2020.106309

Chapter 4
Digitalization, Automation, and Agricultural Labor: Tasks, Roles, and Inequality

Abstract This chapter examines the effects of digitalization and Artificial Intelligence on the structure of agricultural labor, interpreting agriculture as a space of co-evolution between human capabilities and intelligent systems. Drawing on a task-based perspective and the framework of "augmented automation," it shows that the introduction of robotics, advanced sensing technologies, and data-driven platforms does not simply substitute human labor, but recomposes tasks along a continuum from routine manual activities to functions with high cognitive intensity. The diffusion of intelligent systems gives rise to new hybrid roles at the interface between agronomic processes and digital infrastructures, while contributing to the polarization of skills and responsibilities within farms and agri-food value chains. From a distributive perspective, the digital transition interacts with pre-existing inequalities related to gender, generation, migrant status, and territorial position, producing a stratified access to technologies and employment opportunities. The final section discusses policy implications, with particular emphasis on inclusion and reskilling measures, hybrid ecosystems, and multi-actor partnerships aimed at promoting more equitable employment outcomes.

Keywords Agricultural labor · Digital agriculture · Skills and polarization · Digital divide

4.1 Introduction

The introduction of digital technologies into agriculture has reactivated a long-standing debate on the relationship between innovation and labor, placing a sector historically grounded in manual work, ecological variability, and tacit knowledge at the center of a profound organizational and cognitive transformation (Bawden, 1991; Castells, 1996; Kloppenburg, 2005). Understanding this transformation requires an interdisciplinary theoretical framework that integrates labor economics, the sociology of innovation, organizational studies, and contributions specifically focused on digital agriculture.

A. Apicella, *Artificial Intelligence in Agriculture*,
https://doi.org/10.1007/978-3-032-26580-7_4

A first point of reference is Keynes's (1933) reflection on *technological unemployment*, which interprets the capacity of technology to reduce labor demand as a process that may unfold more rapidly than the creation of new jobs. This issue was subsequently revisited by Frey and Osborne (2017), who show how digitalization reshapes the structure of occupations. Alongside these contributions, the task-based perspective proposed by Arntz et al. (2016) has highlighted that occupations are composed of heterogeneous activities, some of which are more readily automatable than others, suggesting that understanding automation requires shifting the analytical focus from the "job" as such to its functional decomposition.

This interpretive lens is particularly effective in the agricultural context. Production processes unfold within biologically variable environments, characterized by climatic uncertainty, ecological interdependencies, and seasonal rhythms that constrain standardization and limit the feasibility of full automation. Research on agricultural automation shows that sectoral activities are distributed along a continuum of manual and cognitive tasks, as well as routine and non-routine operations (Marinoudi et al., 2021). Robotic technologies prove especially effective in repetitive and physically demanding operations, while simultaneously generating new functions related to supervision, control, calibration, and process monitoring, thereby reshaping work organization and increasing the technical and managerial complexity of agricultural activities (Rotz et al., 2019).

The shift toward data-driven production systems represents a further critical juncture of transformation. Sensors, Internet of Things (IoT) networks, real-time monitoring systems, predictive models, and machine learning platforms jointly contribute to creating an environment in which decision-making capacity increasingly depends on the integration of information generated by digital infrastructures (Jha et al., 2019). Howard and Lincoln (2023) propose a multilevel interpretation of this reorganization, distinguishing between changes in the workplace, in the nature of work, and in the workforce. This transition does not merely entail a redistribution of tasks; it introduces new modes of human–machine interaction that shape novel operational sequences and redefine the responsibilities associated with production processes.

The perspective of "augmented automation" helps to interpret this dynamic. According to Tschang and Almirall (2021), Artificial Intelligence (AI) does not fully replace human labor; rather, it reconfigures its structure by automating the most codifiable components while expanding the human role in interpretive and context-dependent activities. This form of modularization generates simultaneous processes of operational simplification and increased articulation of supervisory and decision-making tasks, with differentiated effects on the configuration of job roles (Daum, 2025).

Alongside techno-organizational aspects, a substantial body of research highlights the socio-institutional dimension of automation. Apicella (2025) shows that the introduction of AI can alter hierarchies of expertise and modes of coordination, thereby reconfiguring relationships within production contexts. These impacts are strongly mediated by digital infrastructures, public policies, and organizational capabilities (Omotayo et al., 2025). Within this framework, digitalization may also redefine the symbolic relations through which value is attributed to different forms of contribution to the production process, in some cases reinforcing vulnerabilities and inequalities (Ogunyiola, 2025). At a broader scale, technological change in agriculture is embedded in trajectories of structural transformation that involve productivity dynamics, internal labor mobility, and the reorganization of agri-food value chains (Christiaensen et al., 2021).

Taken together, these approaches converge in interpreting agricultural automation as a multilevel phenomenon governed by logics of substitution, complementarity, and transformation. The intersection between intelligent technologies and production contexts characterized by strong environmental heterogeneity generates new tasks, responsibilities, and organizational configurations. Agriculture thus emerges as an advanced laboratory for the co-evolution of knowledge, technology, and labor.

The theoretical framework outlined in this section provides the analytical tools needed to examine, in the following sections, the reconfiguration of work activities (Sect. 4.2), the emergence of new forms of inequality (Sect. 4.3), and strategies for a fair employment transition (Sect. 4.4). Accordingly, this chapter focuses on the effects of digitalization on the structure of agricultural work and on the distribution of employment opportunities. The dimension of digital skills and the training processes that support these transformations will be examined in a systematic manner in Chap. 5.

4.2 Transformations of Roles and Tasks in Smart Agriculture

The adoption of AI and robotics marks a phase of profound restructuring of agricultural work, embedded within the broader process of digitalization of agri-food systems (Shepherd et al., 2020). This evolution aligns with the trajectory outlined by Christiaensen et al. (2020), who interpret digitalization as a new technological wave centered on information management. Whereas earlier transformations primarily enhanced the physical capacity of agricultural labor, the current cycle strengthens the cognitive dimension of production processes, reshaping the nature of decision-making and the composition of operational activities.

At the same time, the structure of agricultural employment is embedded in a context of increasing articulation of agri-food systems. Estimates from the Food and Agriculture Organization (FAO) of the United Nations indicate that in 2019 approximately 857 million people were employed in primary agriculture and an additional 375 million in non-agricultural segments of the value chain, for a total of 1.23 billion workers (Davis et al., 2023). Rather than contracting, the sector has expanded the range of functions located upstream and downstream of production, increasingly taking the form of an ecosystem in which the ability to integrate and coordinate information flows becomes a key determinant of efficiency and competitiveness.

Within agricultural enterprises, the introduction of AI generates multiple forms of task reconfiguration. Documented applications—ranging from decision-support systems based on predictive models and multi-source data (Jha et al., 2019) to smart sensing technologies used in water, nutrient, and plant protection management (Amini & Rahmani, 2023; Lakshmi & Corbett, 2020)—reduce the uncertainty that characterizes many agronomic decisions and shift part of operational monitoring to digital and robotic systems. As a result, everyday work increasingly moves away from direct field interventions toward functions centered on supervising automated processes, controlling operational parameters, and assessing the consistency between data outputs and actual agronomic conditions.

Robotics further contributes to the reorganization of work tasks. The technologies discussed by Javaid et al. (2023)—including harvesting robots, autonomous soil management systems, computer vision platforms, and integrated precision sowing solutions—do not eliminate human involvement but instead reshape its role. Attention increasingly shifts toward managing interactions with intelligent systems, calibrating automated devices, and addressing operational anomalies that arise in day-to-day functioning.

At a broader level, digitalization drives an organizational restructuring that extends across the entire farm. Studies such as those by Rotz et al. (2019) and Ryan (2023) show that the introduction of automated systems reshapes operational hierarchies and expands coordination functions: work is increasingly distributed between biological and digital processes, requires the management of heterogeneous data flows, and unfolds through operational sequences in which technical, operational, and decision-making activities become tightly interdependent. Agriculture thus emerges as a hybrid space in which manual tasks coexist with functions oriented toward control, validation, and the management of intelligent systems.

Overall, the ongoing transition is redefining the role of agricultural labor, making it less centered on physical execution and increasingly oriented toward process management and the regulation of automated systems. Smart agriculture does not merely replace specific tasks; it reorganizes the internal logic of work, reshaping the distribution of operational responsibilities and the structure of job roles across the agri-food value chain.

4.2.1 Substitution and Fragmentation of Operational Work

The most visible dynamic of the digital transition concerns the selective substitution of manual and repetitive tasks. Analyses by Marinoudi et al. (2021) indicate that around 70% of the agricultural domain shows a high potential for robotization, as the activities involved—accounting for nearly 81% of the workforce—are largely standardizable and characterized by low decision-making variability.

Applied studies confirm the rapid advancement of the technologies involved. The intelligent sensing systems documented by Amini and Rahmani (2023) support water and nutrient management, while the solutions discussed by Javaid et al. (2023) and

Omotayo et al. (2025)—including mobile robots, drones, and predictive systems—are assuming an increasingly prominent role in monitoring activities, in the modulation of crop treatments, and in the early detection of plant diseases. Automation does not eliminate entire occupations; rather, it operates at the level of tasks, decomposing work into functional units characterized by different degrees of automatability (Acemoglu & Restrepo, 2019). Within this configuration, human operators are progressively repositioned in roles centered on the coordination of automated processes, verifying the consistency between digital outputs and actual agronomic conditions.

The gap between the potential of automation and its actual implementation remains substantial and reflects underlying structural differences. Bazargani and Deemyad (2024) show that larger firms or those with greater capital availability adopt autonomous robots and decision-support systems more rapidly, whereas small-scale enterprises—often lacking adequate digital infrastructures—remain anchored to manual processes. Davis et al. (2023) further confirm the pronounced structural heterogeneity of global agricultural employment, showing that more than 857 million people are engaged in primary agriculture and that, in low-income countries, the sector accounts for over 60% of total employment. This distribution highlights how the effective capacity to adopt automated technologies is strongly conditioned by deep disparities in productive structures and in the organization of work.

This heterogeneity is embedded within a broader recomposition of work along agri-food value chains. Christiaensen et al. (2020) show that the gradual reduction of direct field activities is accompanied by the expansion of new functions in maintenance services, data management, and logistics. In low-income countries, this process fosters the emergence of models of the servitization of mechanization, in which shared mechanical and digital services create new employment opportunities for technicians and specialized operators (Van Loon et al., 2020).

The transformation is also socio-territorial in nature. Bowen and Morris (2019) document the divide between "connected" and "marginal" agricultural systems, in which unequal access to digital infrastructures generates differentiated employment trajectories. The adoption of intelligent technologies tends to concentrate in better-equipped contexts, thereby amplifying pre-existing differences in productivity and in the organization of work.

Operational transformations also carry identity-related implications. Holm et al. (2024) observe that the progressive replacement of traditional embodied practices with digital interfaces alters the meaning attributed to agricultural work, weakening the centrality of corporeality while strengthening functions oriented toward control, verification, and algorithmic mediation.

Overall, technological substitution does not eliminate labor but rather redesigns its structure, content, and distribution. Agriculture is shifting from an organization centered on physical execution to a configuration in which interaction with automated systems, process verification, and the coordination between digital models and real ecological conditions become central elements. This constitutes the first level of the transformation of agricultural labor and sets the stage for the emergence of new forms of task articulation, which are examined in the following analysis.

4.2.2 *Emergence of Hybrid Roles and New Cognitive Value Chains*

The diffusion of technologies based on AI does not merely transform the execution of existing tasks but also introduces new professional functions situated within activity domains enabled by digitalization (Vardhan et al., 2025). Smart agriculture thus configures an ecosystem in which humans, machines, and digital infrastructures operate through advanced forms of complementarity. Within this context, Marinoudi et al. (2021) show that the tasks least exposed to automation do not coincide with traditional roles, but rather with activities characterized by high decision-making complexity and an increasing reliance on digital information, thereby creating space for profiles positioned at the interface between agronomic processes and information systems.

The technologies described by Javaid et al. (2023)—including intelligent sensors, predictive models, drones, and mobile robots—generate functions that did not previously belong to established professional profiles. The management of heterogeneous information flows, the calibration of intelligent systems, the analysis of algorithmic anomalies, and the integration of biological parameters with computational indicators together constitute a set of activities that reorganizes the distribution of operational responsibilities within agricultural enterprises. Lakshmi and Corbett (2020) interpret these processes within a digital value-creation framework, emphasizing that productive efficiency derives from the stable integration of technological and biological dimensions. In parallel, Bazargani and Deemyad (2024) observe the gradual formation of an information-oriented workforce, which has become a central feature of more highly digitalized firms.

This recomposition concerns not only the content of activities but also their organization. The integration of AI-based systems fosters forms of coordination that involve agronomists, technicians, and analysts, reshaping professional interdependencies and requiring more articulated collaborative structures (Bhat et al., 2025). Pallathadka et al. (2023) describe a process of progressive codification of empirical knowledge, through which farmers' tacit experience is translated into digital representations, predictive models, and analytical procedures, generating new activities centered on the systematic management and interpretation of information.

The expansion of activities that are not strictly agricultural further confirms these trends. Davis et al. (2023) show that a growing share of employment within agri-food systems is concentrated in support services—technical advisory, digital system maintenance, data analysis, and logistics—indicating a significant diversification of professional profiles. The mapping proposed by Binversie and Van Deurzen (2016) shows that traditional functions such as mechanics, farm management, or environmental advisory services provide the foundation for new profiles oriented toward interaction with intelligent devices and digital infrastructures.

These activities are distributed along a cognitive value chain articulated into three interdependent levels: data generation through sensors and autonomous machines; data processing and modeling through AI techniques; and applied interpretation within decision-making processes. As noted by Rotz et al. (2019) and Ryan (2023), the growing centrality of data introduces new organizational criticalities, as the concentration of digital infrastructures among a limited number of actors may constrain the autonomy of agricultural enterprises and intensify informational asymmetries.

Overall, the emergence of hybrid roles signals a profound transformation in the structure of agricultural labor. Firms increasingly rely on profiles operating at the intersection of agronomic activities and digital processes, coordinating information flows, supervising automated systems, and integrating computational models into production decisions. This evolution reorganizes activity chains across the entire value chain, expanding non-manual functions and redefining professional interdependencies within digitalized agri-food systems.

4.2.3 Organizational Recomposition and the Polarization of Skills

Agricultural digitalization is profoundly transforming the organizational structures of the sector, redefining how knowledge, decision-making, and coordination are produced and distributed. Analyses of emerging digital infrastructures show that the growing mediation of activities through platforms, information systems, and data networks is giving rise to an economy based on integrated information flows, in which the orchestration of information becomes a central component of production processes (Rotz et al., 2019; Wolfert et al., 2017). Within this context, firms are no longer merely users of machines but rather nodes within a techno-organizational ecosystem in which human activities and autonomous systems interact on a continuous basis.

This transformation generates an increasing polarization of work functions. Some activities shift toward tasks related to the coordination of digitalized processes, the management of intelligent systems, and the supervision of information flows, while others remain centered on manual operations characterized by low decision-making intensity. This divide primarily reflects firms' unequal capacity to access technological capital and to participate in digital networks. As observed by Bazargani and Deemyad (2024), the decline in young labor and the limited availability of digital infrastructures among smaller enterprises further accentuate the gap between those who govern innovation processes and those who remain positioned in marginal operational segments.

The implications are particularly evident in contexts characterized by high levels of informality. According to FAO analyses (Davis et al., 2023), in many middle-income countries more than 70% of agricultural workers operate within informal circuits, with limited opportunities to access digital networks and to be integrated into the emerging functions associated with automated systems. This results in a double vulnerability: exclusion from innovation processes and marginalization within value chains, as digitalization tends to favor actors endowed with technical resources and organizational capacities.

In parallel, the governance of agricultural activities undergoes significant transformation. The growing integration of digital platforms into planning, monitoring, and resource management embeds work within technical protocols and algorithmic architectures. Ryan (2023) highlights how standards, interfaces, and digital configurations become decisive elements shaping firms' ability to participate in technological transformation, while Holm et al. (2024) draw attention to the issue of shared responsibility between human operators and autonomous systems, so that the delegation of operational functions to machines remains compatible with transparency and safety.

From a sociological perspective, a significant paradox emerges. The reduction of physical labor enabled by automation is accompanied by an intensification of control exercised through digital systems and algorithmic models. Work becomes less material but more tightly constrained by the interfaces and technical protocols that mediate production processes; autonomy no longer coincides with direct command over operations, but rather with the capacity to interact with and negotiate the technologies that orchestrate these processes.

Overall, digitalization produces an ambivalent organizational recomposition. On the one hand, it increases process complexity and the efficiency of activities; on the other, it introduces new lines of exclusion linked to the distribution of technical resources, control over data, and access to digital infrastructures. The challenge lies in translating these asymmetries into forms of coordination capable of integrating actors, devices, and information systems within more inclusive work configurations.

From this perspective, the transformation of agricultural labor takes differentiated forms across the operational, technical, analytical, and organizational dimensions of work activities. The evidence discussed shows that the introduction of AI does not produce a single direction of change, but rather a plurality of processes ranging from the partial automation of manual tasks to the emergence of functions oriented toward information management and the coordination of digital systems. Table 4.1 synthesizes these dynamics by relating the main categories of tasks to the effects documented in the literature and to the modes—substitution, complementarity, or recomposition—through which digitalization redesigns the structure of agricultural labor.

4.3 Gender and Generational Inequalities in Digital Agricultural Labor

Digitalization in agriculture is reshaping work organization by redistributing operational responsibilities and decision-making authority. These changes alter access to employment opportunities and do not unfold in a neutral setting: long-standing inequalities in economic resources, digital infrastructure, and support services shape rural actors' ability to engage with emerging production models, often leading to

Table 4.1 Task dimensions and modes of transformation of agricultural labor under AI and digitalization

Dimension	Examples of tasks / roles	Effects of AI and digitalization	Type of transformation	Sources
Operational–manual	Harvesting, irrigation, weeding, fertilization	Automation through agricultural robots, sensors, computer vision, and predictive systems	Partial substitution— reduction of physical labor and automation of repetitive tasks	Javaid et al. (2023), Marinoudi et al. (2021)
Supervisory–technical	Monitoring, maintenance, and calibration of autonomous robots and digital systems	Anomaly management, coordination of automated processes, human–machine interfacing	Complementarity—human supervision of intelligent systems	Javaid et al. (2023), Marinoudi et al. (2021)
Analytical–informational	Advanced monitoring, multi-source data integration, model-based diagnostics	Transformation of empirical knowledge into digital representations and analytical procedures	Hybridization—expansion of analytical and interpretive activities	Javaid et al. (2023), Pallathadka et al. (2023)
Organizational–managerial	Digital process planning, interdisciplinary coordination, farm data management	Orchestration of intelligent platforms and management of information flows	Organizational recomposition—evolution of technical and managerial roles	Binversie and Van Deurzen (2016), Davis et al. (2023), Rotz et al. (2019)

an uneven distribution of the benefits and burdens of digital transformation (Asai & Antón, 2024).

Within this framework, gender and age emerge as two dimensions along which asymmetries are particularly pronounced (Aranguri et al., 2025; Hirpa Tufa et al., 2022; Wayagi et al., 2025). Differences in access to devices and connectivity, familiarity with digital tools, and positioning within decision-making structures shape actors' capacity to interact with intelligent systems and data platforms. Territorial variation in adoption costs, the availability of technical services, and control over information flows tend to consolidate the advantages of farms endowed with greater economic and organizational capital, thereby reproducing pre-existing power relations (Hackfort, 2021).

Gender inequalities emerge most clearly in contexts characterized by limited mobility, heavy domestic workloads, and restricted access to digital devices (FAO, 2024). These constraints limit women's participation in activities that require interaction with digital systems and intelligent platforms, contributing to their underrepresentation in monitoring, supervisory, and automated process management functions. Women's knowledge, practices, and responsibilities are not always recognized within information systems, which tend to reflect already unbalanced ownership structures and institutional arrangements (World Bank, 2008). A similar dynamic characterizes the generational dimension. The adoption of digital technologies requires the ability to interact with complex infrastructures, manage data, and navigate technical interfaces. In territories marked by an aging workforce or limited support services, these requirements constitute significant barriers for older farmers, favoring the selective integration of younger cohorts into more highly digitalized roles (Asai & Antón, 2024).

The two dimensions reinforce one another when access to digital technologies depends on material resources and organizational capacities that are unevenly distributed. High costs, inadequate connectivity, limited access to devices, and restricted control over data favor the concentration of benefits among farms already integrated into digital markets (Hackfort, 2021). This results in differences in job quality, training opportunities, and positioning within decision-making processes, with implications for generational continuity and the distribution of power along agri-food value chains.

Digitalization thus emerges as a socio-technical transformation that reshapes roles, responsibilities, and employment opportunities, rather than as a purely technological advance. Its outcomes depend on territories' capacity to provide adequate infrastructures, support services, and fair conditions of access to digital technologies. Attention to inequality dynamics makes it possible to grasp how the digital transition may either exacerbate existing vulnerabilities or, conversely, foster rebalancing processes when supported by appropriate institutional and organizational resources.

4.3.1 Digital Divide and Differential Access to Resources

Digital transformation in agriculture unfolds within a landscape of structural inequalities that condition rural territories' capacity to adopt and effectively use advanced technologies. Access to connectivity, communication infrastructures, and technical support services remains uneven, generating significant differences in the ability to deploy data-driven and automated tools. These disparities are particularly evident in agri-food systems, where a substantial share of the rural population lacks the resources required for the continuous use of digital services. The resulting constraints tend to be more pronounced for women and economically disadvantaged groups, reinforcing existing patterns of exclusion in access to digital innovation (Fisher-Post, 2025).

These material asymmetries are closely intertwined with the structure of agricultural production. Inequality within the sector reflects the distribution of firm-level capital and property-based income, factors that systematically advantage enterprises endowed with greater financial resources while constraining the investment capacity of small-scale farms (Fisher-Post, 2025). Digitalization therefore takes root in an already segmented landscape, in which the ability to adopt new devices, software, and monitoring systems depends directly on ownership structures and capital endowments. Alongside economic disparities, long-standing territorial differences further shape patterns of digital adoption. Evidence from several European contexts points to regions characterized by weak infrastructures and limited access to technical services, which already face structural difficulties in integrating into productive networks and innovation circuits. In such areas, the uptake of digital technologies tends to be slower and concentrated among a small number of firms, thereby widening the divide between central and peripheral territories (Schuh et al., 2019).

The digital divide, however, extends beyond material access to technologies. The reorganization of data-driven production processes entails work functions that require continuous interaction with intelligent systems, digital monitoring activities, and the management of information flows. The uneven distribution of these functions generates an increasing segmentation between workers positioned in information-intensive roles and those engaged in executive or seasonal tasks, who face limited opportunities to be incorporated into digitalized processes (Ryan, 2023). These divergences give rise to a form of functional separation that shapes differential access to the opportunities created by digitalization.

Digital technologies also reshape local knowledge regimes by introducing new dependencies on external platforms and data management systems that are not always controlled by rural actors. Analyses of socio-technical inequalities show that the diffusion of innovation is often governed by power structures that determine which forms of knowledge are recognized and valorized and which remain marginal (Bronson, 2019). Within this context, the capacity to retain local control over data and infrastructures becomes a critical factor, as it affects not only productive efficiency but also the ability to influence decision-making processes and development strategies (Hackfort, 2021).

Participation in the digital transition also depends on the institutional systems that support rural communities (Klerkx et al., 2019). Access to technical services, support networks, and organizational structures capable of accompanying innovation represents a critical resource for absorbing the economic and operational costs associated with technological adoption. Where such systems are weak or fragmented, the opportunities generated by digitalization tend to concentrate among actors already endowed with resources and organizational capacity, increasing the risk of exclusion for vulnerable workers and territories (Asai & Antón, 2024).

Overall, these dynamics delineate a multilayered digital divide that combines infrastructural, economic, functional, and institutional dimensions. The fracture between "connected" and "marginal" forms of agriculture concerns not only the use of technologies, but also the capacity to participate in the production, control, and interpretation of the information that shapes agricultural development. In the absence of territorial strategies capable of reducing these asymmetries, digitalization risks reflecting and amplifying pre-existing inequalities.

4.3.2 Youth and Generational Transition

The aging of the agricultural workforce constitutes a structural trend that significantly affects the sector's capacity to absorb processes of digitalization (Daberkow & McBride, 2003; Roberts et al., 2004). European projections point to a gradual decline in total employment alongside an increase in the average age of farm operators, indicating a slowdown in generational turnover and growing difficulties in integrating younger cohorts into production structures (European Commission, 2024). These dynamic conditions the adoption of digital technologies, as the reorganization of production processes requires actors able to operate on a stable basis within farm systems that integrate digital platforms, autonomous machinery, and complex information flows.

Within this context, young people occupy an ambivalent position. On the one hand, they tend to display greater familiarity with digital tools and a significant innovative potential; on the other, they face material and institutional barriers that limit their access to the more advanced segments of agricultural activity (FAO, 2022). Access to land, credit, and stable employment opportunities remains highly unequal, reflecting ownership constraints and structural barriers that shape the ability of younger generations to enter the sector and to assume decision-making roles (Asai & Antón, 2024).

Youth employment trajectories are also marked by heightened instability. Studies on rural labor markets show that young workers often experience discontinuous pathways characterized by seasonal contracts, high mobility, and difficulties in consolidating stable professional positions (Asai & Antón, 2024; IFAD, 2019). This precarity limits their access to the most digitalized firm-level processes, which tend to be concentrated in enterprises endowed with stronger technical and organizational resources. The outcome is an asymmetric distribution of emerging functions: more structured and strategic activities are located within highly capitalized farms, while many young workers remain confined to executive tasks or positions marked by low continuity.

The combination of entry barriers, employment instability, and the concentration of opportunities within better-equipped enterprises leads to a selective integration of younger generations into innovation processes. The result is a growing segmentation between firms that incorporate young workers into central roles within the digital transition and territories in which youth participation remains marginal, with limited capacity to influence the governance of technological systems.

These inequalities are intertwined with institutional and territorial differences. Access to advisory services, adequate infrastructures, and local support systems constitutes a decisive factor in sustaining the entry of younger generations into the agricultural sector (Klerkx et al., 2019). In the absence of such conditions, digitalization risks consolidating a form of modernization without generational renewal, in which technological innovation advances alongside a declining capacity of young people to assume active and transformative roles within rural systems (Asai & Antón, 2024).

4.3.3 Gender Gap and Female Leadership

The digital transition of agriculture unfolds in a context in which women continue to face constrained access to productive resources, support services, and decision-making arenas. These disparities do not represent historical residues, but rather structural features of contemporary rural systems: land ownership is often insecure or fragmented, access to credit requires guarantees that are difficult to obtain, and advisory services tend to address male members of family farms, who are treated as the "natural" interlocutors of institutional structures (World Bank, 2008). Under such conditions, the capacity to invest in digital infrastructures or to assume leadership roles remains severely limited.

The diffusion of digital technologies does not automatically mitigate these asymmetries. In many rural contexts, the use of management platforms, information systems, or online services encounters specific obstacles, including limited access to devices, logistical constraints related to mobility, and time restrictions stemming from the persistent gendered division of domestic labor (FAO, 2023). Digitalization may thus widen the gap between farms endowed with capital, institutional recognition, and integration into market networks, and those in which women's participation remains concentrated in less formal positions with fewer opportunities for investment.

The functioning of agricultural knowledge systems further contributes to reinforcing these disparities. Participation in producer groups, rural networks, and information circuits constitutes a decisive channel for accessing innovation and influencing collective strategies. However, social norms and organizational constraints often limit women's presence in these spaces, reducing their ability to contribute to the definition of production priorities and to local governance arrangements (FAO,

2023). Exclusion from such networks weakens women's decision-making role and restricts their visibility within agri-food value chains.

Inequalities also emerge at the institutional level. Although some studies point to positive effects of women's participation in rural development processes, female representation within the arenas responsible for shaping modernization strategies remains fragile (FAO, 2023). Limited access to public services, low representation in leadership structures, and the absence of adequate support instruments contribute to maintaining a gap between women's potential role in agricultural governance and their actual influence over decision-making processes (Asai & Antón, 2024).

A significant share of women's work also continues to lack formal recognition. Activities that are central to farm functioning—such as livestock care, post-harvest operations, or informal market management—often remain outside official statistics and digital recording systems, which tend to capture only operations associated with formal farm ownership (World Bank, 2008). As management models shift toward data-driven approaches, this invisibility risks being further intensified.

At the same time, there are trajectories in which digitalization opens new possibilities for women's participation and leadership. In contexts where women have access to adequate material resources, support services, and recognized institutional spaces, they assume central roles in the introduction of organizational innovations, in process management, and in the definition of firm-level strategies (FAO, 2023). These experiences indicate that female leadership is not merely an equity objective, but a key component in strengthening the capacity of agricultural systems to coordinate, adapt, and innovate.

Overall, digitalization can function either as an amplifier of inequalities or as a lever for rebalancing, depending on the material, institutional, and organizational conditions within which it unfolds. Gender thus emerges as a structural dimension of agricultural transformation: not an ancillary issue to innovation, but a determining factor shaping its distribution, its effects, and its long-term sustainability.

4.3.4 Migrant Labor and Systemic Vulnerability

Migrant labor constitutes a structural component of contemporary agri-food systems. In many high-intensity production contexts, the functioning of value chains depends on seasonal and temporary workers from abroad, who are primarily employed in operational phases and during periods of peak activity (de Haas et al., 2020; Rye & Scott, 2018). This configuration reflects both the contraction of local labor supply and the growing difficulty faced by farms in recruiting workers willing to take on tasks characterized by strong seasonal pressure and limited employment continuity (Ryan, 2023).

Digitalization does not affect production techniques alone but also contributes to redefining the position of migrant workers within the hierarchy of agricultural tasks. Automation introduces a sharper division between activities oriented toward the supervision of digitalized processes and support activities that are essential to operational continuity (Rotz et al., 2019). The latter tend to be concentrated among migrant workers, who are employed in segments characterized by lower decision-making autonomy and more intermittent contractual arrangements (Schuh et al., 2019). The result is a form of functional segmentation in which innovation concentrates in a limited set of central positions, while executive work remains assigned to more.

The precarity of migrant workers is further intensified by the widespread diffusion of informal employment relations. In many agricultural economies, a substantial share of labor falls outside fully protected arrangements, with consequences for income stability, organizational security, and access to protective services (Davis et al., 2023). Linguistic barriers, constrained mobility, and uncertain legal status further limit migrant workers' ability to engage with rural institutions and to improve their position within production processes (Asai & Antón, 2024).

The growing diffusion of digital platforms for task management introduces new forms of organizational dependency. The centralization of decision-making capacity among actors with access to digital systems and information flows (Cimino et al., 2024) can widen the gap between those who control technologies and those who remain confined to operational activities. In this scenario, the position of migrant workers risks becoming further subordinated, as control over technologies increasingly overlaps with control over labor structures (Hackfort, 2021).

These dynamics illustrate how the digital transition can interact with pre-existing asymmetries, reinforcing the vulnerability of workers already exposed to fragile contractual conditions and limited bargaining power. In the absence of adequate protection mechanisms and institutional inclusion, digitalization risks translating into the reproduction of disparities rather than their mitigation.

Overall, migrant labor emerges as a sensitive node within agricultural transformation: essential to the functioning of value chains yet systematically positioned in subordinate segments of the labor structure. Digitalization makes more explicit the need to address these vulnerabilities as an integral part of productive reorganization, recognizing that the quality of innovation also depends on the capacity of firms and territorial systems to ensure fair, transparent, and stable conditions for all actors involved.

4.4 Policies for a Fair Employment Transition

Agricultural digitalization profoundly reshapes work organization, widening the distance between high cognitive–intensity functions and operational tasks, while intensifying inequalities linked to gender, generation, and socio-economic conditions. In this context, transition policies concern not only the adoption of advanced technologies, but also the creation of conditions that enable actors to participate in emerging productive arrangements. Access to data, the quality of digital infrastructures, institutional capacity, and the presence of cooperative networks all influence the extent to which innovation can be translated into employment opportunities.

This section examines four dimensions through which these dynamics can be interpreted: the reduction of asymmetries in access to knowledge and technologies (Sect. 4.1); instruments for inclusion and reskilling (Sect. 4.2); and the construction of multi-actor ecosystems and partnerships (Sect. 4.3);

4.4.1 From Fragmentation to Equity in Knowledge and Access to Technologies

Agricultural digitalization calls for an expanded understanding of a "just transition," one that encompasses not only the management of potential employment reductions but also the equitable distribution of the conditions that enable participation in the new cognitive organization of production (Benegiamo et al., 2023; Rijswijk et al., 2021). Digitalization reshapes the geography of decision-making control by assigning a central role to access to data, digital infrastructures, and technologies. In the absence of these prerequisites, modernization tends to consolidate stratification in the capacity to influence production processes, drawing a distinction between those who govern digital systems and those who remain confined to predominantly operational functions (Hackfort, 2021).

Innovation policies display differentiated trajectories depending on institutional and territorial contexts. As Asai and Antón (2024) emphasize, effective strategies must be place-based, since the diversity of production structures, labor regimes, and infrastructural endowments makes a uniform model of modernization unfeasible. In industrialized countries, policy attention focuses primarily on data regulation, the definition of responsibilities along digitalized value chains, and the protection of productive capital. In middle-income countries, by contrast, the central challenges concern labor formalization, access to basic infrastructures, and the construction of minimum conditions for non-unequal participation in innovation.

The convergence of AI, robotics, remote sensing, and biotechnologies profoundly reorganizes the distribution of control over information and strategic functions within agricultural systems. The primary risk lies in the concentration of decision-making capacity among actors endowed with strong organizational and infrastructural power. According to the World Economic Forum (2025), these technologies require complex ecosystems—including data governance arrangements, digital networks, communication infrastructures, and interdisciplinary research—if their benefits are not to remain confined to the most highly capitalized firms.

Reducing informational fragmentation entails the construction of shared spaces for coordination and learning. Hackfort (2021) interprets digitalization as a socio-technical process that can generate new asymmetries, whose mitigation depends on actors' capacity to co-produce knowledge and organizational arrangements. Such spaces make it possible to contextualize innovation, adapt it to local ecological and social conditions, and integrate situated agricultural knowledge into the decision-making logics of digitalized systems.

From this perspective, labor represents a structural dimension of transformation. As Dedieu (2019) observes, technical innovations do not merely alter production processes but also redefine the professional worlds that sustain them. Policies oriented toward a fair transition must therefore recognize agricultural labor as a constitutive component of the innovation ecosystem, rather than as a variable to be addressed solely through compensatory measures.

Within this framework, a fair employment transition takes the form of a negotiated process aimed at building a shared cognitive and organizational infrastructure. Policies that integrate data governance, equitable access to technologies, and the valorization of local resources constitute essential conditions for ensuring that digitalization functions as a driver of inclusion, rather than consolidating new lines of segmentation within rural systems.

4.4.2 Instruments for Inclusion and Reskilling

The digital transformation of agricultural systems requires instruments capable of reducing the structural barriers that limit access to technologies, data, and organizational infrastructures. Digitalization redistributes activities and responsibilities along the value chain, and the ability to participate in its more strategic segments depends on the availability of material resources, territorial connections, and adequate forms of institutional support (Dedieu, 2019; OECD, 2025). In many contexts, the distance between actors endowed with high organizational capacity and farms with limited resources fuels gaps that are reflected in job quality and in the ability to assume roles within decision-making structures (Ryan, 2023).

Three lines of intervention are particularly relevant for supporting equitable access to digitalized systems.

1. Strengthening Technical and Organizational Support Services

The heterogeneity of territorial endowments makes the presence of support services essential for facilitating technology adoption and the management of digital systems. Place-based approaches, as suggested by Asai and Antón (2024), reduce the distance between innovation and rural contexts, thereby enabling the participation of farms with fewer resources. These services do not replace agricultural labor; rather, they enhance its capacity to interact with platforms and with the coordination mechanisms that govern production.

2. **Economic and Institutional Instruments to Reduce Barriers to Technology Access**

The ability to adopt digital solutions depends on the availability of instruments capable of easing initial costs and capital constraints, which are particularly burdensome for small producers and workers in vulnerable conditions (Davis et al., 2012; Šūmane et al., 2018; Van den Berg & Jiggins, 2007). Measures that integrate technical support, proximity services, and forms of economic assistance strengthen rural actors' capacity to access technologies without being excluded from productive networks.

3. **Territorial Platforms and Shared Infrastructures**

The development of territorial hubs and collaborative platforms makes it possible to share technological resources that would otherwise be accessible only to large-scale enterprises. These arrangements, often developed through public–private partnerships, also enable small-scale farms to use digital analytics systems, remote sensing, and deep-tech solutions, thereby broadening the social base of digitalization (Nxumalo & Chauke, 2025; Stojanova et al., 2022; World Economic Forum, 2025). Beyond cost reduction, such ecosystems foster coordination among actors and facilitate information circulation, which constitutes a core component of data-driven agricultural systems.

Taken together, these instruments contribute to the construction of a shared organizational infrastructure that supports equitable participation in the digital transition. Inclusion does not emerge as an additional objective of modernization, but rather as a necessary condition for ensuring that the socio-technical reorganization of agriculture does not amplify pre-existing inequalities.

4.4.3 Hybrid Ecosystems and Multi-Actor Partnerships

The effectiveness of policies for the digital transition depends on the capacity to build hybrid ecosystems in which public institutions, firms, and territorial actors share responsibilities, resources, and design capabilities. Digitalization introduces socio-technical transformations that require coordinated forms of governance, capable of integrating heterogeneous bodies of knowledge and adapting them to territorial specificities. From this perspective, the place-based approach emphasized by Asai and Antón (2024) highlights the importance of aligning technical arrangements, territorial services, and institutional configurations in order to support inclusive innovation processes.

Living labs constitute one of the core components of such ecosystems. As highlighted by McPhee et al. (2021), they operate as "in vivo" experimental environments in which farmers, researchers, and public decision-makers collaborate to develop solutions under real operating conditions. Iterative experimentation fosters the emergence of contextualized innovations capable of integrating professional expertise and local knowledge, and contributes to building the territorial capacities required for the governance and management of digitalized systems.

Alongside living labs, multi-actor platforms play a significant role in coordinating the technological transition. The involvement of farmers, technicians, start-ups, and public institutions facilitates the adaptation of technologies to local needs, the identification of organizational barriers, and the testing of solutions calibrated to different contexts (Nesheim et al., 2021; Poti & Joy, 2022). The convergence of AI, robotics, distributed sensors, and remote observation systems expands the scope for intervention, but also requires cooperative data management regimes, interoperability standards, and shared infrastructures, as indicated by the World Economic Forum (2025).

The construction of public–private–community partnerships represents a further lever for strengthening inclusion and equitable access to innovation processes (Aseete et al., 2023; van Ewijk et al., 2024). Evidence on the functioning of rural networks shows that the involvement of diverse actors broadens the social base of innovation, fostering a more balanced distribution of the opportunities generated by digitalization (FAO, 2023). Such partnerships enable the sharing of resources, the reduction of informational asymmetries, and the support of modernization processes aligned with territorial needs.

Taken together, hybrid ecosystems, living labs, and multi-actor platforms operate as essential infrastructures for an inclusive digital transition. They enable innovation to be articulated as a collaborative process and help mitigate disparities in access to knowledge and resources, thereby strengthening the capacity of agricultural systems to adapt to complex technological transformations.

4.5 Conclusions

Agricultural digitalization profoundly redefines the organization of work, transforming the relationship between operational activities, professional knowledge, and technological tools. The emergence of automated systems, data infrastructures, and intelligent devices shifts the center of labor activity toward functions of interpretation, supervision, and technical coordination, without diminishing the centrality of human contribution. Agricultural labor thus takes the form of a continuous interaction among situated knowledge, algorithmic models, and complex production environments.

The analysis developed in this chapter shows how these processes give rise to heterogeneous professional configurations, in which traditional tasks are recomposed alongside emerging roles linked to information management and the operation of automated systems. Their distribution is not uniform: socio-economic conditions, gender, age, migrant status, and territorial positioning shape the ability to access technologies, to interact with new digital tools, and to participate in the decision-making processes that accompany them. The result is the emergence of lines of inequality that reflect—and in some cases amplify—fractures already present within rural systems.

The digital transition therefore does not take the form of a linear pathway, but rather of a set of trajectories shaped by institutional capacities, local resources, and the organization of innovation networks. Within this framework, cooperative ecosystems, living labs, and multi-actor platforms acquire a growing role, as they enable the integration of heterogeneous forms of knowledge, the experimentation of context-specific solutions, and the construction of collective learning processes.

Overall, agricultural labor in the era of AI emerges as a space of co-evolution between human capabilities and intelligent systems. The quality of this co-evolution depends on the capacity to valorize the plurality of forms of knowledge embedded in territories and to build organizational configurations capable of supporting broad and differentiated participation in emerging production regimes.

These transformations place digital skills at the center of the analysis, highlighting their multilevel articulation and the policies required to support their development. These issues are addressed in Chap. 5, which provides a dedicated examination of the main international frameworks and proposes an interpretive model of skills for digital agriculture.

References

Acemoglu, D., & Restrepo, P. (2019). Automation and new tasks: How technology displaces and reinstates labor. *The Journal of Economic Perspectives: A Journal of the American Economic Association, 33*(2), 3–30. https://doi.org/10.1257/jep.33.2.3

Amini, M., & Rahmani, A. (2023). Agricultural databases evaluation with machine learning procedure. *Australian Journal of Engineering and Applied Science, 8*(6), 39–49.

Apicella, A. (2025). Automation in agriculture: Occupational trends, worker outcomes, and labor market implications. *International Journal of Academic Research in Business and Social Sciences, 15*(8). https://doi.org/10.6007/ijarbss/v15-i8/26128

Arangurí, M., Mera, H., Noblecilla, W., & Lucini, C. (2025). Digital literacy and technology adoption in agriculture: A systematic review of factors and strategies. *AgriEngineering, 7*(9), 296. https://doi.org/10.3390/agriengineering7090296

Arntz, M., Gregory, T., & Zierahn, U. (2016). *The risk of automation for jobs in OECD countries: A comparative analysis*. (OECD Social, Employment and Migration Working Papers, No. 189). OECD Publishing. https://doi.org/10.1787/5jlz9h56dvq7-en

Asai, M. & Antón, J. (2024). *Social issues in agriculture in rural areas* (OECD Food, Agriculture and Fisheries Papers No. 212). OECD Publishing. https://doi.org/10.1787/fec15b38-en

Aseete, P., Barkley, A., Katungi, E., Ugen, M. A., & Birachi, E. (2023). Public-private partnership generates economic benefits to smallholder bean growers in Uganda. *Food Security, 15*(1), 201–218. https://doi.org/10.1007/s12571-022-01309-5

Bawden, R. J. (1991). Systems thinking and practice in agriculture. *Journal of Dairy Science, 74*(7), 2362–2373. https://doi.org/10.3168/jds.s0022-0302(91)78410-5

Bazargani, K., & Deemyad, T. (2024). Automation's impact on agriculture: Opportunities, challenges, and economic effects. *Robotics, 13*(2), 33. https://doi.org/10.3390/robotics13020033

Benegiamo, M., Corrado, A., & Fama, M. (2023). Agricultural digitalisation and just transition: a framework for the analysis. *Rivista Di Economia Agraria, 78*(2), 5–17. https://doi.org/10.36253/rea-14491

Bhat, I. A., Ansarullah, S. I., Ahmad, F., Amir, S., Sidana, S., Sinha, A., Yazdani, G., et al. (2025). Leveraging artificial intelligence in agribusiness: a structured review of strategic management practices and future prospects. *Discover Sustainability, 6*(1). https://doi.org/10.1007/s43621-025-01260-3

Binversie, L. & Van Deurzen, C. (2016). *Exploring agricultural careers*. University of Wisconsin–Madison Division of Extension.

Bowen, R., & Morris, W. (2019). The digital divide: Implications for agribusiness and entrepreneurship. Lessons from Wales. *Journal of Rural Studies, 72*, 75–84. https://doi.org/10.1016/j.jrurstud.2019.10.031

Bronson, K. (2019). Looking through a responsible innovation lens at uneven engagements with digital farming. *NJAS: Wageningen Journal of Life Sciences, 90–91*(1), 1–6. https://doi.org/10.1016/j.njas.2019.03.001

Castells, M. (1996). *The information age: Economy, society and culture (3 volumes).* Blackwell.

Christiaensen, L., Rutledge, Z. & Taylor, J. E. (2020). *The future of work in agriculture: Some reflections World Bank policy Res* (Working Paper. 9193)

Christiaensen, L., Rutledge, Z., & Taylor, J. E. (2021). Viewpoint: The future of work in agri-food. *Food Policy, 99*(101963), Article 101963. https://doi.org/10.1016/j.foodpol.2020.101963

Cimino, A., Coniglio, I. M., Corvello, V., Longo, F., Sagawa, J. K., & Solina, V. (2024). Exploring small farmers behavioral intention to adopt digital platforms for sustainable and successful agricultural ecosystems. *Technological Forecasting and Social Change, 204*(123436), Article 123436. https://doi.org/10.1016/j.techfore.2024.123436

European Commission. (2024). *EU agricultural outlook, 2024–2035.* European Commission, DG Agriculture and Rural Development, Brussels.

Daberkow, S. G., & McBride, W. D. (2003). Farm and operator characteristics affecting the awareness and adoption of precision agriculture technologies in the US. *Precision Agriculture, 4*(2), 163–177. https://doi.org/10.1023/a:1024557205871

Daum, T. (2025). Digitalization and skills in agriculture. *Outlook on Agriculture, 54*(2), 171–181. https://doi.org/10.1177/00307270251336474

Davis, B., Mane, E., Gurbuzer, L.Y., Caivano, G., Piedrahita, N., Schneider, K., Azhar, N., Benali, M., Chaudhary, N., Rivera, R., Ambikapathi, R. & Winters, P. (2023). *Estimating global and country-level employment in agrifood systems* (FAO Statistics Working Paper Series, No. 23–34). FAO. https://doi.org/10.4060/cc4337en

Davis, K., Nkonya, E., Kato, E., Mekonnen, D. A., Odendo, M., Miiro, R., & Nkuba, J. (2012). Impact of farmer field schools on agricultural productivity and poverty in East Africa. *World Development, 40*(2), 402–413. https://doi.org/10.1016/j.worlddev.2011.05.019

de Haas, H., Castles, S., & Miller, M. J. (2020). *The age of migration* (6th ed.). Guilford Publications.

Dedieu, B. (2019). Transversal views on work in agriculture. *Cahiers Agricultures, 28*, 8. https://doi.org/10.1051/cagri/2019008

FAO. (2022). Rural youth action plan. *Rome.* https://doi.org/10.4060/cc0583en

FAO. (2023). The status of women in agrifood systems. *Rome.* https://doi.org/10.4060/cc5343en

FAO. (2024). *Gender gap in agricultural labour productivity: A cross-country comparison.* https://doi.org/10.4060/cc9118en

Fisher-Post, M. (2025). *Inequality and agricultural structural change: Evidence from macro and microdata, 1950-present* (WIDER Working Paper Series wp-2025–5). World Institute for Development Economic Research (UNU-WIDER).

Frey, C. B., & Osborne, M. A. (2017). The future of employment: How susceptible are jobs to computerisation? *Technological Forecasting and Social Change, 114*, 254–280. https://doi.org/10.1016/j.techfore.2016.08.019

Hackfort, S. (2021). Patterns of inequalities in digital agriculture: A systematic literature review. *Sustainability, 13*(22), 12345. https://doi.org/10.3390/su132212345

Hirpa Tufa, A., Alene, A. D., Cole, S. M., Manda, J., Feleke, S., Abdoulaye, T., & Manyong, V. (2022). Gender differences in technology adoption and agricultural productivity: Evidence from Malawi. *World Development, 159*(106027), Article 106027. https://doi.org/10.1016/j.worlddev.2022.106027

Holm, S., Pedersen, S. M., & Tamirat, T. W. (2024). Robots in agriculture – A case-based discussion of ethical concerns on job loss, responsibility, and data control. *Smart Agricultural Technology, 9*(100633). https://doi.org/10.1016/j.atech.2024.100633

Howard, J., & Lincoln, J. M. (2023). Future of work in agriculture. *Journal of Agromedicine, 28*(1), 1–4. https://doi.org/10.1080/1059924X.2022.2137615

IFAD. (2019). *Creating opportunities for rural youth 2019.* Rural Development Report.

Javaid, M., Haleem, A., Khan, I. H., & Suman, R. (2023). Understanding the potential applications of Artificial Intelligence in Agriculture Sector. *Advanced Agrochem, 2*(1), 15–30. https://doi.org/10.1016/j.aac.2022.10.001

Jha, K., Doshi, A., Patel, P., & Shah, M. (2019). A comprehensive review on automation in agriculture using artificial intelligence. *Artificial Intelligence in Agriculture, 2*, 1–12. https://doi.org/10.1016/j.aiia.2019.05.004

Keynes, J. M. (1933). Economic possibilities for our grandchildren. *Essays in Persuasion* (pp. 358–373). Macmillan.

Klerkx, L., Jakku, E., & Labarthe, P. (2019). A review of social science on digital agriculture, smart farming and agriculture 4.0: New contributions and a future research agenda. *NJAS: Wageningen Journal of Life Sciences, 90–91*(1), 1–16. https://doi.org/10.1016/j.njas.2019.100315

Kloppenburg Jr, J. R. (2005). *First the seed: The political economy of plant biotechnology*. Univ of Wisconsin Press.

Lakshmi, V., & Corbett, J. (2020). How artificial intelligence improves agricultural productivity and sustainability: A global thematic analysis. In *Proceedings of the Annual Hawaii International conference on system sciences*. https://doi.org/10.24251/hicss.2020.639

Marinoudi, V., Lampridi, M., Kateris, D., Pearson, S., Sørensen, C. G., & Bochtis, D. (2021). The future of agricultural jobs in view of robotization. *Sustainability, 13*(21), 12109. https://doi.org/10.3390/su132112109

McPhee, C., Bancerz, M., Mambrini-Doudet, M., Chrétien, F., Huyghe, C., & Gracia-Garza, J. (2021). The defining characteristics of agroecosystem living labs. *Sustainability, 13*(4), 1718. https://doi.org/10.3390/su13041718

Nesheim, I., Sundnes, F., Enge, C., Graversgaard, M., van den Brink, C., Farrow, L., Tendler, L. (2021). Multi-actor platforms in the water–agriculture nexus: Synergies and long-term meaningful engagement. *Water, 13*(22), 3204. https://doi.org/10.3390/w13223204

Nxumalo, G. S., & Chauke, H. (2025). Challenges and opportunities in smallholder agriculture digitization in South Africa. *Frontiers in Sustainable Food Systems, 9*(1583224). https://doi.org/10.3389/fsufs.2025.1583224

OECD. (2025). The global forum on productivity at 10: Past and future perspectives on reviving productivity growth. *OECD Publishing, Paris,*. https://doi.org/10.1787/ca7295d9-en

Ogunyiola, A. (2025). The changing face of Agrarian labor in the age of artificial intelligence and machine learning: Balancing benefits and risks. *AI & Society, 40*(1), 223–224. https://doi.org/10.1007/s00146-023-01859-y

Omotayo, A. O., Adediran, S. A., Omotoso, A. B., Olagunju, K. O., & Omotayo, O. P. (2025). Artificial intelligence in agriculture: Ethics, impact possibilities, and pathways for policy. *Computers and Electronics in Agriculture, 239*(110927), Article 110927. https://doi.org/10.1016/j.compag.2025.110927

Pallathadka, H., Mustafa, M., Sanchez, D. T., Sekhar Sajja, G., Gour, S., & Naved, M. (2023). Impact of Machine Learning on Management, Healthcare and Agriculture. *Materials Today: Proceedings, 80*, 2803–2806. https://doi.org/10.1016/j.matpr.2021.07.042

Poti, S., & Joy, S. (2022). Digital platforms for connecting actors in the agtech space: Insights on platform development from participatory action research on KisanMitr. *Journal of Indian Business Research, 14*(1), 65–83. https://doi.org/10.1108/jibr-04-2021-0145

Reissig, L., Wiseman, L., & Cockburn, M. (2024). Farmers and their data: Evaluating the swiss conception of data sharing through the lens of digital farming. *Journal of Rural Studies, 111*(103390), Article 103390. https://doi.org/10.1016/j.jrurstud.2024.103390

Rijswijk, K., Klerkx, L., Bacco, M., Bartolini, F., Bulten, E., Debruyne, L., Brunori, G., et al. (2021). Digital transformation of agriculture and rural areas: A socio-cyber-physical system framework to support responsibilisation. *Journal of Rural Studies, 85*, 79–90. https://doi.org/10.1016/j.jrurstud.2021.05.003

Roberts, R. K., English, B. C., Larson, J. A., Cochran, R. L., Goodman, W. R., Larkin, S. L., Reeves, J. M., et al. (2004). Adoption of site-specific information and variable-rate technologies in cotton precision farming. *Journal of Agricultural and Applied Economics, 36*(1), 143–158. https://doi.org/10.1017/s107407080002191x

Rotz, S., Gravely, E., Mosby, I., Duncan, E., Finnis, E., Horgan, M., Fraser, E., et al. (2019). Automated pastures and the digital divide: How agricultural technologies are shaping labour and rural communities. *Journal of Rural Studies, 68*, 112–122. https://doi.org/10.1016/j.jrurstud.2019.01.023

Ryan, M. (2023*). An assessment of the labour and skills shortages in agriculture and the food sector*. OECD Publishing. TAD/CA/APM/WP(2022)12/FINAL.

Rye, J. F., & Scott, S. (2018). International labour migration and food production in rural Europe: A review of the evidence. *Sociologia Ruralis, 58*(4), 928–952. https://doi.org/10.1111/soru.12208

Schuh, B et al. (2019). *Research for AGRI committee – The EU farming employment: current challenges and future prospects*. European Parliament, Policy Department for Structural and Cohesion Policies, Brussels.

Shepherd, M., Turner, J. A., Small, B., & Wheeler, D. (2020). Priorities for science to overcome hurdles thwarting the full promise of the 'digital agriculture' revolution. *Journal of the Science of Food and Agriculture, 100*(14), 5083–5092. https://doi.org/10.1002/jsfa.9346

Stojanova, S., Cvar, N., Verhovnik, J., Božić, N., Trilar, J., Kos, A., & Stojmenova Duh, E. (2022). Rural Digital Innovation Hubs as a paradigm for sustainable business models in Europe's rural areas. *Sustainability, 14*(21), 14620. https://doi.org/10.3390/su142114620

Šūmane, S., Kunda, I., Knickel, K., Strauss, A., Tisenkopfs, T., Rios, I. D. I., Ashkenazy, A., et al. (2018). Local and farmers' knowledge matters! How integrating informal and formal knowledge enhances sustainable and resilient agriculture. *Journal of Rural Studies, 59*, 232–241. https://doi.org/10.1016/j.jrurstud.2017.01.020

Tschang, F. T., & Almirall, E. (2021). Artificial intelligence as augmenting automation: Implications for employment. *The Academy of Management Perspectives, 35*(4), 642–659. https://doi.org/10.5465/amp.2019.0062

Van den Berg, H., & Jiggins, J. (2007). Investing in farmers—the impacts of farmer field schools in relation to integrated pest management. *World Development, 35*(4), 663–686. https://doi.org/10.1016/j.worlddev.2006.05.004

van Ewijk, E., Ataa-Asantewaa, M., Asubonteng, K. O., Van Leynseele, Y. P. B., Derkyi, M., Laven, A., & Ros-Tonen, M. A. F. (2024). Farmer-centred multi-stakeholder platforms: From iterative approach to conceptual embedding. *Journal of the Knowledge Economy, 15*(4), 17077–17107. https://doi.org/10.1007/s13132-023-01661-7

Van Loon, J., Woltering, L., Krupnik, T. J., Baudron, F., Boa, M., & Govaerts, B. (2020). Scaling agricultural mechanization services in smallholder farming systems: Case studies from sub-Saharan Africa, South Asia, and Latin America. *Agricultural Systems, 180*(102792), Article 102792. https://doi.org/10.1016/j.agsy.2020.102792

Vardhan, P. N. H., Badavath, A., & Srivalli, P. (2025). Artificial intelligence and its applications in agriculture: A review. *Environment Conservation Journal, 26*(1), 274–280. https://doi.org/10.36953/ecj.28802904

Wayagi, E. O., Otieno, D. J., Nyikal, R. A., Okello, J. J., & Kawarazuka, N. (2025). Gender-age differences in the use of ICT platforms among potato farmers in Kenya. *Cogent Food & Agriculture, 11*(1). https://doi.org/10.1080/23311932.2025.2568754

Wolfert, S., Ge, L., Verdouw, C., & Bogaardt, M.-J. (2017). Big data in smart farming—a review. *Agricultural Systems, 153*, 69–80. https://doi.org/10.1016/j.agsy.2017.01.023

World Economic Forum. (2025). *Shaping the deep-tech revolution in agriculture.* Insight Report, World Economic Forum.

World Bank. (2008). *Gender in agriculture sourcebook.* World Bank.

Chapter 5
Digital Skills, AI, and Learning Agriculture

Abstract The digitalization of agriculture generates new skill requirements, as interactions with data, platforms, and AI-based systems profoundly reshape decision-making and organizational practices across the sector. This chapter examines major international frameworks on digital competence and AI literacy developed by European and multilateral institutions, discussing their implications for agri-food systems. Building on a comparative analysis of these frameworks and a targeted review of the literature on digital agriculture and smart farming, the chapter proposes a multilevel interpretive model articulated across five dimensions: digital systems thinking and data awareness; continuous and adaptive learning; integration of hybrid knowledge and reflective professional identity; digital collaboration and intelligent communities; and advanced digital literacy and technological mastery of AI. The chapter shows how digitalization fosters the emergence of hybrid agricultural professional profiles positioned at the interface between agronomic knowledge, analytical capacity, and ethical responsibility in the use of data and algorithms. In the concluding section, the concept of learning agriculture is developed as a cognitive ecosystem in which human capital, institutions, and digital infrastructures co-evolve, making skills the central driver of an inclusive and sustainable digital transition.

Keyword Digital literacy · AI literacy · Learning agriculture

5.1 Introduction

Digitalization is transforming agriculture into a knowledge-based system in which Artificial Intelligence (AI), the Internet of Things (IoT), and data analytics reorganize not only production practices but also the ways in which decision environments are interpreted (Ahmed & Shakoor, 2025; Raj & Prahadeeswaran, 2025). In continuity with the discussion developed in Chap. 4, this evolution does not concern the mere introduction of technological tools. Rather, it entails a broader cognitive transformation that reshapes the nature of agricultural labor by increasing the relevance of interpretive activities and the skills required to integrate complex information into

A. Apicella, *Artificial Intelligence in Agriculture*,
https://doi.org/10.1007/978-3-032-26580-7_5

management processes (Klerkx et al., 2019). Digital technologies generate value only when actors possess the capabilities needed to orient their use in a strategic and sustainable manner and to align them with specific ecological and socioeconomic contexts (Daum, 2025; EIP-AGRI, 2020).

This transition, however, unfolds unevenly. In high-income countries, the prevailing challenge lies in updating consolidated skills and adapting education and training systems to a data-oriented economy (Oli et al., 2025). In middle- and low-income countries, attention instead focuses on equitable access to digital infrastructures, the development of basic digital literacy, and the construction of learning ecosystems capable of including small-scale producers (Porciello et al., 2022). In the absence of such conditions, digitalization may generate divergent outcomes: it can trigger processes of deskilling, reducing decision-making autonomy and the value of experiential knowledge, or activate pathways of reskilling and upskilling that expand managerial capabilities and analytical competences (Daum, 2025; Soma & Nuckchady, 2021).

The skills required by digital agriculture are articulated across multiple domains. The European Innovation Partnership for Agricultural Productivity and Sustainability (EIP-AGRI) (2020) identifies six core areas: openness to change, comprehensive management capabilities, communication and collaboration, the ability to connect technologies and processes ("bridging"), digital literacy, and advanced digital skills. Together, these categories describe a shift in agricultural labor from a predominantly operational activity to a collective cognitive process based on the integration of tacit knowledge, data, and computational models (Daum, 2025; Sørensen et al., 2021). The automation of information flows reshapes the "sense–analyze–act" decision cycle, generating the need for hybrid forms of learning that combine direct experience, continuous updating, and informal knowledge exchange (Goller et al., 2021).

At the same time, differential access to skills shapes economic opportunities and participation in digitalized processes. The lack of adequate digital capabilities can widen existing gaps in rural areas, making the development of inclusive human capital a strategic objective for rural development (Cheng et al., 2024). In this context, the conceptual framework of Agricultural Knowledge and Innovation Systems (AKIS) provides a relevant analytical lens to describe the set of actors and relationships that support the generation, circulation, and application of knowledge in agriculture (FAO and World Bank, 2000). Universities, research centers, and extension services act as central nodes within these systems, facilitating learning and innovation processes and contributing to the reduction of information asymmetries (Bampasidou et al., 2024). Major international organizations converge on this perspective: the Food and Agriculture Organization (FAO), the International Fund for Agricultural Development (IFAD), and the World Bank Group promote the development of public digital infrastructures, data governance programs, and investments in training aimed at fostering an inclusive and sustainable adoption of agricultural technologies (Elbehri & Chestnov, 2021; IFAD, 2025; World Bank Group, 2025).

From a microeconomic perspective, digital skills strengthen entrepreneurial capacity, improve market positioning, and enhance farm resilience, even in the presence of significant barriers for young farmers and new entrants (Campi et al.,

2024; Xue et al., 2025). From this standpoint, digitalization constitutes a cognitive, economic, and institutional transformation that elevates knowledge to a shared resource and a prerequisite for the sustainability of agricultural systems. The remainder of the chapter develops this perspective by, first, reviewing the main institutional frameworks on digital and AI-driven skills (Sect. 5.2) and, second, proposing a multilevel interpretive model of skills for digital agriculture (Sect. 5.3), which provides the basis for the concluding reflections on learning agriculture (Sect. 5.4).

5.2 Policy and International Frameworks for Digital and AI Skills in Agriculture

After situating the issue of skills within the broader context of the cognitive transformation of agri-food systems, this section examines the main international frameworks that define standards, shared vocabularies, and objectives for digital and AI literacy. The evolution of digital and AI-related skills in agriculture is embedded in a wider process of international standard-setting for digital literacy, initiated in Europe more than a decade ago. Through the Joint Research Centre (JRC), the European Commission has promoted a pathway aimed at developing a common language to describe, assess, and foster citizens' digital competence (Carretero et al., 2017).

The first version of the Digital Competence Framework for Citizens (DigComp) introduced an innovative understanding of digital competence, conceived not as a purely technical ability but as a form of cognitive, social, and ethical literacy required for active participation in a data-intensive society. This approach was consolidated with DigComp 2.1, which articulates digital competence into five areas—information and data literacy, communication and collaboration, digital content creation, safety, and problem solving—and structures them across eight progressive levels of proficiency (Carretero et al., 2017).

A significant evolution is represented by DigComp 2.2, which updates the framework by incorporating examples of knowledge, skills, and attitudes related to AI, datafication, accessibility, digital sustainability, and hybrid work (Vuorikari et al., 2022). The inclusion of an appendix dedicated to citizens' interactions with algorithmic systems introduces the theme of AI literacy, understood as the capacity to comprehend, interpret, and govern automated processes. This has direct implications for agriculture, where the use of predictive models, decision-support systems, and precision farming applications makes a critical understanding of algorithmic mechanisms increasingly necessary. The integration of DigComp within the Digital Decade and the European Skills Agenda further consolidates its institutional role by defining measurable targets—such as ensuring that 80% of the European population possesses at least basic digital skills by 2030—and by steering Member States toward educational models based on comparable standards.

In parallel, the JRC has extended the competence framework approach to related domains. GreenComp (Bianchi et al., 2022) represents the most ambitious attempt to integrate digital competences with sustainability. Structured around four areas—*embodying sustainability values*, *embracing complexity*, *envisioning sustainable futures*, and *acting for sustainability*—the framework advances a holistic approach to lifelong learning, with particular emphasis on the capacity to understand complex systems, exercise ethical judgment, and envision sustainable development pathways. These competences are especially relevant for digital agriculture, where the interaction between technologies, ecological data, and agri-food processes requires the ability to interpret socio-ecological dynamics and integrate them into decision-making processes.

Taken together, DigComp, DigComp 2.2, and GreenComp outline an evolutionary trajectory that can be summarized in three phases:

1. **2013–2017**: Digital standardization, characterized by the definition of a shared language and comparable levels of proficiency.
2. **2018–2022**: Cognitive and technological integration, marked by the incorporation of AI, datafication, green information and communication technologies, and new application contexts.
3. **From 2022 Onward**: Sustainability and systemic orientation, with the introduction of ecological and value-based competences that extend digital literacy toward forms of "systemic intelligence."

From this perspective, the digital competence of agricultural workers extends beyond the ability to use tools and is instead defined as the capacity to operate within intelligent, sustainable, and interconnected systems.

At the multilateral level, these principles have been taken up and further developed by FAO, which has assumed a central role in translating European frameworks into operational tools for the digital transformation of agri-food systems. FAO initiatives—including the Digital Services Portfolio, the Digital Villages Initiative, and the Digital Agriculture Transformation and Innovation program—promote an integrated approach structured around three dimensions: institutional innovation, digital capacity development, and inclusive data governance. FAO conceptualizes digitalization not as the mere adoption of technologies, but as a cognitive and organizational process grounded in the collective capacity to use data, platforms, and AI-based systems to generate sustainable value (FAO, 2019). Through the Digital Agriculture Strategy Framework, the organization supports countries in the design of national strategies for digital agriculture by providing methodologies for digital maturity assessment, skills planning, and impact measurement (FAO, 2022).

The World Bank contributes to this framework through the report *Digital Skills: Frameworks and Programs*, which distinguishes between digital skills for the general workforce—drawing on DigComp and UNESCO's Global Digital Literacy Framework (UNESCO, 2018a)—and advanced information and communication technology (ICT) skills for technology-oriented professions (Bashir & Miyamoto, 2020). The *Digital Economy for Africa (DE4A)* initiative integrates these principles into a development model structured around five pillars—infrastructure, platforms, digital financial services, entrepreneurship, and skills—and employs diagnostic tools such as the DE4A Scorecards to assess countries' progress. This dynamic perspective recognizes that even traditionally low-tech sectors, such as agriculture, require progressively higher levels of digital skills and the capacity to interact effectively with intelligent systems.

A complementary contribution comes from the Organization for Economic Co-operation and Development (OECD) *Skills Strategy* (2024), which conceptualizes skills as a collective resource to be developed, effectively deployed, and governed through coordinated systems. OECD analyses emphasize the need to integrate digital and AI-related skills into adult learning systems, ensure the quality of digital education, and strengthen interinstitutional cooperation—issues that are particularly salient in agricultural contexts characterized by institutional fragmentation and limited access to advanced educational services. Regional projects and *Skills Strategy Reviews* further underscore the importance of a whole-of-society approach, in which institutions, firms, local communities, and education systems jointly contribute to the governance of human capital.

UNESCO has introduced an additional level of formalization through two key instruments. The *Global Framework of Reference on Digital Literacy Skills*, developed to monitor indicator 4.4.2 of the 2030 Agenda, provides an intercultural structure that harmonizes definitions, descriptors, and proficiency levels, defining digital literacy as the capacity to access, manage, understand, integrate, communicate, and create information in a safe and ethical manner (UNESCO, 2018a). The framework explicitly identifies agriculture as a priority sector for the application of digital skills, highlighting the role of data and mobile platforms in facilitating access to markets and rural services. Complementing this approach, the *ICT Competency Framework for Teachers* structures teacher training across three levels—*knowledge acquisition*, *knowledge deepening*, and *knowledge creation*—and advances a vision of digital education oriented toward knowledge construction and sharing, as well as the ethical use of data and emerging technologies (UNESCO, 2018b).

The framework is further complemented by a forward-looking perspective offered by the World Economic Forum (2025). In the *Future of Jobs Report 2025*, the organization highlights how skills such as AI and big data literacy, systems thinking, cognitive flexibility, resilience, and sustainability awareness are expected to become central to the global workforce. These competences acquire particular relevance in the agricultural sector, where the increasing integration of predictive models, precision technologies, robotics, and decision-support systems demands cognitive and metacognitive capacities capable of governing the complexity of intelligent systems.

Taken together, European and international frameworks outline a global ecosystem of digital and AI-driven skills grounded in convergent principles: the centrality of literacy as a critical capacity to interact with intelligent systems; the integration of technical, cognitive, social, and ethical dimensions; a strong emphasis on inclusion and sustainability; and the adaptability of models to territorial and sectoral specificities. This convergence defines a new paradigm of sustainable digital competence, in which agriculture emerges as an emblematic sector for understanding the interaction between technological transformation, educational innovation, and ecological transition. Table 5.1 synthesizes the main institutional references, the corresponding competence areas, and their specific implications for agriculture and AI.

5.3 Digital Skills and AI: A Multilevel Interpretive Framework

The digital transformation of agriculture cannot be reduced to the adoption of new technologies. It involves a deeper reconfiguration of the forms of knowledge and practice through which agricultural knowledge is generated, interpreted, and governed (Ahmadi et al., 2025; Vahdanjoo et al., 2025; Zhou & Yin, 2023). The diffusion of AI-based systems, advanced sensing technologies, and data-driven platforms has reshaped decision-making processes, shifting the focus from the mastery of individual tools to the capacity to operate within complex informational environments.

In this context, AI tends to increase the cognitive intensity of agricultural work. Rather than simplifying decision-making, it requires actors to develop skills that support the interpretation, validation, and governance of automated decision systems. Human operators are therefore increasingly involved in supervisory, evaluative, and ethically sensitive functions, particularly where algorithmic outputs interact with ecological variability and context-specific knowledge.

From this perspective, digital competence is best understood as a form of systemic intelligence. It integrates cognitive, ethical, and social dimensions and evolves through progressive and situated learning processes, shaped by practice, experience, and interaction within socio-technical agricultural ecosystems.

The development of the interpretive framework proposed in this section is grounded in a two-level methodological approach. First, a comparative analysis was conducted of the main international frameworks addressing digital and AI-related skills, including DigComp 2.2 (Vuorikari et al., 2022), GreenComp (Bianchi et al., 2022), UNESCO's Digital Literacy Global Framework (2018a), FAO's Digital Agriculture Transformation (2019), the OECD Skills Strategy (OECD, 2024), and the World Economic Forum's Future of Jobs Report (2025). This analysis highlights a clear convergence toward multilevel models of digital competence, in which the technical dimension represents only one component of a broader configuration that also encompasses critical, design-oriented, collaborative, and systemic capacities.

Second, this mapping was complemented by a targeted literature review conducted across major international databases, using combined search strings related to digital skills, AI literacy, training, and digitalization processes in agriculture. Priority was given to contributions published over the past 5 years, in order to capture recent developments in AI-based systems and digitalization processes in agriculture, with particular attention to empirical evidence and theoretical models addressing AI in agriculture, digital agriculture, smart farming, precision agriculture, and rural innovation systems. The review included studies examining technical, cognitive, and

Table 5.1 Comparison of the main international frameworks on digital and AI-driven skills. Source: author's elaboration based on (EU, FAO, World Bank, OECD, UNESCO, and World Economic Forum 2013–2025)

Organization/framework	Year	Main focus	Structure and competence areas	Relevance for agriculture and AI	Strategic orientation
EU—DigComp 2.1/2.2 (JRC)	2017 / 2022	Citizens' digital competence	Five areas: information and data literacy, communication and collaboration, digital content creation, safety, problem solving; eight proficiency levels	Introduces extensions for AI literacy and provides the conceptual basis for sector-specific frameworks (e.g., education, agricultural labor)	Digital literacy, active citizenship, European interoperability
EU—GreenComp	2022	Sustainability and transversal competences	Four areas, twelve competences (values, complexity, sustainable futures, transformative action)	Connects digital literacy and sustainability in agro-ecological processes and digital farming practices	Ecological transition and lifelong learning
FAO—Digital Agriculture Transformation	2019	Systemic digitalization of agriculture	Three pillars: institutional innovation, digital capacity development, inclusive data governance	Defines digital agriculture as a cognitive and multilevel ecosystem integrating AI, data, and digital services	Inclusive innovation, data governance, multilateral cooperation
World Bank—Digital Skills Framework (DE4A)	2020	Digital skills for emerging economies	Two levels: basic digital skills (inspired by DigComp/ UNESCO) and advanced ICT skills; diagnostic tools (scorecards)	Adapts European and UNESCO frameworks to national contexts, relevant for agricultural sectors with low digital maturity	Inclusive development, reduction of the digital divide, capacity building
OECD—skills strategy	2012–2024	Governance of skills systems	Three dimensions: skills development, effective use of skills, governance	Promotes a whole-of-society approach; includes modules on digital skills and AI in agricultural lifelong learning policies	Alignment of training, innovation, and labor policies

(continued)

Table 5.1 (continued)

Organization/framework	Year	Main focus	Structure and competence areas	Relevance for agriculture and AI	Strategic orientation
UNESCO— DLGF / ICT CFT v3	2018	Global digital education	DLGF: framework for SDG 4.4 (digital literacy); ICT CFT v3: three levels (knowledge acquisition, deepening, creation) and six professional areas	Global reference for equity, access, AI, and rural inclusion; explicit application to food-related sectors	Digital literacy as a universal right and a lever for development
World economic forum—future of jobs report	2025	Emerging skills and the digital transition	Key skills: AI and big data literacy, systems thinking, resilience, sustainability awareness	Highlights the impact of AI on agricultural employment, hybrid skills, and adaptive capacities	Forward-looking vision of human capital and labor markets

socio-organizational skills, as well as analyses focused on the role of educational institutions, extension services, and digital platforms in supporting learning and skill formation.

The integration of documentary analysis and the literature review made it possible to construct a coherent interpretive framework, in which agricultural human capital is conceived as an evolving cognitive system that co-produces innovation together with digital technologies. This perspective informed the structuring of the multilevel framework, ensuring consistency with ongoing transformations in agri-food systems and with the orientations promoted by major international organizations.

Level 1—Digital Systems Thinking and Data Awareness

The first level concerns the ability to read agriculture as a complex informational ecosystem, characterized by continuous data flows generated by sensors, platforms, predictive models, and collaborative networks. This dimension echoes the information and data literacy area of DigComp and the systemic perspective advanced by GreenComp, as well as the emphasis on systems thinking highlighted by the World Economic Forum. In agricultural contexts, it includes the capacity to interpret time series, geospatial maps, agro-environmental indicators, and algorithmic outputs as integral components of decision-making processes.

Level 2—Continuous and Adaptive Learning

The second level refers to the capacity for continuous learning, through which knowledge and practices are regularly updated in response to technological change. This dimension is central to UNESCO frameworks (2018a), to OECD strategies on lifelong learning, and to FAO programs aimed at strengthening the digital capacity of small-scale producers. Digital agriculture, characterized by rapidly evolving technologies, requires a model of ongoing training that enables actors to remain aligned with emerging tools, platforms, and standards.

Level 3—Integration of Hybrid Knowledge and Reflective Professional Identity

The third level highlights the reconfiguration of professional roles in agriculture, where agronomic, digital, managerial, and analytical competences are progressively integrated. This perspective is reflected in FAO orientations that frame digital agriculture as a cognitive ecosystem, as well as in DigComp 2.2, which distinguishes technical proficiency from the capacity to create digital content and solutions. At this level, digital competence acquires a reflective dimension: agricultural workers interpret data in light of experience, negotiating meanings, practices, and responsibilities within contexts increasingly shaped by AI.

Level 4—Digital Collaboration and Intelligent Communities

The fourth level concerns the capacity to operate within collaborative networks and intelligent communities. DigComp identifies digital collaboration as a core competence area; FAO articulates this dimension through initiatives such as the Digital Villages Initiative; and the OECD highlights its role in interinstitutional governance.

In agricultural contexts, communities of practice, cooperative platforms, and shared information systems become spaces for the distributed production of knowledge.

Level 5—Digital Literacy and Advanced Technological Mastery

The fifth level integrates technical, ethical, and strategic competences in the management of advanced digital technologies, including AI-based systems. This dimension draws on DigComp 2.2 contributions on AI literacy, on the skills identified by the World Economic Forum in relation to AI and big data literacy, and on FAO and World Bank orientations concerning the responsible use of AI in agri-food systems. At this level, digital competence becomes the capacity to interpret, evaluate, and govern predictive models; algorithmic decision systems; and data-driven platforms in a conscious and sustainable manner.

The multilevel framework outlined above describes an evolutionary pathway that moves from awareness of the informational system to full responsibility in the use of AI. Digital competence emerges as a form of advanced human capital, in which technical knowledge, reflective capacity, ethical judgment, and data mastery are intertwined within a continuous learning ecosystem. From this perspective, digital agriculture is not merely a space for technological adoption, but a cognitive laboratory in which people design, interpret, and steer innovation, contributing to the generation of shared and sustainable value.

5.3.1 Digital Systems Thinking and Data Awareness

Digital systems thinking represents the foundational competence of smart agriculture, as it enables actors to read the production system as a complex informational ecosystem structured around continuous data flows. In line with the Level 1 of the proposed framework, this competence concerns awareness of how data generated by sensors, platforms, predictive models, and collaborative networks are interconnected and embedded within agricultural decision processes.

Digitalization, in this sense, does not correspond to a simple automation of tasks. It entails a cognitive shift that requires the ability to recognize interdependencies, relate heterogeneous data sources, and interpret informational signals within contexts characterized by uncertainty, variability, and ecological complexity (Veraart & Blok, 2025). Data awareness thus becomes a prerequisite for informed decision-making, enabling actors to situate algorithmic outputs, indicators, and digital representations within broader system dynamics rather than treating them as isolated or self-sufficient inputs.

Empirical evidence on skill requirements in the agricultural sector confirms this perspective. Aletdinova et al. (2021) show that digitalization increases the centrality of cognitive and metareflective abilities, including critical thinking, complex analysis, and cognitive flexibility, which are necessary to interpret climatic, agronomic, and market data and to operate effectively within digitalized production environments. These capacities constitute a cognitive threshold through which actors connect data, knowledge, and experience, transforming empirical observation into informed judgment.

Luo (2025) shows that the integration of IoT sensors, mobile applications, and analytical platforms supports the development of situated data literacy by improving access to information and the quality of day-to-day decision-making. From this perspective, data-driven technologies function as cognitive mediators: they extend farmers' capacity to observe, interpret, and adapt, contributing to the construction of knowledge that is more structured, timely, and context-sensitive.

This evolution can be interpreted through the SAMR model (Substitution–Augmentation–Modification–Redefinition), which describes levels of digital transformation in learning practices (Puentedura, 2020). Zakharov et al. (2021) show that the more advanced stages ("modification" and "redefinition") involve a reorganization of cognitive activities. From an interpretive standpoint, this suggests that advanced uses of data do not merely increase efficiency but alter the very form of agricultural knowledge.

Digital systems thinking therefore constitutes the first level of the multilevel framework outlined in this chapter: the foundation through which agricultural actors develop an integrated understanding of production processes and acquire the capacity to navigate complex informational ecosystems. It provides the prerequisite for subsequent levels of digital competence oriented toward continuous learning, the integration of knowledge domains, and the responsible mastery of AI.

5.3.2 Continuous and Adaptive Learning

The digital transformation of agriculture requires a reconceptualization of human capital as an evolving cognitive system, capable of learning in a continuous, reflective, and adaptive manner. In a context marked by rapid innovation and ongoing organizational change, competence can no longer be understood as a stable condition; rather, it takes the form of a permanent process of updating that keeps knowledge, practices, and digital tools aligned over time (Cesco et al., 2023; Veraart & Blok, 2025). Learning thus becomes the infrastructure that sustains the cognitive viability of digitalized agricultural systems.

The literature confirms this requirement. Aletdinova et al. (2021) identify lifelong learning as a core pillar of digital competitiveness, showing how continuous training enables human capital to adapt to emerging technological dynamics. In the context of agricultural extension, Asante (2025) highlights that the gap between theoretical knowledge and operational skills can be addressed only through flexible training models capable of integrating sensing technologies, robotics, and machine learning systems. From this perspective, learning does not represent a simple technical update, but a process of cognitive and operational adaptation.

A complementary perspective is provided by Zakharov et al. (2021), who emphasize the need for upskilling programs and psycho-pedagogical support to accompany professionals through the digital transition. Their analysis highlights the role of reflective learning and sustained educational guidance as key sources of resilience in the face of technological change. Efremova et al. (2023) reinforce this view by introducing the concept of *digital didactics*: a pedagogical architecture grounded in human–machine interaction and experiential learning, in which educators act as facilitators of personalized digital environments and promoters of critical reflexivity.

Empirical evidence further indicates that the main barrier to agricultural digitalization is cognitive in nature. Subaeva et al. (2020) show that low levels of digital literacy, resistance to change, and insufficient continuous training represent the most significant obstacles in the transition toward digital agriculture. The authors propose a dual- and network-based training model, grounded in cooperation among universities, firms, and institutions, aimed at developing transversal competences—such as analysis, creativity, teamwork, and adaptability—that are essential for fostering a form of informed digital citizenship in agriculture.

At the institutional level, Tu et al. (2025) show that building a digital workforce requires a shared and multilevel competence framework. Drawing on the experience of 151 Vietnamese universities, the authors demonstrate that a Digital Competency Framework inspired by the European DigComp can structure learning across seven competence areas and five levels of proficiency, conceiving competence as a dynamic process shaped by iterative feedback cycles. Michailidis et al. (2024) emphasize that training in precision agriculture should promote transition-oriented competences that integrate technology into decision-making and organizational processes, moving beyond a purely training-based approach. Through the development of a Digital Competency Index for agricultural extension professionals, Mukherjee et al. (2025) further confirm the multidimensional nature of digital competence, which combines information management, communication, and ethical responsibility.

Finally, the collaborative dimension of learning emerges clearly from recent studies. Stampfl et al. (2025) show that media competence directly influences attitudes toward online training and preferences for hybrid formats, suggesting that effective learning is grounded in the interaction between practical experience, peer collaboration, and reflexivity. Khudyakova et al. (2023) confirm this perspective by conceptualizing continuous training as an open system articulated through dynamic networks that connect universities, firms, and production communities.

Overall, this second level of the multilevel framework shows that agricultural digitalization requires a culture of lifelong learning in which knowledge and technology co-evolve. Continuous and adaptive learning enables the integration of knowledge domains, the redefinition of professional roles, and the preparation of the ground for the emergence of a hybrid and reflective agricultural professionalism capable of governing digital complexity.

5.3.3 Integration of Hybrid Knowledge and Reflective Professional Identity

At the third level of the framework, digitalization is understood as a force that reshapes not only production techniques but the very structure of agricultural professionalism. Within digital ecosystems, competences are no longer organized into separate domains; instead, they are progressively integrated into forms of practical and reflective knowledge that combine experience, analytical capacity, and the critical use of technology (Cheng et al., 2024; Ji & Zhuang, 2023).

At this level, farmers, technicians, and advisors act as cognitive mediators between data, territory, and innovation. Their professional identity is constructed through the continuous interpretation of digital information in relation to situated knowledge and contextual constraints, within shared knowledge spaces in which technology functions as a common language rather than a purely instrumental tool.

Empirical evidence shows that this hybrid form of professionalism depends, first and foremost, on operators' ability to articulate practical knowledge with basic digital competences. Abdulai et al. (2023) demonstrate that skills such as mobile phone use, Internet access, participation in farmer groups, and interaction with extension services significantly shape the very possibility of accessing digital services. This finding indicates that the hybridization of knowledge is not an abstract process, but one that is firmly rooted in specific material and cognitive conditions. Digital inclusion therefore emerges as a prerequisite for the development of more advanced forms of agricultural professionalism.

Within agricultural extension systems, this dynamic is particularly evident. Asante (2025) shows that farm advisors operate at the intersection between innovation and rural contexts, performing translation and mediation functions that enable agricultural communities to appropriate emerging technologies. Digital competence therefore does not coincide with technical mastery alone; it also entails interpretive and relational capacities oriented toward contextualization.

At a more general level, digital transformation entails a shift from an executive form of professionalism toward a project-oriented and reflective one. Analyzing the evolution of digital didactics through the SAMR model, Zakharov et al. (2021) show that the introduction of technologies leads to a redefinition of learning and decision-making processes.

This trajectory is further developed by Charatsari et al. (2022), who use the concept of *responsible professionalism* to describe the emerging identity of farm advisors. The dimensions of translation, facilitation, visioning, and reflection delineate a form of professionalism grounded in autonomy, responsibility, and shared meaning-making. In a subsequent contribution, Charatsari et al. (2023a) identify three training domains for future advisors—technocentric, future-oriented, and farmer-centric—making explicit the multidimensional nature of digital professionalism.

The educational dimension also contributes to the construction of reflective professional identities. Efremova et al. (2023) show that digital didactics fosters awareness and responsibility, transforming learning into a mechanism for cognitive recomposition. In parallel, within the field of precision agriculture, Michailidis et al. (2024) demonstrate that emerging professional profiles must integrate data analysis, information management, and strategic capacities, overcoming the traditional separation between technical and managerial functions.

Overall, the integration of hybrid knowledge represents an evolutionary threshold in digital agricultural professionalism: a process of cognitive reconfiguration that brings together technical competences, relational capacities, and ethical judgment. Reflexivity acquires a social dimension, as it enables actors to orient change within cooperative and technologically complex contexts. On this basis, the next level of the framework builds, focusing on digital collaboration and intelligent communities, where knowledge extends beyond individual boundaries and becomes a form of collective construction.

Box 5.1 the Evolution of Agricultural Professional Roles in the AI Era

Digital transformation does not merely introduce new technologies into agricultural systems; it redefines the professional grammar of work, giving rise to hybrid roles that integrate agronomic, digital, and organizational competences. These professional profiles do not replace traditional roles but rather reconfigure them within a socio-technical ecosystem in which data, sensors, and intelligent systems co-produce value together with human actors.

The profiles presented in Table 5.2 do not constitute an exhaustive list, but rather an interpretive map of emerging functions. They are intended to clarify how digitalization reshapes the cognitive division of labor and the training pathways required to support this reorientation.

Table 5.2 Emerging roles and the reconfiguration of digital agricultural work

Professional role	Key competences	Main functions
Data agronomist	Agronomic data analysis, predictive modeling, sensor and database management	Interprets field data to optimize irrigation, nutrition, and yields
AI maintenance specialist	Mechatronics, predictive diagnostics, calibration of agricultural robots	Manages maintenance and safety of autonomous systems; liaises with technology providers
Digital field technician	Precision agronomy, GIS, sensing technologies, drones	Integrates geospatial data and climate models to support operational decisions
Platform manager	Data governance, cybersecurity, system interoperability	Coordinates information flows among farms, platforms, and the supply chain
Agri-education facilitator	Digital pedagogy, upskilling and reskilling	Promotes continuous training and digital inclusion in rural areas
Farm data manager	Integrated analysis of farm data, digital crop planning, interoperable system management	Supports the transition from traditional management to data-driven planning
Agro-systems coordinator	Interdisciplinary management of automated processes, coordination of technical–scientific teams	Facilitates interaction among operators, technologists, and digital service providers

The Data Agronomist embodies the convergence between agronomic knowledge and analytical capacity. By interpreting data from sensors, drones, and digital platforms, this role translates information into operational decisions related to irrigation, nutrition, and crop management, ensuring continuity between empirical observation and digital modeling.

The AI Maintenance Specialist safeguards the reliability of autonomous systems. By integrating mechatronics, predictive diagnostics, and operational safety, this role ensures the coherent functioning of robots and intelligent machines, shifting maintenance from a predominantly corrective activity to a cognitively oriented process focused on prevention and the supervision of algorithmic flows.

The Digital Field Technician maintains the link between the physical environment and the digital production infrastructure. Through competences in sensing technologies, GIS, and drones, this role collects and validates geospatial and environmental data that feed decision models and support precision crop management.

The Platform Manager operates on the governance side of complex digital systems. This role manages security, transparency, and consistency of information flows across farms, platforms, and value chains, helping to define the conditions for data access, use, and sharing.

The Agri-education Facilitator underscores the importance of the training dimension. This role designs upskilling and reskilling pathways, supports the acquisition of digital competences, and fosters the development of learning networks in rural contexts.

The Farm Data Manager consolidates data as a strategic resource. By coordinating interoperability among information systems, ensuring database quality, and integrating economic, agronomic, and logistical information, this role facilitates the shift from traditional management models to data-driven planning.

Finally, the Agro-systems Coordinator represents the intermediate organizational level of transformation. By coordinating interdisciplinary teams, integrating automated processes, and aligning technical innovation with managerial practices, this role ensures the operational coherence of the entire production system.

Taken together, these roles delineate an agricultural workforce increasingly oriented toward the integration of practical knowledge and digital capability. Smart agriculture does not replace traditional knowledge; rather, it recomposes it into cooperative forms between human operators and automated systems, in which information becomes the primary vector of value creation.

5.3.4 Digital Collaboration and Intelligent Communities

Digital competence develops within collaborative networks that transform learning into a social, distributed, and situated process. In agriculture, digitalization makes cooperation a structural component of innovation: farmers, technicians, and institutions co-produce knowledge through practices of exchange, reciprocity, and trust that enable technologies to be interpreted in context and aligned with local needs (Cesco et al., 2023; Charatsari et al., 2023b). Learning is therefore not an individual outcome, but an emergent product of interactions that sustain the collective capacity to use, adapt, and govern complex digital systems.

Empirical evidence shows that local networks represent a decisive factor in the adoption of digital technologies. Abdulai et al. (2023) find that participation in digital services is facilitated by membership in farmer groups, interaction with extension officers, and the presence of informal support channels, indicating that social capital directly shapes digital inclusion. In contexts characterized by limited infrastructural provision, such networks take on a substitutive role *vis-à-vis* formal institutions: Jena and Tigga (2023) show that experienced farmers, local retailers, and community groups constitute the primary infrastructure for learning and for the diffusion of digital innovations.

From a skills perspective, Archibong (2025) shows that information and data literacy, communication and collaboration, and problem solving—three core areas of DigComp—are significant predictors of youth engagement in agriculture. Beyond facilitating the use of technologies, collaborative competences enable collective learning processes and the construction of shared meanings, which are essential for addressing digitalized agricultural contexts characterized by high informational complexity.

The collaborative dimension also extends to institutional networks. Subaeva et al. (2020) propose a training structure based on cluster–network that integrate universities, firms, and regional institutions, showing how interorganizational cooperation fosters cognitive innovation and the co-design of digital solutions. Similarly, Tu et al. (2025) highlight that systematic collaboration between universities and the productive sector represents a strategic node for building skills ecosystems and communities of practice oriented toward digital transformation.

Alongside territorial contexts, digital platforms configure new environments for collaborative learning. Stampfl et al. (2025) show that engagement in online training depends on media competence and that well-designed e-learning environments foster interaction, motivation, and mutual trust. From this perspective, digital learning operates as a social space in which individual experiences and professional practices are transformed into collective knowledge.

In contexts of the Global South, digital collaboration also assumes an empowerment function. Macharia and Obuya (2025) show that community digital champions play a crucial role in facilitating technology use among small-scale producers, strengthening their autonomy, decision-making capacity, and participation in digital markets. Human mediation thus emerges as an essential component of intelligent communities, within which technology acts as a catalyst for collective empowerment.

Taken together, this body of evidence shows that digital collaboration constitutes the relational dimension of systemic competence: a web of practices, values, and infrastructures that connects individuals, institutions, and territories. Networks—formal and informal, territorial and digital—function as epistemic spaces in which agricultural knowledge is negotiated, shared, and continuously regenerated. This fourth level of the framework introduces the collective component of digital human capital, paving the way for the subsequent level devoted to digital literacy and technological mastery, where attention shifts from cooperation to the conscious governance of intelligent systems.

5.3.5 Digital Literacy and Advanced Technological Mastery

Digital literacy represents the threshold through which agricultural human capital fully enters the paradigm of digitalization. It marks the transition from an instrumental use of technologies to a reflective form of mastery, in which technical knowledge, critical awareness, and ethical responsibility converge into a multilevel competence capable of orienting innovation and governing its impacts (Ji & Zhuang, 2023). From this perspective, digital literacy does not consist of a simple set of operational skills; rather, it constitutes an extended cognitive capacity that enables operators to evaluate, contextualize, and purposefully use complex digital systems.

Recent literature converges in recognizing this articulated nature of digital literacy. Aletdinova et al. (2021) interpret digital literacy as a transversal competence that combines technical abilities with critical evaluative capacity, showing that competitiveness in the digital agricultural economy derives from a balance between efficiency of use and an understanding of the socio-technical effects of innovation. This perspective is confirmed by Archibong (2025), who finds that information and data literacy, communication and collaboration, and problem solving—core areas of DigComp—are significant predictors of youth engagement in the agricultural sector. Asante (2025) further emphasizes that the growing adoption of robotics, drones, and AI-based systems calls for advanced forms of technological mastery, in which technical capability is integrated with strategic vision and decision-making capacity.

The reflective dimension emerges with force in pedagogical research. Efremova et al. (2023) define digital didactics as the integration of technical mastery, critical awareness, and ethical responsibility, advancing a conception of digital competence as a civic and professional practice oriented toward the assessment of the impacts of innovation. Mukherjee et al. (2025) reinforce this interpretation through a Digital Competency Index articulated across multiple dimensions—information management, communication, problem solving, and ethical awareness—which highlights the normative nature of digital maturity and underscores its connection with processes of responsible decision-making.

The international landscape confirms convergence toward an evolutionary model of digital competence. Tu et al. (2025) show that Asian frameworks and DigComp 2.2 delineate a continuum of mastery structured across levels, ranging from basic instrumental use to the capacity to design, evaluate, and govern complex digital systems. Petropoulos et al. (2025) extend this perspective to the bioeconomy, highlighting the role of data management, digital collaboration, and ethical responsibility as key entrepreneurial competences for a sustainable transition.

In European contexts, technological maturity appears closely connected to the capacity to assess the risks and benefits associated with digitalization. Reissig and Siegrist (2025) show that positive perception, trust, and acceptance of technologies depend on education levels and the robustness of digital skills, indicating that literacy functions as a cognitive and social mediator of adoption processes. From this perspective, critical judgment of digital tools constitutes an integral component of technological mastery.

The social dimension of digital literacy emerges strongly in rural contexts. Luo (2025) highlights how the integration of data-driven technologies with situated training strengthens trust and awareness in the use of information. Macharia and Obuya (2025) show that digital literacy functions as a mechanism of collective empowerment, through the role of community digital champions who act as knowledge mediators. Jena and Tigga (2023) confirm that digital competence is rooted in access to information and cognitive networks, while Giorgio et al. (2024) show that the digital maturity of European agricultural systems depends on the integration of skills, information infrastructures, and institutional governance. Finally, Chowdhury et al. (2025) emphasize that AI can contribute to reducing the digital divide only if accompanied by targeted inclusion policies, making AI literacy an indispensable dimension of contemporary digital competence.

Overall, technological mastery represents the most advanced level of the multilevel framework outlined in this chapter: a form of cognitive and value-based maturity in which skills, data, and governance converge within a unified ecosystem. Digital literacy thus evolves into a strategic capacity to orient innovation toward objectives of sustainability, equity, and transparency, closing the framework's cycle and integrating systemic awareness, continuous learning, reflective professionalism, and digital collaboration into a coherent vision of agricultural transformation in the era of AI.

5.4 Conclusions

The trajectory developed in this chapter has shown that the digitalization of agriculture cannot be interpreted as a simple process of technological adoption, but rather as a cognitive, professional, and institutional reconfiguration involving the entire agri-food ecosystem. Digital skills constitute the invisible infrastructure of this transition: an evolving set of capacities that, from the most elementary levels of data interpretation to the reflective mastery of AI, defines the very possibility of participating in the new knowledge-based agriculture.

The proposed multilevel framework has highlighted that these competences develop along a progressive trajectory. Digital systems thinking enables agriculture to be interpreted as an interconnected informational ecosystem; continuous and adaptive learning provides the cognitive structure needed to accompany change; the integration of hybrid knowledge and a reflective professional identity redefines operators' roles and functions; digital collaboration and intelligent communities demonstrate that innovation is an inherently collective process; finally, digital literacy and technological mastery represent the most advanced outcome of this evolution, in which technical capability, ethical responsibility, and informed judgment converge into a competence for governing innovation.

Taken together, these levels delineate an agricultural human capital capable of thinking and acting within intelligent environments, translating data, technologies, and relationships into sustainability-oriented decisions. Digitalization thus emerges as a process of co-evolution among people, institutions, and information infrastructures, in which competence becomes the driving force through which agriculture can address the environmental, economic, and social challenges of the coming decades.

The analysis conducted suggests that agricultural digitalization does not simply require more technology, but rather more knowledge, stronger learning capacities, denser forms of cooperation, and a governance of innovation capable of valuing the ethical and inclusive dimensions of ongoing transformations. The proposed framework therefore provides a foundation for orienting educational policies, institutional strategies, and training programs toward the construction of a learning agriculture: a system capable of learning alongside technology and of steering it toward forms of sustainable productivity, social equity, and long-term resilience.

References

Abdulai, A.-R., Kc, K. B., & Fraser, E. (2023). What factors influence the likelihood of rural farmer participation in digital agricultural services? experience from smallholder digitalization in Northern Ghana. *Outlook on Agriculture, 52*(1), 57–66. https://doi.org/10.1177/00307270221144641

Ahmadi, S., Amendolagine, V., & LaSala, P. (2025). Unpacking the impacts of digitalization of knowledge transfer in agri-food sector, through sociotechnical systems theory: a systematic literature review. *Agricultural and Food Economics, 13*(1). https://doi.org/10.1186/s40100-025-00393-3

Ahmed, N., & Shakoor, N. (2025). Advancing agriculture through IoT, Big Data, and AI: A review of smart technologies enabling sustainability. *Smart Agricultural Technology, 10*(100848), Article 100848. https://doi.org/10.1016/j.atech.2025.100848

Aletdinova, A. A., Bakaev, M. A., & Astapchuk, V. A. (2021). Intelligent analysis of digital economy competencies in agriculture labor. *IOP Conference Series. Materials Science and Engineering, 1019*(1), 012046. https://doi.org/10.1088/1757-899x/1019/1/012046

Archibong, E. M. (2025). Digital literacy and agricultural engagement among youth in Akwa Ibom State, Nigeria: A Study Using the Digital Competence Framework. *Indian Research Journal of Extension Education, 25*(4), 33–41. https://doi.org/10.54986/irjee/2025/oct_dec/33-41

Asante, I. K. (2025). Digital technologies competencies and training needs of agricultural extension agents. *African Journal of Rural Development, 9*(4), 376–389.

Bampasidou, M., Goldgaber, D., Gentimis, T., & Mandalika, A. (2024). Overcoming 'Digital Divides': Leveraging higher education to develop next generation digital agriculture professionals. *Computers and Electronics in Agriculture, 224*(109181), Article 109181. https://doi.org/10.1016/j.compag.2024.109181

Bashir, S., & Miyamoto, K. (2020). *Digital skills: Frameworks and programs.* World Bank.

Bianchi, G., Pisiotis, U., Cabrera Giraldez, M., (2022). GreenComp—The European sustainability competence framework. In M. Bacigalupo & Y. Punie (Eds.), EUR 30955 EN, Publications Office of the European Union. ISBN 978–92–76–46485–3, https://doi.org/10.2760/13286, JRC128040.

Campi, M., Asai, M., McFadden, J., Pindado, E., & Rosburg, A. (2024). *The Evolving profile of new entrants in agriculture and the role of digital technologies.* OECD Food, Agriculture and Fisheries Papers No. 209. OECD Publishing. https://doi.org/10.1787/d15ea067-en

Carretero, S., Vuorikari, R., & Punie, Y. (2017). *DigComp 2.1: The digital competence framework for citizens with eight proficiency levels and examples of use.* EUR 28558 EN, https://doi.org/10.2760/38842

Cesco, S., Sambo, P., Borin, M., Basso, B., Orzes, G., & Mazzetto, F. (2023). Smart agriculture and digital twins: Applications and challenges in a vision of sustainability. *European Journal of Agronomy: The Journal of the European Society for Agronomy, 146*(126809), Article 126809. https://doi.org/10.1016/j.eja.2023.126809

Charatsari, C., Lioutas, E. D., Papadaki-Klavdianou, A., Michailidis, A., & Partalidou, M. (2022). Farm advisors amid the transition to Agriculture 4.0: Professional identity, conceptions of the future and future-specific competencies. *Sociologia Ruralis, 62(*2), 335–362. https://doi.org/10.1111/soru.12364

Charatsari, C., Michailidis, A., Francescone, M., De Rosa, M., Aidonis, D., Bartoli, L., & Lioutas, E. D. (2023a). Do agricultural knowledge and innovation systems have the dynamic capabilities to guide the digital transition of short food supply chains? *Information (Basel), 15*(1), 22. https://doi.org/10.3390/info15010022

Charatsari, C., Michailidis, A., Lioutas, E. D., Bournaris, T., Loizou, E., Paltaki, A., & Lazaridou, D. (2023b). Competencies needed for guiding the digital transition of agriculture: Are future advisors well-equipped? *Sustainability, 15*(22), 15815. https://doi.org/10.3390/su152215815

Cheng, C., Gao, Q., Ju, K., & Ma, Y. (2024). How digital skills affect farmers' agricultural entrepreneurship? An explanation from factor availability. *Journal of Innovation & Knowledge, 9*(2), Article 100477. https://doi.org/10.1016/j.jik.2024.100477

Chowdhury, K., Rahman, M. A., Mallik, S. K., Chowdhury, L. N., & Nova, N. A. (2025). Bridging the global digital divide in agriculture: The role of AI in equitable technology access. *International Journal of Sustainable Development and Planning, 20*(6), 2469–2481. https://doi.org/10.18280/ijsdp.200616

Daum, T. (2025). Digitalization and skills in agriculture. *Outlook on Agriculture, 54*(2), 171–181. https://doi.org/10.1177/00307270251336474

Efremova, N., Tsoy, N., & Platonova, I. (2023). The problems of digital training of specialists for the agro-industrial complex. *E3S Web of Conferences, 381*, 01088. https://doi.org/10.1051/e3sconf/202338101088

EIP-AGRI. (2020). *New skills for digital farming: Final report*. European Innovation Partnership for Agricultural Productivity and Sustainability. European Commission.

Elbehri, A., & Chestnov, R. (2021). *Digital agriculture in action – Artificial intelligence for agriculture*. Food and Agriculture Organization of the United Nations (FAO) and International Telecommunication Union (ITU).

FAO & World Bank. (2000). *Agricultural Knowledge and Information Systems for Rural Development (AKIS/RD)*. Strategic vision and guiding principles. FAO.

FAO. (2019). *Digital agriculture transformation and innovation: transforming ideas into value in a sustainable way for #ZeroHunger*. Information Technology Division.

FAO. (2022). *Digital agriculture: AgriFin 7th annual learning event Presentation*. FAO.

Giorgio, A., Penate Lopez, L. P., Bertoni, D., Cavicchioli, D., & Ferrazzi, G. (2024). Enablers to digitalization in Agriculture: A case study from Italian field crop farms in the Po River Valley, with insights for policy targeting. *Agriculture, 14*(7), 1074. https://doi.org/10.3390/agriculture14071074

Goller, M., Caruso, C., & Harteis, C. (2021). Digitalisation in agriculture: Knowledge and learning requirements of German dairy farmers. *International Journal for Research in Vocational Education and Training, 8*(2), 208–223. https://doi.org/10.13152/ijrvet.8.2.4

IFAD. (2025). *Advancing IFAD's digital agriculture vision for rural transformation (2025–2030)*. International Fund for Agricultural Development. IFAD.

Jena, P., & Tigga, A. S. (2023). Digital competency in agriculture sector- an outlook in Indian context. *International Journal of Environment and Climate Change, 13*(5), 224–230. https://doi.org/10.9734/ijecc/2023/v13i51763

Ji, S., & Zhuang, J. (2023). The impact path of digital literacy on farmers' entrepreneurial performance: Based on survey data in Jiangsu province. *Sustainability, 15*(14), 11159. https://doi.org/10.3390/su151411159

Khudyakova, E., Shitikova, A., Stepantsevich, M. N., & Grecheneva, A. (2023). Requirements of modern Russian agricultural production for digital competencies of an agricultural specialist. *Education Sciences, 13*(2), 203. https://doi.org/10.3390/educsci13020203

Klerkx, L., Jakku, E., & Labarthe, P. (2019). A review of social science on digital agriculture, smart farming and agriculture 4.0: New contributions and a future research agenda. *NJAS: Wageningen Journal of Life Sciences, 90–91*(1), 1–16. https://doi.org/10.1016/j.njas.2019.100315

Luo, M. (2025). Enhancing agricultural knowledge and digital literacy of farmers through data-driven technology integration. *International Journal of Information and Communication Technology, 26*(10). https://doi.org/10.1504/ijict.2025.10070827

Macharia, J., & Obuya, C. (2025). The effect of digital literacy skills on rural kenyans' smallholder farmers' livelihoods. In M. Cunningham & P. Cunningham (Eds.), *IST-Africa 2025 Conference Proceedings* (pp. 1–12). IST-Africa Institute and IIMC.

Michailidis, A., Charatsari, C., Bournaris, T., Loizou, E., Paltaki, A., Lazaridou, D., & Lioutas, E. D. (2024). A first view on the competencies and training needs of farmers working with and researchers working on precision agriculture technologies. *Agriculture, 14*(1), 99. https://doi.org/10.3390/agriculture14010099

Mukherjee, S., Padaria, R. N., Burman, R. R., Nikam, V. R., Velayudhan, P. K., Mahra, G. S., & Ghosh, B. (2025). Development and standardisation of a digital competency index for extension professionals of India: A principal component analysis approach. *Agricultural Research*. https://doi.org/10.1007/s40003-025-00865-4

OECD. (2024). *OECD skills strategy projects—assessment, recommendations and reviews*. OECD Centre for Skills.

Oli, D., Gyawali, B., Acharya, S., & Oshikoya, S. (2025). Factors influencing learning attitude of farmers regarding adoption of farming technologies in farms of Kentucky, USA. *Smart Agricultural Technology, 10*(100801), Article 100801. https://doi.org/10.1016/j.atech.2025.100801

Petropoulos, D., Deirmentzoglou, G. A., Apostolopoulos, N., Paris, B., Michas, D., Balafoutis, A. T., & Moreira da Silva, J. F. (2025). Digital and entrepreneurial competencies for the bioeconomy: Perceptions and training needs of agricultural professionals in Greece, Italy, Portugal, and Sweden. *Agriculture, 15*(10), 1106. https://doi.org/10.3390/agriculture15101106

Porciello, J., Coggins, S., Mabaya, E., & Otunba-Payne, G. (2022). Digital agriculture services in low- and middle-income countries: A systematic scoping review. *Global Food Security, 34*(100640), Article 100640. https://doi.org/10.1016/j.gfs.2022.100640

Puentedura, R. R. (2020). *SAMR—A research perspective*. http://hippasus.com/rrpweblog/archives/2020/01/SAMR_AResearchPerspective.pdf

Raj, M., & Prahadeeswaran, M. (2025). Revolutionizing agriculture: a review of smart farming technologies for a sustainable future. *Discover Applied Sciences, 7*(9). https://doi.org/10.1007/s42452-025-07561-6

Reissig, L., & Siegrist, M. (2025). From the attitude towards digitalisation in agriculture to the acceptance of future agricultural technologies. *Smart Agricultural Technology, 12*(101095), Article 101095. https://doi.org/10.1016/j.atech.2025.101095

Soma, T., & Nuckchady, B. (2021). Communicating the benefits and risks of digital agriculture technologies: Perspectives on the future of digital agricultural education and training. *Frontiers in Communication, 6*. https://doi.org/10.3389/fcomm.2021.762201

Sørensen, L. B., Germundsson, L. B., Hansen, S. R., Rojas, C., & Kristensen, N. H. (2021). What skills do agricultural professionals need in the transition towards a sustainable agriculture? *A Qualitative Literature Review. Sustainability, 13*(24), 13556. https://doi.org/10.3390/su132413556

Stampfl, R., Prodinger, M., & Prodinger, J. (2025). Innovative paths to education: The effect of digital media on agricultural training in Austria. *Social Sciences & Humanities Open, 12*(101654), Article 101654. https://doi.org/10.1016/j.ssaho.2025.101654

Subaeva, A. K., Nizamutdinov, M. M., & Mavlieva, L. M. (2020). Changes of the agricultural staff potential in the transition to digital agriculture. *BIO Web of Conferences, 17*, 00178. https://doi.org/10.1051/bioconf/20201700178

Tu, D. T., Linh, B. T. H., Truong, N. H. X., Nguyet, T. T. M., & Linh, H. M. (2025). Digital workforce training: An empirical study of higher education institutions in Vietnam. *Multidisciplinary Reviews, 8*(11), 2025347. https://doi.org/10.31893/multirev.2025347

UNESCO. (2018b). ICT competency framework for teachers—version 3. UNESCO Publishing. ISBN 978-92-3-100285-4.

UNESCO. (2018a). *A global framework of reference on digital literacy skills for indicator 4.4.2.* UIS Information Paper No. 51

Vahdanjoo, M., Sørensen, C. G., & Nørremark, M. (2025). Digital transformation of the agri-food system. *Current Opinion in Food Science, 63*(101287), Article 101287. https://doi.org/10.1016/j.cofs.2025.101287

Veraart, R., & Blok, V. (2025). Digitalisation of agri-food systems: A paradigm shift? *Journal of Agricultural & Environmental Ethics, 38*(3). https://doi.org/10.1007/s10806-025-09954-4

Vuorikari, R., Kluzer, S. and Punie, Y. (2022). *DigComp 2.2: The digital competence framework for citizens, EUR 31006 EN*. Publications Office of the European Union. ISBN 978–92–76–48882–8, https://doi.org/10.2760/115376, JRC128415

World Bank Group. (2025). *Digital agriculture roadmap playbook.* World Bank.

World Economic Forum. (2025). *Future of jobs report 2025.* World Economic Forum.

Xue, X., Gao, J., & Xu, S. (2025). The impact and mechanism of digital economy on agricultural development resilience: evidence from China. *Frontiers in Sustainable Food Systems, 9*(1574461). https://doi.org/10.3389/fsufs.2025.1574461

Zakharov, K., Komarova, A., Baranova, T., & Gulk, E. (2021). Information literacy and digital competence of teachers in the age of digital transformation. *E3S Web of Conferences*, 273, 12077. https://doi.org/10.1051/e3sconf/202127312077

Zhou, R., & Yin, Y. (2023). Digital agriculture: Mapping knowledge structure and trends. *IEEE Access: Practical Innovations, Open Solutions, 11*, 103863–103880. https://doi.org/10.1109/access.2023.3315606

Chapter 6
Governing Artificial Intelligence in Agriculture: Institutions, Infrastructures, and Future Scenarios

Abstract This chapter examines how the integration of Artificial Intelligence (AI) is reshaping agri-food systems as socio-technical infrastructures in which data, algorithms, and institutions co-produce both value and risk. AI governance is framed as the coordination of algorithm design, data regimes, regulatory frameworks, and human capabilities. The first part analyzes key governance dimensions: data quality, bias, and fairness; transparency, explainability, and accountability; privacy and informational rights; and systemic security, interoperability, and data governance. The interplay among European instruments (GDPR, the AI Act, and the Data Act), OECD principles, and sectoral initiatives is discussed in relation to power asymmetries, lock-in dynamics, and digital divides that shape AI adoption in agriculture. The second part applies the Generic Foresight Process Framework to develop three scenarios to 2045—conservative, transformative, and regressive—generated by the interaction between enabling capacities and the quality of socio-technical governance. Building on these scenarios, the chapter proposes a 2025–2045 roadmap structured into three phases (digital and occupational foundations; socio-technical integration; inclusive scalability and systemic resilience), complemented by a mapping of actors and responsibilities. The chapter concludes by proposing SDG-oriented metrics and by showing that AI impacts ultimately depend on the development of inclusive, transparent, and accountable governance arrangements.

Keywords I governance · Scenario analysis · Digital inclusion · SDG metrics

6.1 Introduction

The increasing integration of Artificial Intelligence (AI) into agri-food systems is redefining how knowledge is produced, evaluated, and used, transforming agriculture into a context characterized by high informational and decision-making intensity (Finger, 2023; Veraart & Blok, 2025). As discussed in Chap. 5, this transition does not concern digital technology adoption alone; rather, it deeply involves the reorganization of labor, the distribution of skills, and the ways in which actors participate

A. Apicella, *Artificial Intelligence in Agriculture*,
https://doi.org/10.1007/978-3-032-26580-7_6

in value generation. AI thus emerges as a structural component of the agricultural ecosystem, capable of influencing operational choices, management models, and coordination dynamics along the value chain.

The impact of such systems depends crucially on the socio-technical context within which they are designed, implemented, and used. The literature shows that AI can promote efficiency, resilience, and sustainability in agricultural systems only when supported by governance arrangements capable of ensuring transparency, equity, security, and the centrality of human oversight (Jouanjean et al., 2020; Wirtz et al., 2022). In the absence of adequate supervisory mechanisms, informational asymmetries, technological dependencies, and the heterogeneity of digital infrastructures may translate into concentrations of decision-making power, the exclusion of more vulnerable actors, and the erosion of digital rights.

International institutions converge in placing governance at the center of the evolution of AI. The OECD Recommendation (OECD, 2025) defines principles for the trustworthy, safe, and inclusive use of AI, while the European regulatory framework—from the General Data Protection Regulation (GDPR) to the AI Act and the Data Act—introduces binding requirements concerning data quality, algorithmic transparency, human oversight, the protection of informational rights, and the interoperability of digital infrastructures (European Commission, 2016, 2023, 2024). In parallel, organizations such as FAO and the World Bank emphasize the need for integrated policies that combine infrastructural investment, institutional capacity, and skills development, so that agricultural digitalization can generate widespread and sustainable benefits (FAO, 2019; World Bank Group, 2025).

In this perspective, analyzing the governance of AI means adopting a systemic view that goes beyond the technical perimeter of the algorithm to include social relations, information regimes, institutional configurations, and material conditions that shape its impacts. The chapter structures this analysis along three complementary axes: (i) the principles, risks, and instruments of algorithmic governance and digital rights (Sect. 6.2); (ii) the technological infrastructures and enabling policies required to support a trustworthy digital ecosystem in agricultural systems (Sect. 6.3); and (iii) a foresight-oriented perspective on long-term scenarios and a roadmap defining responsibilities, instruments, and metrics to guide the transition toward ethical, inclusive, and sustainable AI models by 2045 (Sect. 6.4).

The overall objective is to provide an integrated framework for interpreting the ongoing transformation, clarifying the technical, institutional, and regulatory conditions under which AI can become a driver of economic, social, and environmental sustainability in contemporary agri-food systems.

6.2 Algorithmic Governance and Digital Rights

The governance of AI in agri-food systems constitutes a critical domain in which technical, legal, and socio-institutional considerations converge. The adoption of predictive models and data-driven platforms generates new forms of informational value, while simultaneously producing vulnerabilities and asymmetries that require reliable regulatory and infrastructural frameworks (Cesco et al., 2023; Veraart & Blok, 2025). The quality of AI outcomes depends not only on algorithmic performance, but also on the broader set of rules, contracts, and infrastructures that shape their design, implementation, and use (Wirtz et al., 2022).

A first critical issue concerns the distribution of informational power. Studies on data governance show that farmers' ability to benefit from the data they generate depends less on formal ownership than on the effective exercise of rights of access, portability, reuse, and refusal (Jouanjean et al., 2020). Opaque contractual conditions, dependence on proprietary platforms, and limited interoperability can produce forms of technological lock-in that are difficult to renegotiate, constraining decision-making autonomy and bargaining capacity (Kosior, 2020). A governance approach grounded in user participation and the clarity of informational rights therefore becomes essential.

These dynamics are compounded by infrastructural vulnerabilities: data quality and integrity, network continuity, the reliability of sensing systems, and the coherence of cloud–edge architectures directly affect the accuracy, robustness, and timeliness of AI-supported decisions (Gupta et al., 2020; Wang & Cai, 2022). Fragmented digital ecosystems, based on incompatible standards or non-interoperable platforms, can amplify systemic risks and consolidate dominant positions, thereby reducing resilience and adaptive capacity.

The European regulatory framework addresses these issues by defining specific requirements for data-based systems. The GDPR establishes foundational principles—transparency, data minimization, privacy by design, and the rights of data subjects, including the right to contest fully automated decisions—that constitute the basis of digital rights (European Commission, 2016). The AI Act builds on these principles by introducing obligations related to data quality, technical documentation, human oversight, risk management, and traceability for systems classified as high impact (European Commission, 2024). The Data Act instead targets contractual asymmetries by making effective the user's right to access data generated by connected products and to share them with third parties under fair, secure, and interoperable conditions, thereby fostering the creation of open agricultural data spaces (European Commission, 2023).

While the regulatory dimension provides important foundations for steering the development of AI, it may not fully exhaust the conditions required for its effective adoption. Trust emerges as a decisive factor: perceptions of fairness, protection, and inclusion strongly influence operators' willingness to integrate intelligent systems into decision-making processes (Sadjadi & Fernández, 2023). Tools for explainability, accountability mechanisms, human oversight in critical decisions, and the coherence of organizational practices are central to building such trust (Wu & Zhong, 2025). In contexts characterized by limited infrastructural capacity, these elements must also be accompanied by strategies of frugal digitalization, capable of operating under resource constraints and of promoting technological inclusion in less-equipped rural areas (Govindan, 2024).

Overall, the governance of agricultural AI requires a polycentric approach that coordinates digital rights, infrastructures, standards, risk models, social practices, and market configurations within an integrated framework oriented toward transparency, equity, security, and sustainability. This implies considering the entire life cycle of systems—from data generation and quality to algorithmic design, from contractual arrangements to technical infrastructures, and through to processes of supervision and accountability.

The following sections examine these issues by articulating them into four operational dimensions: data quality, bias, and fairness (Sect. 6.2.1); transparency, explainability, and accountability (Sect. 6.2.2); privacy, data ownership, and privacy-preserving solutions (Sect. 6.2.3); and systemic security, interoperability, and data governance (Sect. 6.2.4). Together, these dimensions constitute the analytical pillars through which the reliability and sustainability of AI systems applied to agriculture can be assessed.

6.2.1 Data Quality, Bias, and Fairness

Data quality, representativeness, and access regimes constitute the essential epistemic conditions for the development of trustworthy AI systems in agri-food contexts. The effectiveness of predictive models depends not solely on algorithmic design, but on how data are collected, curated, and documented, in ways that reflect the heterogeneity of agricultural systems and pedoclimatic environments (Dara et al., 2022). From this perspective, fairness emerges as a systemic property: it is not an isolated attribute of the algorithm, but the outcome of data production processes capable of equitably representing territories, practices, and socio-technical conditions (Jouanjean et al., 2020; Ryo, 2022).

Dataset representativeness constitutes the first critical issue. Empirical evidence shows that a large share of the datasets used in digital agriculture originates from highly infrastructured contexts, concentrated on crops and conditions that are relatively homogeneous (Heider et al., 2025). This results in models that are less generalizable and more context-sensitive, with lower performance in areas characterized by lower levels of digitalization or greater environmental variability (Garske et al., 2021; Rauch et al., 2025). The consequence is a form of distributive unfairness: systems that are underrepresented in datasets are often also those that derive fewer benefits from the adoption of AI.

A second level concerns asymmetries in data management and access. The concentration of technical and infrastructural capabilities in the hands of a limited number of actors can restrict the availability of diverse data and affect the epistemic quality of models (Kosior, 2020). In this respect, contractual choices, the availability of shared standards, and interoperability mechanisms directly shape the capacity of algorithms to reflect the complexity of agri-food value chains. The obligations introduced by the Data Act, which recognize users' rights to access and share data generated by connected devices, aim to mitigate these imbalances and to foster a more open and pluralistic ecosystem (European Commission, 2023).

Data quality is also shaped by cognitive and infrastructural factors. Differences in digital skills, connectivity constraints, and disparities in technical capacities can lead to incomplete or inaccurate datasets, amplifying structural biases, particularly in more vulnerable rural contexts (Wu & Zhong, 2025). These dynamics confirm that fairness is not an objective that can be achieved through algorithmic adjustments alone, but rather requires structural investments in data production, infrastructures, and professional capacities.

The European regulatory framework reinforces an epistemic understanding of data quality as an enabling condition for reliable AI systems in agriculture. In particular, the AI Act explicitly links the trustworthiness of high-risk systems to the use of appropriate, representative, and adequately documented datasets throughout the entire development lifecycle, acknowledging that data distortions undermine the validity of algorithmic inferences (European Commission, 2024). On a complementary level, the GDPR affects the personal component of agricultural data by imposing principles of accuracy and accountability in data processing, with direct implications for the integrity of informational inputs (European Commission, 2016). OECD principles further contribute to this perspective by emphasizing data governance models oriented toward robustness and bias mitigation (OECD, 2025). Taken together, these instruments anchor AI fairness not in ex post algorithmic adjustments, but in the structural conditions under which data are produced and governed.

Ultimately, data governance oriented toward quality and representativeness constitutes a prerequisite for reducing systemic biases and ensuring that agricultural AI contributes not only to productive efficiency, but also to equity and the sustainability of agri-food systems.

6.2.2 Transparency, Explainability, and Accountability

Transparency and explainability constitute central dimensions of algorithmic governance in agri-food systems, as they determine actors' ability to understand, evaluate, and control intelligent technologies embedded in production processes (Chen et al., 2023). In sectors characterized by high ecological variability, heterogeneous infrastructures, and unevenly distributed digital skills, the opacity of AI systems can amplify pre-existing informational asymmetries, reducing users' decision-making autonomy, undermining trust, and hindering the informed adoption of innovation (Girmay et al., 2025). Such opacity manifests both in the limited visibility of data collection, transformation, and use logics (Dara et al., 2022), and in the complexity of technical architectures that integrate sensors, IoT networks, analytical platforms, and predictive models into distributed infrastructures that are difficult to reconstruct ex post (Garske et al., 2021; Gupta et al., 2020). An additional institutional and contractual dimension further compounds these issues: opaque terms of use, proprietary practices, and limited clarity regarding data access and sharing arrangements can consolidate imbalances of informational power in favor of a small number of dominant actors (Jouanjean et al., 2020; Kosior, 2020).

In this context, explainability takes on strategic significance. Understanding not only model outputs, but also the relationships, assumptions, and inferences that generate them, is essential in a sector in which contextual knowledge remains decisive for interpreting recommendations. Explainable AI techniques provide useful tools for increasing the intelligibility of complex models, reducing the cognitive distance between intelligent systems and end users, and enhancing farmers' capacity to critically assess operational predictions (Shams et al., 2024). However, explainability is not a purely technical attribute: perceptions of opacity can discourage data sharing, slow technology adoption, and amplify forms of distrust, particularly in contexts characterized by limited digital skills or weak infrastructures (Sadjadi & Fernández, 2023). As highlighted by Wu and Zhong (2025), transparency and interpretability represent socio-technical prerequisites for effective collaboration between humans and intelligent systems.

Alongside transparency and explainability, accountability constitutes the third pillar of algorithmic governance. In digitalized agricultural systems, the informational value chain involves a plurality of actors—developers, data providers, platform integrators, and end users—who contribute, in different ways, to the production, transformation, and application of data. In the absence of systematic documentation, audit trails, and shared logging mechanisms, it becomes difficult to reconstruct the origin of a predictive error, identify the stage at which an anomaly emerged, or determine who should be held responsible for a harmful outcome (Dara et al., 2022; Novelli et al., 2024). The complexity of cloud–edge architectures, the fragmentation of information pipelines, and the lack of common risk assessment metrics further intensify this uncertainty, resulting in the transfer of responsibilities and burdens toward less-equipped actors—particularly farmers—who often lack the technical or contractual tools needed to fully assess the implications of the systems they adopt. Algorithmic accountability is therefore not an exclusively legal attribute; it is a socio-technical property that requires robust documentary infrastructures, verifiable processes, clearly defined roles, and an equitable distribution of responsibilities across the entire system life cycle.

In the domain of transparency and explainability, regulatory frameworks primarily shape users' ability to understand and evaluate AI systems embedded in agricultural processes. The AI Act introduces obligations related to documentation, traceability, and human oversight for high-risk systems, thereby strengthening the intelligibility of algorithmic decisions and enabling informed control by operators (European Commission, 2024). The GDPR complements this approach where personal data are involved, limiting the use of fully automated decision-making and imposing information duties to safeguard the decisional autonomy of data subjects (European Commission, 2016). Also from this perspective, transparency and explainability are not merely technical requirements, but socio-technical conditions that make accountability possible along decision chains increasingly mediated by intelligent systems.

Taken together, these dimensions show that process transparency, decision explainability, and actor accountability constitute indispensable conditions for the equitable, trustworthy, and sustainability-oriented adoption of agricultural AI. Only systems that are interpretable, traceable, and supported by practices of shared responsibility can enable an integration of AI that values experiential knowledge, mitigates risks, and distributes the benefits of digital transformation more equitably.

6.2.3 Privacy, Data Ownership, and Privacy-Preserving Solutions

The pervasive digitalization of agri-food systems has significantly expanded the volume and variety of data generated by sensors, intelligent machines, management platforms, and mobile applications. This transformation assigns data a central role not only in decision-making processes, but also in shaping power relations and the distribution of benefits along the AI value chain (Rahaman et al., 2024; Zha, 2020). Empirical evidence nevertheless shows that the expansion of agricultural data collection and processing practices is accompanied by growing uncertainty among operators, particularly with regard to secondary data uses, the degree of contractual transparency, and the possibility that data may be exploited without fair returns or meaningful participation in decision-making processes (Dembani et al., 2025). The issue therefore concerns not only privacy protection in a narrow sense, but also the broader socio-technical structure that governs access to data, their transformation, and the redistribution of informational value.

A critical issue concerns the legal and epistemic ambiguity associated with data ownership regimes in agriculture. As noted by Kosior (2020), applying the notion of "ownership" to data is intrinsically problematic: what determines actors' effective ability to benefit from the digital ecosystem is not formal title, but the exercise of substantive rights—access, reuse, objection, and negotiated sharing—that enable control over the information life cycle. This ambiguity is reflected in farmers' perceptions: limited transparency of digital contracts, informational asymmetries, and dependence on proprietary platforms can foster distrust and reduce willingness to share data (Sadjadi & Fernández, 2023). A broader interpretation of these dynamics is offered by Wu and Zhong (2025), who argue that digital agricultural systems risk configuring forms of digital extractivism: farmers contribute decisively to the generation of informational value, yet retain limited control over downstream data uses and derive only marginal economic or decision-making returns linked to AI.

The issue of privacy and informational rights directly concerns the distribution of power and value within digitalized agricultural systems. The GDPR establishes the reference framework for the protection of fundamental rights when agricultural data can be linked to identified or identifiable individuals, imposing principles of purpose limitation, data minimization, and privacy by design that shape the design of platforms and information architectures (European Commission, 2016). By contrast, the Data Act addresses structural asymmetries typical of digital agriculture by granting users effective rights of access to and portability of data generated by connected devices, while countering discriminatory contractual practices (European Commission, 2023). These provisions aim to narrow the gap between data generation and data control, creating the conditions for more equitable models of information sharing and value creation. In this context, privacy-preserving solutions play an enabling role by allowing data use in ways that are compatible with rights protection and with more informed participation by agricultural operators.

However, equitable and sustainable data governance also requires technical solutions capable of embedding protection from the earliest stages of system design. Robust anonymization techniques, federated learning, homomorphic encryption, granular access controls, and decentralized architectures can serve as key tools to reduce exposure to re-identification risks, preserve the confidentiality of sensitive information, and enable data use in ways that are consistent with the principles of privacy by design and data sovereignty. The integration of such solutions into contractual arrangements, digital infrastructures, and interoperability policies could help strengthen actors' trust, reduce informational asymmetries, and create the conditions for more informed and participatory data sharing.

Overall, privacy, informational rights, and privacy-preserving solutions constitute essential components of AI governance oriented toward inclusion and sustainability. Ensuring that farmers retain effective control over informational flows not only protects their fundamental rights but also represents a structural condition for equitable participation in the value generated by digital systems. This perspective sets the stage for the discussion of systemic security, interoperability, and data governance, which are examined in the following section.

6.2.4 Systemic Security, Interoperability, and Data Governance

The security of AI systems applied to agriculture must be understood as an emergent property of socio-technical ecosystems characterized by complex interdependencies among digital infrastructures, operational practices, and environmental conditions (Ali et al., 2024; Chen et al., 2023). In a sector marked by technological heterogeneity; ecological variability; and growing reliance on sensor networks, cloud platforms, and distributed architectures, vulnerabilities rarely remain confined to individual components: local failures, software errors, or cyber compromises can propagate along the digital value chain and generate non-linear effects on agricultural activities and the continuity of critical services. Evidence indicates that the robustness of intelligent systems depends on the ability of models and devices to operate under variable conditions, manage uncertainty, and withstand attacks that include data flow manipulation, interference across network layers, or the injection of misleading information (Dara et al., 2022). The fragmented nature of agricultural IoT networks amplifies these risks: sensors and machinery sourced from different manufacturers, non-uniform updates, and inconsistent standards expand the attack surface and complicate the timely detection of anomalies (Gupta et al., 2020). Within this context, risk assumes a systemic character, as technical, infrastructural, and organizational vulnerabilities tend to combine and generate distributed impacts across the entire digital ecosystem (Wu & Zhong, 2025).

Alongside challenges related to security and robustness, interoperability constitutes a decisive factor for ensuring operational continuity, data quality, and the transparency of decision-making processes. In agriculture, the coexistence of sensors, intelligent machinery, management platforms, predictive models, and cloud services makes the need for shared technical and semantic standards particularly evident (López-Morales et al., 2020). The literature shows that the absence of interoperability generates not only inefficiencies but also dataset fragmentation, difficulties in traceability, and barriers to the integration of information flows, with direct implications for prediction quality and for the ability to ensure accountability along the decision chain (Rauch et al., 2025). Such fragmentation may also foster forms of technological lock-in: closed platforms, proprietary protocols, and limited data portability reduce farmers' decision-making autonomy and reinforce dominant positions in digital markets (Garske et al., 2021; Kosior, 2020).

Lack of interoperability also affects security. Uncoordinated updates, incompatible architectures, and heterogeneous protocols create uneven attack surfaces, complicate vulnerability management, and increase the likelihood that localized breaches will propagate across interconnected systems (Gupta et al., 2020). Interoperability therefore assumes a socio-technical dimension, requiring not only engineering solutions but also institutional convergence on rules governing data access, use, and sharing, as well as investments in resilient and adaptable edge–cloud infrastructures. These needs are particularly salient in rural areas characterized by unstable connectivity (Rauch et al., 2025; Sadjadi & Fernández, 2023).

At the systemic level, data governance constitutes the mechanism through which security, interoperability, and informational rights are coordinated within digitalized agricultural ecosystems. In contexts characterized by heterogeneous infrastructures and complex interdependencies among sensors, platforms, and predictive models, security cannot be treated as a property of individual components; rather, it emerges from the overall coherence of technical and organizational architectures. OECD principles emphasize the need for systems that are robust, traceable, and subject to risk management proportional to their application context, providing a framework for integrating security and interoperability within a long-term perspective (OECD, 2025). In the absence of governance arrangements capable of aligning technical standards, institutional responsibilities, and data-sharing practices, vulnerabilities tend to propagate along the digital value chain, reinforcing dependencies and undermining the resilience of the agri-food system as a whole.

Taken together, systemic security, interoperability, and data governance constitute inseparable dimensions of an algorithmic governance approach oriented toward resilience, transparency, and equity. Only by recognizing the interdependent nature of technical, infrastructural, and institutional vulnerabilities it is possible to build digital agricultural ecosystems capable of supporting an adoption of AI that is reliable, inclusive, and consistent with the sustainability and stability objectives of contemporary agri-food value chains.

6.3 Scenarios 2045 and Operational Roadmap: Methodological Approach

The use of foresight scenarios represents a well-established technique for analyzing complex systems characterized by high uncertainty, socio-technical interdependencies, and non-linear evolutionary trajectories. In such contexts, scenarios do not serve a predictive function; rather, they provide a structured space in which to explore a range of plausible futures; make explicit the assumptions that shape change; and identify enabling conditions, constraints, and potential bifurcation points (Amer et al., 2013; Schoemaker, 1995). The evolution of AI in agri-food systems—shaped by the dynamic interaction of technological, institutional, socio-economic, and environmental factors—constitutes a paradigmatic non-linear domain, in which scenario analysis is particularly useful for extending the cognitive horizon and supporting the formulation of resilient strategies. In this chapter, scenarios are constructed to represent plausible trajectories of AI development in contemporary agri-food systems, without assuming a specific geographical focus, and integrate evidence drawn from literature on agricultural digitalization processes.

The strategic foresight literature highlights how scenarios foster both the expansion of anticipatory capacity and processes of collective learning: they make divergent assumptions visible, facilitate dialogue among actors, and support long-term strategic conversations (Bishop et al., 2007). From this perspective, the scenarios proposed here do not aim to depict the future of agri-food systems in 2045, but rather to outline alternative configurations of the digitalization of agri-food system, designed to illuminate emerging trade-offs, opportunities, and vulnerabilities.

6.3.1 Methodological Framework: The Generic Foresight Process Framework

Scenario construction is based on the Generic Foresight Process Framework (GFPP) developed by Voros (2003). The GFPP structures the foresight process into four interdependent and iterative phases:

1. **Scanning (inputs)**—the systematic collection of weak signals; established trends; and relevant technological, institutional, and socio-economic drivers.

2. **Sensemaking (analysis and interpretation)**—the interpretation of signals through structural analysis, thematic clustering, and the reconstruction of causal relationships among variables.
3. **Prospection**—the exploration of plausible futures through the combination of drivers and critical uncertainties, leading to the definition of the generative logics of the scenarios.
4. **Strategic outputs**—the derivation of strategic implications, which in this chapter take the form of the 2025–2045 operational roadmap.

In the present analysis, the scanning and sense-making phases enabled the identification of the key factors shaping the evolution of agricultural AI, including technological maturity, digital infrastructures, data governance, institutional capacity, skill levels, digital inclusion, and territorial resilience. The prospection phase led to the formulation of three scenarios for 2045, while the strategic outputs provide the foundation for the roadmap presented in Sect. 6.4. The transition from scenarios to the roadmap is achieved through the identification of robust policy levers, conditional options, and priority investments that remain coherent across alternative trajectories.

6.3.2 Drivers, Critical Uncertainties, and Generative Logics

Scenario construction follows the methodological distinction between drivers and critical uncertainties, which is central to the approach developed by Schoemaker (1995):

- **Drivers (driving trends)**: relatively stable directions of change, such as the evolution of sensing technologies, the digitalization of farm management practices, the development of cloud–edge architectures, and the growing demand for transparency and sustainability.
- **Critical Uncertainties**: high-impact variables whose direction and intensity remain uncertain, including levels of public and private investment, institutional capacity, platform interoperability, the diffusion of digital skills, and the maturity of data governance arrangements.

The combined analysis of these elements, consistent with the systematic approaches described by Bishop et al. (2007), led to the identification of two interpretive axes that synthesize the system's evolutionary dynamics:

1. **Enabling capacities** (infrastructures, standards, technical services, and training).
2. **Quality of socio-technical governance** (data management models, inclusion, distribution of capabilities, and relationships among actors).

The intersection of these two variables constitutes the generative matrix of the three scenarios developed in the following section, which correspond to distinct regimes of the digital agri-food system rather than to variations in intensity along a single trajectory.

6.3.3 Typological Positioning of the Scenarios

The classification adopted in this chapter is consistent with the framework proposed by van Notten et al. (2003), which conceptualizes scenarios along three dimensions—purpose, process design, and content—specified through fourteen characteristics, including the degree of normativity, the temporal perspective (forecasting or backcasting), the nature of the data used (qualitative or quantitative), and the representation of change dynamics (trends, uncertainties, and discontinuities).

Within this typology, the scenarios developed in the chapter primarily belong to the category of descriptive scenarios with an exploratory orientation, constructed on the basis of qualitative evidence and aimed at mapping plausible futures. At the same time, they incorporate an evaluative component that places them in a hybrid zone between exploration and normativity, in line with the literature on so-called hybrid scenario forms.

More specifically:

- **Scenario A—Conservative**: aligned with the logic of trend-based descriptive scenarios, characterized by incremental innovation and a limited capacity for systemic transformation.
- **Scenario B—Transformative**: comparable to highly enabling exploratory configurations, with a strong emphasis on interoperability, open infrastructures, and digital inclusion; a typology consistent with scenarios oriented toward systemic collaboration.
- **Scenario C—Regressive**: close to discontinuity scenarios with degenerative outcomes, in which the combination of infrastructural vulnerabilities, lock-in dynamics, and institutional weakness generates trajectories of erosion of socio-technical capacities.

This typological positioning ensures methodological coherence and enables a structured comparison of the trajectories, making explicit the logic underlying the evolutionary divergences represented by the scenarios.

6.3.4 Function of Scenarios in the Digital Agri-food Governance Process

Scenarios do not constitute a merely descriptive exercise, but rather an operational tool that makes it possible to:

- identify strategic levers to strengthen the resilience and inclusiveness of agri-food systems;
- highlight emerging risks related to fragmentation, lock-in dynamics, skills polarization, and infrastructural dependencies;
- compare alternative models of data governance and digital infrastructure governance;

- guide public and private investments toward trajectories consistent with sustainability, technological autonomy, and territorial development.

Consistent with the strategic outputs phase of the GFPP, the scenarios therefore serve as the analytical foundation for the 2025–2045 roadmap presented in Sect. 6.4.2, which articulates priorities, responsibilities, and operational metrics for the digitalization of agri-food systems.

6.4 Scenarios Extended to 2045

Scenario A—Conservative: Incremental Innovation and Persistent Fragmentation

In this scenario, over the 2025–2045 period, the diffusion of AI in agriculture follows predominantly incremental trajectories, largely consistent with currently mature technical solutions. Tools based on computer vision, predictive models for irrigation and fertilization, multispectral drones, IoT sensor systems, and agro-environmental monitoring networks gradually consolidate, supporting operational improvements and more timely decision-making (Jha et al., 2019; Kisliuk et al., 2023; Sharma et al., 2022). This evolution reflects both the growing technical stability of these applications and the persistence of uneven adoption across territories and farm types.

The benefits are evident: greater agronomic precision, reduced resource waste, the expansion of decision-support systems, and the increasing digitalization of farm management practices (Rauch et al., 2025). However, these advantages tend to concentrate among farms with stronger infrastructural conditions and higher investment capacity, while gaps related to connectivity, access to cloud services, availability of advanced sensing technologies, and technical support persist. Empirical evidence indicates that small-scale producers continue to face significant difficulties in adopting complex digital solutions due to high upfront costs, limited digital skills, and the scarce availability of accompanying support services (High et al., 2025; Mhlanga, 2021; World Economic Forum, 2025).

The fragmentation of digital architectures represents an additional constraint. The absence of shared standards, the proliferation of proprietary platforms, and limited interoperability keep data integration costs high and exacerbate informational asymmetries among actors along the value chain. These dynamics are further reinforced by technological dependencies on cloud providers and their integrated ecosystems, which constrain the development of open and flexible digital infrastructures (CAST, 2025; Elbehri & Chestnov, 2021; van der Vlist et al., 2024). Public actors and value chain organizations primarily play an incremental facilitative role, without being able to substantially reshape existing institutional and market architectures.

Employment effects are moderate but ambivalent. The automation of certain repetitive tasks reduces the physical burden of work, while demand increases for operational digital skills related to the management of dashboards, sensors, and predictive models. However, uneven access to training and support services risks excluding workers with lower skill levels, thereby reinforcing pre-existing socio-technical vulnerabilities (High et al., 2025; Klerkx and Rose, 2020).

Overall, the conservative scenario outlines a future characterized by real but systemically limited innovation: technologies enhance productive efficiency, yet the persistence of infrastructural, organizational, and skill-related gaps prevents these advances from achieving a transformative scale. Adoption progresses, but it does not substantially alter the structural conditions that constrain the equitable diffusion of AI in agricultural systems, nor does it significantly reshape the distribution of decision-making power along the value chain.

Scenario B—Transformative: Open Infrastructures, Digital Inclusion, and Workforce Upskilling

Over the 2025–2045 period, in this scenario, AI evolves as a structural component of a socio-technical ecosystem capable of sustaining widespread innovation, interoperability, and inclusive participation. The dynamic is no longer fragmented or confined to individual firms; instead, it is grounded in the coordinated development of open infrastructures, shared standards, and data platforms designed to facilitate cooperation among public and private actors.

At the infrastructural level, a central role is played by interoperable platforms dedicated to agricultural data, supported by quality standards, shared documentation protocols, and transparent governance mechanisms. As highlighted by recent analyses of agricultural digitalization, these conditions aim to overcome current fragmentation and enable the integration of heterogeneous data originating from sensors, remote sensing, drones, and predictive systems (CAST, 2025; Elbehri & Chestnov, 2021). Within this context, shared infrastructures such as AI Factories and living labs consolidate, enabling co-development, experimentation, and localization of solutions, while reducing adoption costs and complexity for farms of different sizes (Rauch et al., 2025). This trajectory is grounded in the capacity of coalitions among public administrations, research centers, technology firms, and producer organizations to define shared rules governing data use, infrastructural investment, and the distribution of benefits.

Integration does not concern the farm level alone but extends across the entire agri-food value chain. End-to-end interconnection among sensors, predictive models, robotics, drones, and traceability systems enables more coordinated process management, with potential benefits in terms of production optimization, waste reduction, logistical efficiency, and responsiveness to climatic and market variables (Ben Ayed & Hanana, 2021; Kisliuk et al., 2023). The value chain thus takes shape as an adaptive system, grounded in shared information flows and more integrated decision-making processes.

From an employment perspective, this trajectory opens significant opportunities for workforce upskilling. New professional roles emerge—digital agronomists, data technicians, predictive systems operators, and robotics and drone maintenance specialists—requiring advanced combinations of agronomic, computational, and analytical skills (High et al., 2025; World Economic Forum, 2025). Agricultural extension services assume a strategic role in mediating between local knowledge and algorithmic capabilities, supporting processes of interpretation, validation, and contextualization of recommendations generated by AI. Continuous training becomes an integral component of organizational models, contributing to the mitigation of skill polarization risks. A critical element lies in the capacity to translate complex outputs—derived from predictive models, multispectral imagery, and neural networks—into comprehensible and context-specific operational recommendations, as emphasized in the applied literature on computer vision, drones, and big data (Sharma et al., 2022). Despite its strongly enabling character, this trajectory is not free of tensions, particularly regarding the allocation of investment costs, data protection, and the risk of new forms of dependency on digital infrastructures regarded as essential.

Overall, the transformative scenario outlines a future in which AI contributes to narrowing digital divides, upgrading skills, strengthening productive resilience, and supporting sustainable development objectives, particularly in areas related to innovation, decent work, the reduction of inequalities, and environmental sustainability (Mhlanga, 2021; Vinuesa et al., 2020). This trajectory exhibits a high transformative potential, but it requires substantial investment and strong institutional coordination to realize these opportunities at a systemic scale, as well as regulatory and monitoring mechanisms capable of governing the new asymmetries that may emerge in a highly digital-intensive context.

Scenario C—Regressive: Technological Polarization, Infrastructural Dependencies, and Labor Precarization

In this scenario, agricultural systems derive only marginal benefits from AI due to infrastructural fragilities, technological dependencies, and inadequate governance arrangements. The lack of coordination between public and private actors, persistent institutional fragmentation, and underinvestment in digital infrastructures give rise to an ecosystem marked by inefficiencies, vulnerabilities, and widening inequalities. Over the period 2025–2045, the combination of discontinuous investment patterns, weak regulatory capacity, and external shocks further erodes trust in institutions responsible for governing agricultural digitalization, fostering the concentration of technological power in the hands of a limited number of global actors.

At the technological and infrastructural level, advanced applications such as autonomous robotics, deep learning systems, complex predictive models, and multi-source analytics platforms require high data quality, sustained maintenance capacity, and robust digital architectures. In the absence of these prerequisites, such solutions prove difficult to implement or scale, generating negative effects on operational costs and process efficiency (Jha et al., 2019). Perceived complexity, high investment requirements, and maintenance challenges further reinforce reluctance toward adoption, particularly among small-scale producers and farms with limited digital capabilities (Sharma et al., 2022).

These constraints are compounded by a growing dependence on global cloud service providers and proprietary platforms. Such configurations can generate forms of technological lock-in (van der Vlist et al., 2024), limiting the autonomy of agricultural systems and their capacity to develop solutions adapted to local contexts. Analyses of global digital dynamics further indicate that the concentration of technological power in a small number of actors increases exposure to systemic vulnerabilities and risks of structural dependency (UNCTAD, 2025). As a result, territorial actors—including public institutions and professional organizations—experience a progressive erosion of their steering capacity, while critical decisions concerning infrastructures and data are effectively outsourced to extra-territorial private actors.

The effects on labor are particularly problematic. The substitution of certain manual tasks occurs in contexts that lack adequate training and reskilling pathways, contributing to a polarization between a small group of highly qualified profiles and a large share of workers with insufficient or outdated skills. The absence of robust training infrastructures and effective extension services further amplifies the socio-technical exclusion of rural territories and less qualified workers (Klerkx and Mhlanga, 2021; Rose, 2020). The increasing delegation of decisions to opaque algorithmic systems may also foster processes of deskilling, a risk widely recognized in debates on general-purpose technologies (Howard, 2019), especially when mechanisms for human interpretation, contextualization, and validation of outputs are lacking. Combined with unstable market dynamics and fragile governance arrangements, these factors may contribute to new forms of precarization of agricultural labor (UNCTAD, 2025).

At the systemic level, this trajectory is associated with increasing economic and environmental vulnerabilities, the concentration of technological power in a small number of global providers, the widening of territorial disparities, and a growing risk of divergence from sustainable development objectives—particularly those related to decent work, the reduction of inequalities, and environmental sustainability (Vinuesa et al., 2020). Taken together, these dynamics delineate an ecosystem that is unable to harness the potential of AI and is instead prone to processes of structural dependency and innovative regression. This scenario differs from the conservative one not merely in the intensity of its criticalities, but in the distinct configuration of technological and institutional power that underpins it.

Table 6.1 synthesizes the defining features of the three trajectories by comparing key structural dimensions, including enabling capacities, governance configurations, levels of digital integration, modes of adoption, skill profiles, equity of access, and the degree of qualitative alignment with the Sustainable Development Goals (SDGs). The comparison serves as an analytical bridge to the 2025–2045 operational roadmap, highlighting enabling conditions that cut across the different scenarios. Alignment with the SDGs is reported in qualitative terms, based on the theoretical and empirical linkages discussed throughout the chapter.

Table 6.1 Summary of the three scenarios to 2045

Dimension	Scenario A	Scenario B	Scenario C
Enabling capacities	Intermediate	High	Low
Governance	Fragmented	Coordinated	Weak
Digital integration	Limited	High	Low
Adoption	Selective	Widespread	Residual
Skills	Uneven	Strengthened	Polarized
Equity	Persistent gaps	Reduced gaps	Widening gaps
SDGs alignment	Partial	High	Weak

6.4.1 The Logic of the Trajectories to 2045

The scenarios described represent three plausible configurations of the evolution of AI in agri-food systems, generated by the interaction between enabling capacities and socio-technical governance models. Although they originate from shared conditions—such as infrastructural heterogeneity, increasing environmental pressure, and the acceleration of digital innovation—they diverge in the ability of institutional, economic, and territorial actors to translate the potential of AI into social, productive, and environmental value. Each trajectory corresponds to a distinct combination of the two interpretive axes: intermediate enabling capacities and fragmented governance in the conservative scenario; high enabling capacities and coordinated governance in the transformative scenario; and weak enabling capacities and fragile governance, accompanied by a strong concentration of technological power, in the regressive scenario. The synthetic descriptors associated with the scenarios reflect this reading and also incorporate an assessment of the trajectories in light of sustainability objectives.

Scenario A—Conservative: "Growth Without Transformation"

In this trajectory, innovation advances in continuity with currently consolidated technologies. The adoption of computer vision tools, IoT sensing, and decision-support systems expands gradually, generating localized improvements in agronomic precision and waste reduction. However, infrastructural barriers, data fragmentations, and skill asymmetries prevent systemic scalability.

The result is an evolution characterized by tangible but unevenly distributed benefits, with limited effects on overall resilience and inclusion dynamics. Public and private actors tend to reproduce existing arrangements, favoring incremental interventions that do not challenge the structure of value chains or the distribution of decision-making capacities.

Scenario B—Transformative: "Inclusive and Adaptive Innovation"

This trajectory reflects the convergence of infrastructural investment, open standards, transparent data governance, and digital inclusion policies. Edge–cloud infrastructures, interoperable data spaces, and collaborative ecosystems such as AI Factories and living labs enable end-to-end integration of processes across the value chain.

The availability of continuous training pathways, digital extension services, and new hybrid professional profiles supports widespread adoption and enhances the capacity to contextualize algorithmic recommendations.

This scenario maximizes the impact of AI on productivity, sustainability, and the reduction of disparities, provided that stable coalitions among public institutions, technology firms, and producer organizations are able to negotiate shared rules on data, standards, and investment, and to manage the distributive conflicts that accompany transformative processes.

Scenario C—Regressive: "Technology Without Enabling Capacities"

In this configuration, the absence of adequate infrastructures, shared standards, and effective governance severely constrains the implementation of advanced technologies. Machine learning solutions, robotics, and multi-source analytics fail to scale, generating inefficiencies and increasing operational costs.

Dependence on global platforms reinforces technological lock-in, while the lack of training services and algorithmic mediation mechanisms leads to skill polarization, labor precarization, and widening territorial disparities.

This trajectory illustrates how AI can contribute to regressive dynamics when institutional capacities and infrastructures are misaligned, and when the erosion of regulatory capacity on the part of public institutions allows a small number of technological actors to assume a de facto regulatory role, redefining the conditions of access to infrastructures and data.

6.4.2 Operational Roadmap 2025–2045

The scenarios outlined above show that the evolution of AI in agriculture depends on cumulative processes involving infrastructures, skills, organizational models, and data governance arrangements. These trajectories are neither linear nor deterministic: they reflect the interaction between territorial conditions, institutional capacities, and the availability of technical resources. The proposed roadmap translates these dynamics into a sequence of progressive interventions structured across three interconnected temporal phases. The 2025–2045 horizon makes it possible to capture the long-term temporality of socio-technical transitions, which require extended cycles of investment, technological maturation, and institutional consolidation.

2025–2030—Digital and Occupational Foundations

The first phase aims to establish the basic enabling conditions. Evidence shows that infrastructural gaps, discontinuous connectivity, and data fragmentation constitute critical barriers to the adoption of digital technologies, particularly in less-served rural contexts (CAST, 2025; Mhlanga, 2021). Priorities include strengthening communication networks, developing reliable edge–cloud architectures, and creating interoperable repositories supported by quality standards and shared procedures for documentation and access (Elbehri & Chestnov, 2021; Rauch et al., 2025).

In parallel, it is necessary to strengthen foundational training. Digital literacy programs, capacity-building initiatives, and training pathways focused on the use of drones, computer vision systems, IoT sensing technologies, and decision-support systems help reduce the gap between technological availability and effective use. Particular attention to small-scale producers and groups most exposed to digital inequalities is essential to prevent the technological transition from consolidating pre-existing vulnerabilities (High et al., 2025; Sharma et al., 2022; World Economic Forum, 2025). Table 6.2 summarizes the strategic objectives, key actions, actors, and expected outcomes characterizing the 2025–2030 phase focused on establishing digital and occupational foundations.

2030–2035—Socio-Technical Integration and New Professional Profiles

The second phase places coordinated integration of infrastructures and actors at the center of the transition. During this period, AI Factories, living labs, and territorial experimentation spaces gain prominence, enabling co-development, local adaptation of solutions, and structured collaboration among research institutions, technology firms, and farms (Rauch et al., 2025). The introduction of shared standards for interoperability, security, and transparency helps reduce fragmentation across information systems and strengthens trust in data-sharing practices (CAST, 2025; UNCTAD, 2025).

At the labor level, this phase requires an expansion of reskilling and upskilling programs to support the emergence of hybrid professional profiles with competencies in data management, the maintenance of automated systems, and the operational

Table 6.2 Phase 2025–2030: Digital and occupational foundations

Dimension	Content
Strategic objectives	Reduce the rural digital divide; build basic digital infrastructures for AI; strengthen digital literacy and operational skills
Key actions	Investments in connectivity and edge–cloud architectures; launch of interoperable repositories supported by quality standards; digital literacy programs and operational training on core digital solutions
Key actors	Public institutions and rural development agencies; training providers and extension services; farms and professional organizations
Expected outcomes	Initial adoption of basic digital technologies; improvement in operational skills; reduction of territorial and infrastructural gaps

interpretation of algorithmic outputs (High et al., 2025; World Economic Forum, 2025). Generative systems and advisory tools tailored to local agro-ecological and linguistic contexts can improve access to advanced services and enhance decision quality.

A further element concerns the progressive integration of Digital Management Support Tools (DMST), namely, digital tools for territorial coordination and the shared management of resources, into local governance processes. These instruments support alignment between agricultural, environmental, and territorial development policies (Rauch et al., 2025). Table 6.3 outlines the strategic objectives, key actions, actors, and expected outputs defining the 2030–2035 phase centered on socio-technical integration and the emergence of new professional profiles.

2035–2045—Inclusive Scalability and Systemic Resilience

The third phase focuses on the scalability of intelligent solutions and the consolidation of systemic resilience. In this period, agricultural extension networks and intermediary actors play a decisive role in translating algorithmic outputs into operational practices, reducing the risk of socio-technical exclusion, particularly in peripheral and less-equipped contexts (High et al., 2025; World Economic Forum, 2025).

During this period, tools for monitoring employment-related risks associated with automation, together with anticipatory governance approaches, become increasingly important in assessing the impact of AI on work, job quality, and the distribution of skills, in line with analyses of general-purpose technologies (Howard, 2019; UNCTAD, 2025).

At the same time, public–private models oriented toward digital sovereignty and the reduction of dependencies on proprietary platforms consolidate, supported by the development of open infrastructures, the promotion of shared standards, and the expansion of spaces for collaborative innovation (Rauch et al., 2025; UNCTAD, 2025; van der Vlist et al., 2024). The progressive alignment of technological trajectories with the SDGs is reinforced by assessment tools that integrate environmental, social, and economic dimensions (Vinuesa et al., 2020). Table 6.4 presents the

Table 6.3 Phase 2030–2035: Socio-technical integration and new professional profiles

Dimension	Content
Strategic objectives	Integrate technologies and services into coordinated ecosystems; foster co-development and local adaptation of solutions; promote advanced skills and hybrid professional profiles
Key actions	Activation of AI Factories, living labs, and territorial experimentation spaces; introduction of shared standards for interoperability, security, and transparency; advanced reskilling and upskilling programs; implementation of generative models and DMST tailored to local contexts
Key actors	Universities and research centers; technology firms and agri-food startups; digital extension networks; policy makers
Expected outputs	End-to-end integration of digital technologies; enhanced territorial innovation capacity; development of advanced digital professional profiles

strategic objectives, key actions, actors, and extended impacts associated with the 2035–2045 phase focused on inclusive scalability and systemic resilience.

Taken together, the three phases of the roadmap outline a development pathway that acknowledges the cumulative nature of socio-technical transitions and the need to integrate infrastructures, skills, data governance, and institutional capacities. The proposed progression—from digital foundations to resilient scalability—highlights that the effectiveness of AI in agri-food systems depends not only on technological availability, but on the ability of actors to build coherent enabling conditions over time.

The roadmap also emphasizes the importance of intermediary institutions and extension networks, which operate as connective mechanisms between algorithmic capabilities, local knowledge, and decision-making processes. Their role becomes central in ensuring that innovation does not remain concentrated in a limited number of highly infrastructured contexts, but instead diffuses more evenly, contributing to the reduction of territorial disparities and to the qualification of agricultural labor.

The proposed approach also highlights that digital transformation is not neutral: the expansion of infrastructural capacities, the evolution of skills, the quality of data governance, and the degree of participation of local actors give rise to markedly different trajectories, as illustrated by the scenarios. The roadmap therefore represents not only a planning exercise, but an anticipatory tool capable of identifying critical levers, emerging risks, and the coordination conditions required to steer innovation toward inclusive and sustainable outcomes.

Finally, the 2025–2045 articulation provides a coherent temporal framework for assessing the impacts of AI in relation to the SDGs. The integration of environmental, social, and economic dimensions in the scalability phase makes it possible to directly link technological evolution to sustainability challenges, positioning the roadmap as an operational instrument for aligning the digitalization of the agri-food sector with objectives of equity, resilience, and collective well-being. The following section

Table 6.4 Phase 2035–2045: Inclusive scalability and systemic resilience

Dimension	Content
Strategic objectives	Extend intelligent services to peripheral areas; strengthen anticipatory governance and digital sovereignty; align AI development with the SDGs
Key actions	Strengthening digital extension networks and human–AI mediation functions; introduction of systems for monitoring employment-related risks; development of public–private models for open infrastructures and the reduction of technological dependencies; application of environmental, social, and employment impact assessments
Key actors	Policy makers and regulatory agencies; technology firms and digital infrastructure providers; multilateral organizations; research centers
Extended impacts	Resilient and scalable AI ecosystems; reduced infrastructural and technological dependencies; measurable contributions to the SDGs; greater territorial equity and sustainability

further develops these linkages by outlining metrics, responsibilities, and priority actions for monitoring the contribution of AI to the SDGs.

6.4.3 Actors, Responsibilities, and SDG Metrics

The evolution of AI in agri-food systems is closely linked to the capacity of the actors involved to coordinate strategies, investments, and governance arrangements within a complex socio-technical ecosystem. Digital technologies do not operate in isolation: their effectiveness depends on available infrastructures, data quality, the distribution of skills, and the alignment among institutions, firms, and territorial networks. From this perspective, the analysis of actors and their respective responsibilities represents a critical step for understanding the trajectories outlined by the scenarios, while the definition of metrics oriented toward the SDGs makes it possible to monitor over time the direction and quality of the transformations induced by AI.

Actors and Responsibilities in a Multilevel Socio-technical Ecosystem

Public institutions play a decisive role in creating the enabling conditions for digital innovation. Through infrastructural investments, rural connectivity policies, and the regulation of data flows, they contribute to reducing the digital divide and to promoting interoperability standards that limit the fragmentation of information systems (CAST, 2025; Elbehri & Chestnov, 2021; UNCTAD, 2025). Policies supporting innovation also assume a strategic function in mitigating the risks associated with the concentration of computational power and technological dependence on proprietary platforms.

Farms, particularly small- and medium-sized operations, represent a critical node in innovation processes. They do not play a merely adoptive role but actively participate in the production and contextualization of data that feed predictive models and algorithmic systems. The quality, granularity, and continuity of farm-level data directly influence the transferability of applications and their territorial scalability (World Economic Forum, 2025). Collective organizations and producer cooperatives can further expand this capacity by facilitating access to advanced digital services and strengthening the bargaining position of farmers *vis-à-vis* technology providers.

Technology firms and digital infrastructure providers play a central role in the design of AI models, the development of data platforms, and the management of cloud–edge architectures. However, the concentration of expertise and infrastructures in a limited number of actors can generate structural dependencies, particularly in the absence of open standards and effective interoperability mechanisms (CAST, 2025; van der Vlist et al., 2024). The choice between proprietary infrastructures and open solutions therefore becomes strategically significant, as it conditions the ability of territories to develop systems adapted to their specific agricultural contexts.

Agricultural extension networks and advisory services perform a crucial intermediary function. They translate algorithmic outputs into understandable and context-specific operational guidance, mitigating the risk of socio-technical exclusion, particularly in areas characterized by lower levels of digital literacy (Klerkx and Rose, 2020). This mediation is essential to ensure that AI becomes embedded in everyday practices rather than remaining confined to high-technology contexts.

Research institutions and universities contribute to knowledge production, the development of data infrastructures, and the independent assessment of the economic, social, and environmental impacts of AI. Analyses of labor transformations and skill dynamics highlight the importance of structured lifelong learning pathways in preventing deskilling processes associated with automation (Howard, 2019). The capacity of the research sector to generate robust evidence therefore represents a critical factor in guiding policies and strategies along inclusive trajectories.

SDG Metrics as Tools for Evaluation and Governance

The definition of SDG-oriented metrics makes it possible to systematically interpret ongoing transformation processes, fostering forms of governance capable of aligning innovation with sustainability. Metrics related to equity in access to digital technologies—such as connectivity, availability of intelligent devices, and the participation of small producers in training programs—represent key indicators for monitoring progress toward SDGs 1 and 10, which address poverty reduction and the reduction of inequalities (Mhlanga, 2021).

Data quality, openness, and interoperability constitute foundational dimensions for SDGs 9 and 16. Accuracy, granularity, timeliness of updates, and real-time availability are essential criteria for assessing the maturity of information systems and the level of trust in advanced applications (CAST, 2025; World Economic Forum, 2025).

The labor dimension requires indicators capable of capturing not only risks of displacement, but also the emergence of new hybrid professional roles, the effectiveness of reskilling programs, and the capacity of territories to sustain continuous learning processes (Howard, 2019; UNCTAD, 2025). These elements are central to SDG 8, which aims to promote decent work and inclusive economic growth.

For the environmental SDGs—particularly SDGs 2, 12, 13, and 15—metrics related to input-use efficiency, waste reduction, climate resilience, and the capacity of systems to anticipate and mitigate agro-climatic risks are crucial. Evidence shows that, across different contexts, AI can contribute to reducing the use of fertilizers and pesticides, optimizing irrigation, and improving risk management (Ben Ayed & Hanana, 2021; Kisliuk et al., 2023). However, assessment frameworks should also incorporate indicators related to the energy costs and environmental impacts of computational infrastructures, in line with integrated approaches proposed in the literature (Vinuesa et al., 2020).

SDG metrics do not function merely as monitoring tools, but as governance instruments that guide coordination among public actors, technology firms, and territorial organizations. The definition of such indicators makes it possible to render transformation trajectories transparent, facilitate resource allocation, and identify priority areas for intervention. Taken together, they enable an assessment of whether AI is contributing to more inclusive, sustainable, and resilient configurations, or whether it tends instead to reinforce conservative or exclusionary dynamics.

6.5 Conclusions

The digital transition of agriculture is producing a transformation that simultaneously affects technological, cognitive, and institutional dimensions. The diffusion of systems based on AI, advanced sensing technologies, and data-driven management introduces forms of knowledge that do not merely support decision-making, but fundamentally reconfigure it. Agricultural work increasingly takes the form of an interpretive process that requires new modes of observation, new decision-making categories, and new forms of responsibility. Technology does not replace experience; rather, it reorganizes it in ways that demand reflective skills capable of evaluating, contextualizing, and integrating heterogeneous information.

Within the trajectory outlined by this volume, digital transformation emerges as a multilevel phenomenon affecting roles, professional identities, organizational arrangements, and knowledge institutions. Digital skills, discussed in depth in the preceding chapters, function as the invisible infrastructure of this evolution: not merely technical abilities, but systemic capacities that enable actors to steer technologies in informed, predictable, and sustainable ways. The transition toward smart agriculture therefore requires not only the adoption of tools, but the capacity to build cognitive environments in which data acquire meaning and algorithms become an integral component of decision-making processes.

In this sense, AI amplifies the importance of metacognitive and collaborative skills: the ability to interpret model outputs, assess their reliability, recognize the limits of predictability, and understand the informational asymmetries generated within digital systems. Agricultural professionalism is redefined as a hybrid form of professionalism, distributed between humans and machines, between tacit knowledge and analytical capabilities, and between decision-making autonomy and the governance of digital tools. This reconfiguration is not neutral: it reshapes relations of production, affects roles, transforms responsibilities, and redefines the relationship between experience and innovation.

The perspective advanced in this volume underscores the importance of interpreting these processes not in isolation, but through a systemic approach. Digital agriculture develops within information ecosystems that encompass institutions, collaborative networks, production chains, and territorial communities. It is within these spaces that the meanings of data are negotiated, trust and legitimacy are constructed, and standards and skills are defined. The transition therefore depends not only on technological innovations, but on the collective capacity to learn, cooperate, and reflect on the socio-technical implications of automation.

From this analysis emerges the concept of *learning agriculture*: an interpretive model that conceives farmers, technicians, extension services, educational institutions, and digital infrastructures as components of a single cognitive system in co-evolution. Learning agriculture is not a normative objective, but a necessary condition for ensuring that digitalization generates shared and sustainable value. It advances a view of agriculture as a dynamic process in which human capacities and Artificial Intelligences are integrated according to logics of complementarity rather than substitution.

Looking ahead, the primary challenge does not lie in the introduction of ever more sophisticated technologies, but in the construction of individual and collective capacities capable of governing them. The quality of human capital, the transparency of digital systems, data governance, and the accessibility of information infrastructures will become decisive factors for the competitiveness and sustainability of agri-food systems. Public policies, in turn, will be required to support not only technological adoption, but also lifelong learning, digital inclusion, and the creation of institutional environments conducive to knowledge sharing.

In conclusion, AI will not redefine agriculture solely through what it makes possible, but above all through what it requires: new forms of understanding, new responsibilities, and new competencies. Digital transition thus becomes a process of collective learning, in which the capacity to interpret, integrate, and steer innovation represents the fundamental lever for building agricultural systems that are resilient, equitable, and sustainable over the long term.

References

Ali, G., Mijwil, M. M., Buruga, B. A., Abotaleb, M., & Adamopoulos, I. (2024). A survey on artificial intelligence in cybersecurity for smart agriculture: State-of-the-art, cyber threats, artificial intelligence applications, and ethical concerns. *Mesopotamian Journal of Computer Science*,53–103. https://doi.org/10.58496/mjcsc/2024/007

Amer, M., Daim, T. U., & Jetter, A. (2013). A review of scenario planning. *Futures, 46*, 23–40. https://doi.org/10.1016/j.futures.2012.10.003

Ben Ayed, R., & Hanana, M. (2021). Artificial intelligence to improve the food and agriculture sector. *Journal of Food Quality, 2021*, 1–7. https://doi.org/10.1155/2021/5584754

Bishop, P., Hines, A., & Collins, T. (2007). The current state of scenario development: An overview of techniques. *Foresight, 9*(1), 5–25. https://doi.org/10.1108/14636680710727516

CAST. (2025). *AI in agriculture: Opportunities, challenges, and recommendations.* Council for Agricultural Science and Technology, Issue Paper No. 83.

Cesco, S., Sambo, P., Borin, M., Basso, B., Orzes, G., & Mazzetto, F. (2023). Smart agriculture and digital twins: Applications and challenges in a vision of sustainability. *European Journal of Agronomy: THe Journal of the European Society for Agronomy, 146*(126809), Article 126809. https://doi.org/10.1016/j.eja.2023.126809

Chen, H.-Y., Sharma, K., Sharma, C., & Sharma, S. (2023). Integrating explainable artificial intelligence and blockchain to smart agriculture: Research prospects for decision making and improved security. *Smart Agricultural Technology, 6*(100350), Article 100350. https://doi.org/10.1016/j.atech.2023.100350

Commission, E. (2016). Regulation (EU) 2016/679 of the European Parliament and of the Council of 27 April 2016 on the protection of natural persons with regard to the processing of personal data and on the free movement of such data (General Data Protection Regulation). *Official Journal of the European Union, L, 119*, 1–88.

Dara, R., Hazrati Fard, S. M., & Kaur, J. (2022). Recommendations for ethical and responsible use of artificial intelligence in digital agriculture. *Frontiers in Artificial Intelligence, 5*, Article 884192. https://doi.org/10.3389/frai.2022.884192

Dembani, R., Karvelas, I., Akbar, N. A., Rizou, S., Tegolo, D., & Fountas, S. (2025). Agricultural data privacy and federated learning: A review of challenges and opportunities. *Computers and Electronics in Agriculture, 232*(110048), Article 110048. https://doi.org/10.1016/j.compag.2025.110048

Elbehri, A., & Chestnov, R. (2021). *Digital agriculture in action – Artificial intelligence for agriculture. Bangkok: Food and Agriculture Organization of the United Nations (FAO) and International Telecommunication Union (ITU).*

FAO. (2019). *Digital agriculture transformation and innovation: Transforming ideas into value in a sustainable way for #ZeroHunger*. Information Technology Division.

Finger, R. (2023). Digital innovations for sustainable and resilient agricultural systems. *European Review of Agricultural Economics, 50*(4), 1277–1309. https://doi.org/10.1093/erae/jbad021

Garske, B., Bau, A., & Ekardt, F. (2021). Digitalization and AI in European agriculture: A strategy for achieving climate and biodiversity targets? *Sustainability, 13*(9), 4652. https://doi.org/10.3390/su13094652

Girmay, M. B., Droste, J., Deters, H., & Doerr, J. (2025). *Explainability needs in agriculture: Exploring dairy farmers' user personas*. Preprint retrieved from https://doi.org/10.48550/ARXIV.2509.16249

Govindan, K. (2024). How artificial intelligence drives sustainable frugal innovation: A multitheoretical perspective. *IEEE Transactions on Engineering Management, 71*, 638–655. https://doi.org/10.1109/tem.2021.3116187

Gupta, M., Abdelsalam, M., Khorsandroo, S., & Mittal, S. (2020). Security and privacy in smart farming: Challenges and opportunities. *IEEE Access: Practical Innovations, Open Solutions, 8*, 34564–34584. https://doi.org/10.1109/access.2020.2975142

Heider, N., Gunreben, L., Zürner, S., & Schieck, M. (2025). A survey of datasets for computer vision in agriculture. Preprint retrieved from https://doi.org/10.48550/ARXIV.2502.16950

High, C., Singh, N., & Nemes, G. (2025). Artificial intelligence for agricultural extension: Supporting transformative learning among smallholder farmers. *Journal of Development Policy and Practice*, (24551333251345224). https://doi.org/10.1177/24551333251345224

Howard, J. (2019). Artificial intelligence: Implications for the future of work. *American Journal of Industrial Medicine, 62*(11), 917–926. https://doi.org/10.1002/ajim.23037

Jha, K., Doshi, A., Patel, P., & Shah, M. (2019). A comprehensive review on automation in agriculture using artificial intelligence. *Artificial Intelligence in Agriculture, 2*, 1–12. https://doi.org/10.1016/j.aiia.2019.05.004

Jouanjean, M., Casalini, F., Wiseman, L., & Gray, E. (2020). *Issues around data governance in the digital transformation of agriculture: The farmers' perspective*. OECD Food, Agriculture and Fisheries Papers, No. 146, OECD Publishing

Kisliuk, B., Krause, J. C., Meemken, H., Saborío Morales, J. C., Müller, H., & Hertzberg, J. (2023). AI in current and future agriculture: An introductory overview. *KI—Künstliche Intelligenz, 37*(2–4), 117–132. https://doi.org/10.1007/s13218-023-00826-5

Klerkx, L., & Rose, D. (2020). Dealing with the game-changing technologies of Agriculture 4.0: How do we manage diversity and responsibility in food system transition pathways? *Global Food Security, 24*(100347), 100347. https://doi.org/10.1016/j.gfs.2019.100347

Kosior, K. (2020). Economic, ethical and legal aspects of digitalization in the agri-food sector. *Problems of Agricultural Economics, 263*(2), 53–72. https://doi.org/10.30858/zer/120456

López-Morales, J. A., Martínez, J. A., & Skarmeta, A. F. (2020). Digital transformation of agriculture through the use of an interoperable platform. *Sensors (Basel, Switzerland), 20*(4), 1153. https://doi.org/10.3390/s20041153

Mhlanga, D. (2021). Artificial intelligence in the industry 4.0, and its impact on poverty, innovation, infrastructure development, and the Sustainable Development Goals: Lessons from emerging economies? *Sustainability, 13*(11), 5788. https://doi.org/10.3390/su13115788

Novelli, C., Taddeo, M., & Floridi, L. (2024). Accountability in artificial intelligence: What it is and how it works. *AI & Society, 39*(4), 1871–1882. https://doi.org/10.1007/s00146-023-01635-y

OECD. (2025). *Recommendation of the Council on artificial intelligence (OECD/LEGAL/0449)*. Organisation for Economic Co-operation and Development.

Rahaman, M., Lin, C.-Y., Pappachan, P., Gupta, B. B., & Hsu, C.-H. (2024). Privacy-centric AI and IoT solutions for smart rural farm monitoring and control. *Sensors (Basel, Switzerland), 24*(13), 4157. https://doi.org/10.3390/s24134157

Rauch, B., Matar, R., & Dörr, J. (2025). *AI-enabled Decision-Making Support Tools (AI DMST) for Agriculture: Analysis of market dynamics, technical requirements, and stakeholder perspectives. Study prepared for the European Commission, DG CNECT (Contract EC-CNECT/2024/VLVP/0103)*. Fraunhofer IESE, Kaiserslautern.

European Commission. (2023). *Regulation (EU) 2023/2854 of the European Parliament and of the Council of 22 November 2023 on harmonised rules on fair access to and use of data (Data Act)*. Official Journal of the European Union, L 2023/2854.

European Commission. (2024). *Regulation (EU) 2024/1689 of the European Parliament and of the Council of 13 June 2024 laying down harmonised rules on artificial intelligence and amending certain Union legislative acts (Artificial Intelligence Act)*. Official Journal of the European Union, L 2024/1689.

Ryo, M. (2022). Explainable artificial intelligence and interpretable machine learning for agricultural data analysis. *Artificial Intelligence in Agriculture, 6*, 257–265. https://doi.org/10.1016/j.aiia.2022.11.003

Sadjadi, E. N., & Fernández, R. (2023). Challenges and opportunities of agriculture digitalization in Spain. *Agronomy (Basel, Switzerland), 13*(1), 259. https://doi.org/10.3390/agronomy13010259

Schoemaker, P. J. (1995). Scenario planning: a tool for strategic thinking. *MIT Sloan Management Review*.

Shams, M. Y., Gamel, S. A., & Talaat, F. M. (2024). Enhancing crop recommendation systems with explainable artificial intelligence: A study on agricultural decision-making. *Neural Computing & Applications, 36*(11), 5695–5714. https://doi.org/10.1007/s00521-023-09391-2

Sharma, S., Verma, K., & Hardaha, P. (2022). Implementation of artificial intelligence in agriculture. *Journal of Computational and Cognitive Engineering, 2*(2), 155–162. https://doi.org/10.47852/bonviewJCCE2202174

UNCTAD. (2025). *Technology and innovation report 2025: Inclusive artificial intelligence for development*. United Nations.

van Notten, P. W. F., Rotmans, J., van Asselt, M. B. A., & Rothman, D. S. (2003). An updated scenario typology. *Futures, 35*(5), 423–443. https://doi.org/10.1016/s0016-3287(02)00090-3

Veraart, R., & Blok, V. (2025). Digitalisation of agri-food systems: A paradigm shift? *Journal of Agricultural & Environmental Ethics, 38*(3). https://doi.org/10.1007/s10806-025-09954-4

Vinuesa, R., Azizpour, H., Leite, I., Balaam, M., Dignum, V., Domisch, S., & Fuso Nerini, F. (2020). The role of artificial intelligence in achieving the sustainable development goals. *Nature Communications, 11*(1), 233. https://doi.org/10.1038/s41467-019-14108-y

van der Vlist, F., Helmond, A., & Ferrari, F. (2024). Big AI: Cloud infrastructure dependence and the industrialisation of artificial intelligence. *Big Data & Society, 11*(1). https://doi.org/10.1177/20539517241232630

Voros, J. (2003). A generic foresight process framework. *Foresight, 5*(3), 10–21.

Wang, W., & Cai, Y. (2022). The risk of artificial intelligence embedded in government governance: Mechanism, process, prevention and control. In *Proceedings of the 2022 2nd International*

Conference on Public Management and Intelligent Society (*PMIS 2022*) (pp. 609–616). https://doi.org/10.2991/978-94-6463-016-9_63

Wirtz, B. W., Weyerer, J. C., & Kehl, I. (2022). Governance of artificial intelligence: A risk and guideline-based integrative framework. *Government Information Quarterly, 39*(4), Article 101685. https://doi.org/10.1016/j.giq.2022.101685

World Bank Group. (2025). *Digital agriculture roadmap Playbook*. World Bank.

World Economic Forum. (2025). *Future farming in India: A playbook for scaling artificial intelligence in agriculture*. World Economic Forum.

Wu, P., & Zhong, Y. (2025). Artificial intelligence in sustainable agriculture: Towards a socio-technical roadmap. *Smart Agricultural Technology, 12*(101578), Article 101578. https://doi.org/10.1016/j.atech.2025.101578

Zha, J. (2020). Artificial intelligence in agriculture. *Journal of Physics. Conference Series, 1693*(1), Article 012058. https://doi.org/10.1088/1742-6596/1693/1/012058

Index

A
Accountability, 19, 20, 39, 64, 117, 119–123, 125
Adaptive learning, 93, 101, 103, 104, 111
Adaptive resilience, 49, 56–58, 64
Adoption, 2, 4–6, 8, 9, 11–14, 18, 19, 21, 29, 30, 32, 37, 39–43, 49–64, 71, 73, 78–80, 83, 85, 94, 96, 98, 102, 108, 110, 111, 117–123, 126, 129–135, 140, 141
Agricultural digitalization, 1, 2, 50, 51, 57, 75, 83, 84, 87, 104, 112, 118, 126, 130, 131
Agricultural knowledge, 11, 13, 81, 84, 94, 98, 103, 109
Agricultural labor, 8, 9, 21, 69, 71–73, 75–77, 85, 87, 88, 93, 94, 99, 132, 137
Agricultural systems, 2, 6, 8, 9, 18, 19, 30–32, 35, 39, 41, 43, 50, 56–59, 62–64, 73, 82, 84–87, 95, 103, 106, 111, 118, 120, 122, 123, 130–132, 141
Agri-food systems, 1, 3, 4, 21, 29, 54, 71, 74, 75, 79, 82, 93, 95, 96, 101, 102, 117, 118, 121, 123, 125–129, 133, 137, 138, 141
Agri-food value chain, 5, 9, 10, 13, 16, 30, 33, 39, 50, 57, 64, 69, 71–73, 78, 82, 120, 126, 130
Agro-ecological, 11, 19, 30, 99
Agronomic knowledge, 2, 4, 12, 21, 93, 107
AI Act, 117–119, 121, 122
AI-based solutions, 51, 53, 54, 60, 62
AI literacy, 93, 95, 98, 99, 102, 111
Algorithmic governance, 1, 9, 16, 18, 20, 64, 118, 121, 122, 125
Algorithmic transparency, 2, 21, 54, 118
Analytical capacity, 93, 105, 107
Automatability, 73
Automation, 2, 10, 13, 14, 18, 21, 29–31, 33, 35, 36, 38–42, 56, 58, 62, 69–71, 73, 74, 76, 77, 82, 94, 102, 129, 136, 139, 140

B
Blockchain, 30, 39, 57

C
Climate models, 34, 35, 107
Cloud–edge, 29, 30, 42, 119, 122, 127, 138
Competences, 50–53, 55, 93–111
Complementarity, 37, 71, 74, 76, 77, 141
Computer vision, 10, 12, 14, 16, 18, 30, 32, 33, 35, 36, 38, 40, 72, 77, 129, 131, 133, 135
Connectivity, 8, 19, 21, 30–32, 36, 37, 41, 54, 55, 59, 61, 78, 79, 121, 125, 129, 135, 138, 139
Critical thinking, 102
Cyber-physical, 17, 35, 36, 42

D
Data awareness, 93, 101, 102
Data-driven, 15, 16, 35, 38, 50–52, 55, 69, 70, 79, 82, 86, 98, 102, 103, 107, 108, 110, 118, 140
Datafication, 8, 95, 96

A. Apicella, *Artificial Intelligence in Agriculture*,
https://doi.org/10.1007/978-3-032-26580-7

Data governance, 2, 11, 21, 49, 57, 59, 61–64, 84, 85, 94, 96, 99, 107, 117, 119–121, 124, 125, 127, 128, 134, 137, 141
Data ownership, 9, 20, 120, 123
Data quality, 10, 19, 29, 35, 49, 52, 54, 59, 61, 64, 117–121, 125, 131, 138, 139
Decision-makers, 52, 86
Decision-making, 1, 2, 4, 7–11, 13, 15, 16, 18, 20, 21, 31, 33–37, 42, 50–52, 54, 55, 58–60, 62, 63, 70–72, 74–76, 78–85, 87, 93, 94, 96, 98, 101–105, 109, 110, 117–119, 121–123, 125, 129, 130, 133, 137, 140
Decision-support systems, 19, 32, 33, 59, 72, 73, 95, 97, 129, 133, 135
Deep learning, 10, 15, 17, 18, 34, 35, 38, 131
Deskilling, 94, 132
Diagnosis, 10, 29–31, 33–35, 38–42
Digital agriculture, 16, 33, 34, 36, 50, 69, 88, 93–96, 98, 99, 101, 102, 104, 120, 124, 140
Digital collaboration, 93, 101, 106, 108–111
Digital inequalities, 18, 19, 39, 135
Digital infrastructures, 8, 10–13, 18, 20, 29, 37, 39, 40, 49, 53–55, 58, 59, 61, 64, 69, 70, 73–76, 81, 83, 84, 93, 94, 118, 124, 127–129, 131, 135, 137, 138, 141
Digital literacy, 12, 19, 51, 52, 60, 63, 93–100, 102, 104, 109–111, 135, 139
Digital maturity, 49, 53, 58, 63, 64, 96, 99, 110, 111
Digital platforms, 2, 7–9, 11, 14, 16, 18, 53, 76, 80, 83, 101, 107, 109
Digital rights, 118–120
Digital skills, 11, 19, 21, 60, 71, 88, 94–99, 110, 111, 121, 122, 127, 129, 140
Digital systems thinking, 93, 101–103, 111
Digital technologies, 1, 2, 8, 13, 19, 21, 38, 50, 53–56, 69, 78–81, 94, 101, 102, 108, 117, 135, 136, 138, 139
Digital transformation, 1–3, 13, 18, 21, 29, 39, 42, 50, 78, 79, 85, 96, 98, 103, 105, 106, 109, 123, 137, 140
Digital twins, 12, 16, 17, 32

E

Ecosystem, 1, 11, 15, 29, 30, 34, 37, 40–42, 52, 54, 57, 61–63, 69, 71, 74, 75, 84–87, 93, 94, 97–99, 101–103, 105, 106, 109, 111, 118, 119, 121, 123–126, 129–132, 134, 136–138, 140
Employment, 21, 69, 71, 73, 74, 76, 78, 80–85, 100, 129, 130, 136, 137
Enabling conditions, 18, 19, 37, 51, 121, 126, 132, 135, 137, 138
End users, 11, 20, 61, 122
Environmental factors, 9, 50, 53, 56–58, 126
Environmental impacts, 139
Environmental sustainability, 2, 6, 7, 10, 118, 131, 132
Equifinality, 57
Ethical responsibility, 93, 104, 110, 111
Explainability, 13, 17, 117, 119–123
Explainable AI, 11, 122

F

Fairness, 63, 117, 119–121
Farming practices, 2, 6, 99
Food and Agriculture Organization (FAO), 4–6, 13, 15–20, 59, 61, 71, 75, 78, 80–82, 87, 94, 96, 98, 99, 101, 102, 118
Foresight, 21, 117, 118, 126
Frugal digitalization, 119

G

Gender, 8, 69, 78, 81–83, 87
General Data Protection Regulation (GDPR), 117–119, 121–123
Generalizability, 34, 35, 39, 59
Generative AI, 1, 3, 4, 10–15, 17, 18, 20, 21, 39

H

Human capital, 19, 49, 52, 55, 60, 93, 94, 97, 100–103, 109, 111, 141
Hybrid roles, 69, 74, 75, 106

I

Inequalities, 1, 2, 8, 21, 29, 39, 49, 59–62, 69, 71, 76, 78–83, 86, 87, 131, 132, 139
Institutional capacity, 6, 83, 87, 118, 127, 134, 137
Institutional environment, 54, 141
Intelligent communities, 93, 101, 106, 108, 109, 111

Interoperability, 11, 13, 16, 19, 29, 36, 37, 42, 49, 50, 52, 59, 63, 87, 99, 107, 108, 117–120, 124, 125, 127–130, 135, 136, 138, 139

K
Knowledge-based agriculture, 111

L
Large language models, 12, 14, 17
Large-scale farms, 21, 56–58
Leadership, 49, 52, 53, 55, 81, 82
Learning agriculture, 93, 95, 112, 141
Livestock, 7, 8, 18, 30, 33, 36–38, 40, 50, 82
Living labs, 86, 87, 130, 134–136
Local communities, 63, 97
Lock-in, 60, 63, 117, 119, 125, 128, 132, 134

M
Machine learning, 14–19, 34, 36, 38, 51, 70, 103, 134
Mechanization, 1–7, 9, 13, 14, 21, 35, 73
Monitoring, 2, 10, 16, 29–33, 35–42, 59, 60, 70, 72, 73, 76–79, 129, 131, 136–139
Multi-actor partnerships, 69, 86

N
Networks, 5, 8, 10, 12, 17, 29–31, 37, 38, 52, 54, 55, 57–61, 70, 75, 79–84, 86, 87, 101, 102, 104, 108, 109, 111, 119, 121, 124, 125, 129, 135–140
Neural networks, 10, 11, 15, 17, 33, 34, 36, 131
Non-routine, 70

O
Opacity, 11, 14, 59, 121, 122
Operational tasks, 30, 83
Organisation for Economic Co-operation and Development (OECD), 15–18, 85, 97–99, 101, 117, 118, 121, 125

P
Precision agriculture, 1–3, 7–9, 14, 15, 32, 40, 51, 98, 104, 106
Prediction, 10, 17, 29–31, 34, 35, 38–42, 52, 59, 61, 122, 125
Predictive models, 3, 14, 30, 35, 36, 40, 41, 51, 61, 70, 72, 74, 95, 97, 101, 102, 118, 120, 121, 125, 129–131, 138
Privacy-preserving solutions, 120, 123, 124
Production systems, 3, 5, 6, 19, 39, 40, 42, 61, 70, 102, 108
Professional identity, 93, 105, 101, 111, 140
Professional organizations, 132, 135
Public institutions, 63, 86, 132, 134, 135, 138
Public–private partnerships, 86
Public support, 54, 57

R
Reliability, 12, 14, 35, 36, 42, 58, 59, 64, 107, 119, 120, 140
Representativeness, 59, 64, 120, 121
Reskilling, 69, 84, 85, 94, 107, 108, 132, 135, 136, 139
Responsible design, 49, 62–64
Risk management, 19, 20, 35, 59, 119, 125, 139
Roadmap, 21, 117, 118, 126, 127, 129, 132, 134, 137
Robotic, 29, 30, 36–38, 51, 69–72, 84, 86, 97, 103, 110, 130, 131, 134
Robustness, 8, 10, 32, 33, 37, 110, 119, 121, 124, 125
Routine, 52, 55, 69, 70
Rural innovation systems, 98

S
Safety, 36, 76, 95, 99, 107
Sandboxes, 63
Scalability, 29, 36, 37, 42, 56, 117, 133, 136–138
Scalable efficiency, 49, 56–58, 64
Scenarios, 12, 21, 32, 34, 35, 61, 83, 117, 118, 126–134, 137, 138
Sensing technologies, 3, 7, 29, 31, 35, 36, 42, 51, 54, 69, 72, 98, 103, 107, 127, 129, 135, 140
Servitization, 73
Smallholder, 56–58, 60
Small-scale farms, 8, 79, 86
Socio-cultural, 49, 54, 55, 62
Socio-technical, 1, 3, 9, 20, 49, 57, 64, 78, 79, 84, 86, 98, 106, 110, 117, 118, 120, 122–126, 128, 130, 132–134, 136–140

Standardization, 15, 19, 37, 52, 58, 59, 64, 70, 96
Substitution, 6, 71–73, 76, 77, 103, 132, 141
Supervision, 12, 31, 36, 70, 75, 77, 82, 87, 107, 120
Sustainable Development Goals (SDGs), 100, 117, 132, 133, 136–139
Systemic security, 117, 120, 124, 125

T

Technological mastery, 93, 102, 109–111
Technological unemployment, 70
Technology-Organization-Environment, 49, 50
Territorial resilience, 127
Traceability, 13, 37, 39, 54–56, 58, 62, 119, 122, 125, 130
Transformation, 1–5, 7–13, 21, 29, 31–33, 37, 42, 56, 64, 69–71, 73, 75–78, 82, 83, 85–88, 93, 95–99, 101, 108, 111, 112, 118, 121–123, 128, 133, 138–140
Transparency, 2, 11, 17, 20, 21, 32, 39, 59, 61, 63, 64, 76, 108, 111, 117–123, 125–127, 135, 136, 141

U

UNESCO, 96–101
Upskilling, 94, 103, 107, 108, 130, 135, 136

V

Value-chain dynamics, 53, 55, 62

W

Waste reduction, 130, 133, 139
Workforce, 4, 70, 72, 74, 78, 80, 96, 97, 104, 108, 130
Work organization, 16, 60, 70, 76, 83
Workplace, 70
World Bank, 78, 81, 82, 94, 96, 99, 102, 118
World Economic Forum, 30, 32, 41, 59, 60, 84, 86, 87, 97–102, 129, 131, 135, 136, 138, 139

The manufacturer's authorised representative in the EU is Springer Nature Customer Service Centre GmbH, Europaplatz 3, 69115 Heidelberg, Germany. If you have any concerns regarding our products, please contact ProductSafety@springernature.com

Printed and bound by CPI Group (UK) Ltd, Croydon, CR0 4YY
16/09/2026
02217795-0004